Beirut Radical

Beirut Radical

A Global Microhistory from the Sixties to the Lebanese Civil War

Dylan Baun

I.B. TAURIS
LONDON · NEW YORK · OXFORD · NEW DELHI · SYDNEY

I.B. TAURIS

Bloomsbury Publishing Plc, 50 Bedford Square, London, WC1B 3DP, UK
Bloomsbury Publishing Inc, 1359 Broadway, New York, NY 10018, USA
Bloomsbury Publishing Ireland, 29 Earlsfort Terrace, Dublin 2, D02 AY28, Ireland

BLOOMSBURY, I.B. TAURIS and the I.B. Tauris logo are trademarks
of Bloomsbury Publishing Plc

First published in Great Britain 2025

Cover design: Adriana Brioso
Cover image: Imad Nuwayhid's work badge at Hotel Phoenicia
Intercontinental Beirut, c. 1966. Courtesy of the Nuwayhid family.

A catalogue record for this book is available from the British Library.

A catalog record for this book is available from the Library of Congress.

ISBN: HB: 978-0-7556-5524-3
         PB: 978-0-7556-5528-1
       ePDF: 978-0-7556-5526-7
      eBook: 978-0-7556-5525-0

Typeset by Integra Software Services Pvt. Ltd.
Printed and bound in Great Britain

For product safety related questions contact productsafety@bloomsbury.com.

To find out more about our authors and books visit www.bloomsbury.com
and sign up for our newsletters.

For Imad and all the other radicals

Contents

Figures

Acknowledgments

How does one condense gratitude? Acknowledge in a few pages the magnitude of support they received from hundreds of people over a decade? An impossible task, one I try to fulfill in *Beirut Radical* by introducing in each chapter those who made this book possible.

But for the purposes of a shortened transcript of support, I must start with those for whom without this book would not exist. That is the Nuwayhids. This wonderful family opened their homes and hearts to me over the past eight years and opened me to the life of this book's subject, Imad Nuwayhid. I list them here in the order I met them: Iman Nuwayhid, Walid Nuwayhid, Jawad Nuwayhid, Iyad Nuwayhid, Lina Nuwayhid Hariz, Tala Nuwayhid, Jad Nuwayhid, Salim Nuwayhid, Youssef Nuwayhid, and Rifaat Nuwayhid. For you all, especially Imad's siblings (Jawad, Iyad, Lina, and Salim), this may be a difficult read. However, it is my hope that restoring even a fragment of your brother's memory provides some release.

Next my sincere appreciation to Imad's friends, comrades, and sons and daughters of those radicals: Nabil al-Khishin, Rida Ismael, Gilbert Achcar, Maurice Nahra, Khalid al-Habre, Omar Deeb, and Maya Jalloul. You all provided another angle to Imad's life and tragic death. Thanks to your dedication and assistant, his beliefs and politics live on.

Most of the research for *Beirut Radical* was conducted in Lebanon over the past ten years and is indebted to a host of archives, archivists, and librarians. They include Nami Jafet Memorial Library at the American University of Beirut (including the Archives & Special Collections), the Institute of Palestine Studies, UMAM Documentation and Research, the Arab Center for Architecture (and most notably its President George Arbid), and the Ministry of Tourism (and particularly Rania Abdel Samad). Beyond these more formal archives, Mary Choueiry and Sami Ghazali were crucial to information on Imad's home village and his first job at Hotel Phoenicia Intercontinental.

Imad's story is global, and hence the archival research was global. I thank the staff at the following archives for their indispensable assistant both in person and online: the Special Collections at the University of Miami, the archives at *École Hôtelière de Lausanne* (and its former head archivist Delphine Thonney), Haverford College's Quaker Collections, the Friends Historical Library at Swarthmore College, Hannover Germany's City Archives, and the Libraries and Archival Services of the Ville de Lausanne.

To fund summer travels to these places, I am most grateful to my home institution, the University of Alabama in Huntsville. While more known for aerospace than Middle East history, at every turn UAH financially supported my work. Most importantly was the UAH Humanities Center, which funded research trips in 2018, 2022, and 2023, and a manuscript proposal workshop that was pivotal in readying *Beirut Radical* for publishers. As the research for this book has been a decade in the making, I'd be remiss to acknowledge those other, earlier funders: the University of Arizona, Franklin & Marshall College, and the Southeast Regional Middle East and Islamic Studies Society (SERMESISS).

My colleagues, students, and friends at UAH have always been my sounding board. First and foremost are those associated with my department, the Department of History, and my college, the College of Arts Humanities and Social Sciences. I'd particularly like to thank the following for helping with ideas, writing or research: John Harfouch, Nicole Pacino, Molly Johnson, Joe Conway, John Mohr, John Saunders, Josh Riddle, and Tim Hufford. Also I'd like to recognize several past students, Alexandria Bailey, Phillip Lee, and Coleman Hawkins, who served as research assistants at different phases of this project.

As I wrote the second half of this book in fall 2023, I returned to my intellectual home, Tucson, Arizona, the University of Arizona, and the School of Middle Eastern & North African Studies. Between long writing session, I gave talks, visited classes, and met with those whose feedback I respect the most. Thanks to Leila Hudson, Maha Nassar, Yassen Noorani, Julie Ellison, Maryah Converse, and Jadwiga Pieper Mooney.

The errors in this book are my own, but its refinements over the years are the product of those who have answered my queries, read bits, listened to conference presentations, or provided detailed feedback in the form of workshops. They include Susanne Abou Ghaida, Malek Abisaab, Ziad Abu Rish, Said Abou Zaki, Kristine Alexander, Habib Battah, Orit Bashkin, Matt Buehler, Tylor Brand, Fadi Bardawil, Kim Brengle, Michaelle Browers, Joan Chakar, Mohamad El Chamaa, Sowon Kim Crettex, Agnès Favier, Nate George, Laure Guirguis, Waleed Hazbun, Linda Herrera, Sami Hermez, Elizabeth Holt, Nour Hodeib, al-Tayyib al-Hosni, Idriss Jabari, Richard Jobs, Akram Khatar, Nadim al-Kak, Jeffrey Karam, Maya Mikdashi, Adey Almohsen, Zeina Maasri, Jamil Mouawad, Laila Parsons, Joseph Ben Prestel, Makram Rabah, Jeremy Randall, Mary Jirmanus Saba, Hicham Safieddine, Janina Santer, Yezid Sayigh, Nadya Sbaiti, Cyrus Scayegh, Hannah Elsisi, and James Stocker.

A second book comes from experience of the first. With this knowledge, and the intimate subject matter that lay ahead, I was patient to find the right home for *Beirut Radical*. And I have with I.B. Tauris. My editor, Rory Gormley, believed in this project from the early stages and has seen it through to the end. Thank you for that, as well as Faiza Zakaria for the assistance along the way.

Personal, behind-the-scenes support has been essential to *Beirut Radical* since in beginnings. Most important here is my wife, Nicole. You know this project better than anyone and have always given me the confidence to forge ahead, even if/when you can't say yes or no!

Lastly, to my family, Nicole, Barbara, Bill, Joe, Clint, and Marie, and my closet friends—you all serve as the unofficial dedication of this book. I love and cherish our relationships, and without them, my work would be devoid of the love and care I hope comes through the pages that follow.

However, Imad Nuwayhid is the official dedication and gets the final word. Without you, I simply wouldn't have this book. With you as the guide, I have grown as a scholar, historian, writer, and human. For that I owe you everything.

***

As I wrote these acknowledgments in late 2024, the country I have come to know and love was being destroyed. The sadness, guilt, and cognitive dissonance were unbearable. What does it mean to have the time and freedom to write these thanks when my friends in Lebanon wondered what destruction tomorrow will bring? As you will learn, Imad wanted a free Palestine, and a Lebanon that stood side by side in solidarity. In the end, *Beirut Radical* stands as a testament to Imad's message and those who carry on his legacy. The time is nigh.

Note on Translation and Correspondence

All translations are done by the author with occasional help from native Arabic-speaking friends and colleagues. Any errors, though, are the author's responsibility. I only use diacritics with translated Arabic words or titles, not names, organizations, or groups.

All interviews, in-person conversations, emails, and WhatsApp or Facebook Messenger correspondence were undertaken by the author, and only the author. All correspondences noted as "interviews" were recorded by the author and consented by the interviewees. All "conversations" were consented by the parties I spoke with but were not recorded.

Introduction: A Man, a Martyr, and Claiming Him

The Comrade Martyr, Imad Nuwayhid

Beirut, Fall 2013

This is when I first met the subject of this book. I saw his face and read the words *al-Rafiq al-Shahid 'Imad Nuwayhid*, The Comrade Martyr, Imad Nuwayhid.[1] They were on the front page of the October 29, 1975, edition of the Lebanese Communist Party's newspaper, *al-Nida'*, the Appeal. The picture and text of Imad were placed above two other fallen comrade martyrs: Diyab Ismael and Muhammad Maki.[2]

Over a decade ago, I was working on my dissertation and spending almost every day in the microfilm reading room at the American University of Beirut's main library. Skimming through this October 29, 1975, issue and its frontpage story, I learned that Imad, Diyab, and Muhammad had died in a battle in Beirut the day prior, six months into what would become known as the Lebanese Civil War (1975–90). I turned the handle of the microfilm reader to page 4, as the newspaper instructed me, to learn "about the martyrs."[3] Then I read Imad's obituary, listed first in bullet-point format:

The Martyr Comrade
Imad Nuwayhid

- He was born in Ras al-Matn in 1945.
- He joined the Lebanese Communist Party in 1973.
- He participated in the battle of May 1973 and in every nationalist battle since April 13 [1975].[4]

The Martyr Comrade
Imad Nuwayhid

- He participated in the ranks of unions, especially unions for hotels, restaurants, and amusement parks. The martyr is known for his prowess and devotion in defending the principles of the party and confronting the reactionary conspiracies and Lebanese isolationists.
- He was martyred on Tuesday, October 28, 1975 in the Qantari neighborhood where he was fighting fierce battles against the fascist Kataib gangs on the side of the Joint Forces of the National Movement.

As hard as I try, I can't remember my exact reaction to Imad's obituary.[5] A major theme of my dissertation was the recruitment strategies of parties to the war. I knew that in this instance, like many others, regardless of faction or side during the war, the Lebanese Communist Party was memorializing their "martyrs" who died at the hands of the "enemy," here fighters of the right-wing Kataib Party, in order to compel the living rank and file to take up arms—if they hadn't already—and fight.[6] As one of the 18,500 people killed in the first two years of the war, Imad's death was, sadly, unremarkable.[7] The information on Imad, with a focus on service to the Communist Party, and little on his personal life beyond where he was from, was then one piece of evidence toward my argument of party memorialization *for* recruitment. I believe if this is all I had found on Imad, an archival fragment during the war, through the eyes of a political party turned wartime militia, I would not, and could not, have written this book.

But Imad kept coming back. As I continued scrolling through issues of *al-Nida'* into November and December 1975, I saw funeral notices for Imad, remembrances on Imad written by his comrades, and reports of memorial services turned rallies for Imad. In one research note, I wrote, "*Ok now really, who is Imad? So much dedicated to him.*" In another, "*Imad is your guy.*" I'm not sure if the density of materials for Imad was as amazing as I wrote—or for that matter more than for Diyab or Muhammad—but weeks later, I was introduced to this project's single most important document.

In another room of the main library of American University of Beirut, Archives and Special Collections, I was pointed by the head archivist to a 1980 volume, authored by the Lebanese Communist Party and titled *Shuhada' al-Hizb al-Shuyu'i al-Lubnani 1975–1980: min Ajalak ya Watani, The Martyrs of the Lebanese Communist Party: for your Sake oh my Nation.* Each of its some 300 pages is dedicated to someone affiliated to the Lebanese Communist Party who died in the war.[8] Regardless of whether the person was a young man, woman, older, or a child, the format is the same: picture, birth-to-death years, and biographical information. On page 64, there he was (see Figure 0.1 below).

The entry on Imad included so much more than his *al-Nida'* obituary. It read that he was actually born in 1944—not 1945, as the *al-Nida'* obituary

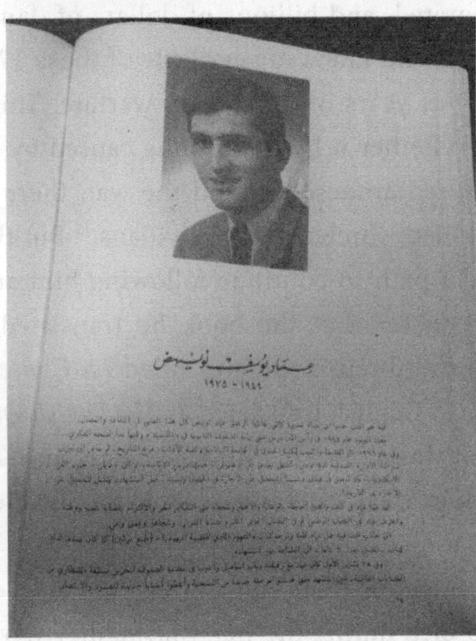

Figure 0.1 First glimpses of Imad Nuwayhid. On the cover of *al-Nida'*, October 29, 1975 (side top left on left), and in *Shuhada' al-Hizb al-Shuyu'i al-Lubnani 1975–1980: Min Ajalak Ya Watani*, 1980. Courtesy of the Lebanese Communist Party.

cited—making him thirty-one at the age of his death in the battle of Qantari on October 28, 1975. He studied law, history, literature, and philosophy at the Lebanese University in the 1960s. I read on. "He worked at Hotel Phoenicia" in Beirut and "traveled to Lausanne [Switzerland] to study hotel administration for a period of two years." I knew Beirut fairly well, so I was familiar with the famous hotel near its waterfront. What I didn't know at the time, and looked up later, was that Phoenicia was part of the US-owned Intercontinental Hotel Corporation, a subsidiary of the once US-owned Pan American Airlines. And while the entry informed me that Imad studied hotel administration, I did not yet know that he attended the most prestigious hospitality school in the world: *École Hôtelière de Lausanne*. Then, I read the following: "From the side of the rifle, Imad carried his pen and translated the book 'A Materialist Understanding for the Jewish Issue.'"[9]

I was blown away. I had been studying the war since undergrad; its causes, rooted in the Lebanese political system that favored Maronite Christians over other groups; its actors, including the Palestinian Liberation Organization, which sought to win support of local leftists toward regional liberation; its costs, including the loss of 170,000 lives, even more injured, displaced, and emigrated, and billions of dollars of damage.[10] However, I had rarely considered, and knew so very little of those 170,000 people who died in the fifteen-plus years of on and off warfare. This was not (solely) due to my naivety. Whether it be the trauma caused by bringing back the dead or state-sponsored amnesia around the war, there was so very little out there on those killed, combatants or civilians.[11] But this note on Imad's translation gave me a path to continue following him and his intellectual work. I learned thereafter that the book he translated, from French to Arabic, was written by Abram Leon and titled *La Conception Matérialiste de la Question Juive* (in English translated as *The Jewish Question: A Marxist Interpretation*). Leon was a Jewish, Polish, Belgian, anti-Zionist, Trotskyist who wrote this book in 1942, only two years before he died as a prisoner at Auschwitz concentration camp.

Simply put, this entry on Imad humanized him and, equally important, others like him who died during the war. Maybe they were not just fighters, or even intellectuals turned fighters. They were young people with lives and career aspirations. Since that fateful day when I first saw a picture of Imad in *al-Nida'*, I have learned that the question of who he was, how people remember him, and what that shows about the Lebanese Civil War is not so simple.

Javier Cercas' book, *Lord of All the Dead*, is instructive here.[12] It follows the story of Cercas' uncle, Manuel Mena, who died in the Spanish Civil War. The book's blurb sets up Cercas' seemingly contradictory inquiries: "Who was this young man? A fascist hero whose memory is an embarrassment to the left-leaning author, or a committed idealist who happened to fall on the wrong side of history?"[13] Similar questions guide *Beirut Radical*: who was Imad Nuwayhid? A leftist intellectual or a self-interested hotel worker? A martyr or a victim? An idealist youth with hopes and dreams that got caught up in the Palestinian cause and the war? Or was he even a fighter at all? And what does all of this mean for how Lebanese carry the war with them today?

It is my hope that by the final pages of this book, I have answered these questions as well as other important ones that Imad's life, death, and legacy have led me to ask. But for the sake of an initial answer, I find that Imad was none of these things alone, but all of them together. Considering Imad as a window into something much larger—grounds for a "global microhistory"—I argue that he represents a generation of what I term "practical radicals;" a global generation who were as invested in their politics as their income while they came of age under a growing American empire. Although much more is known about the former, particularly support for left-wing ideologies in the turbulent 1960s, Imad's life highlights how young people pursued them, equally, alongside their career aspirations. Imad's death in the war, then, shows the twisting path by which some young radicals ceded their autonomy to liberation struggles. Thereafter, and well into the present, multiple actors (political parties, comrades, and family members) battle over the memory of the fallen, claiming individuals like Imad Nuwayhid for their own, rivaling purposes.

Narrating the Dead

Over a decade since I met Imad in the archives, I have met his siblings, cousins, comrades, and admirers. I have been given his published writings, personal letters he wrote, class transcripts, and work ID cards. I have traveled to his school's archive in Lausanne, his company's archive in Miami, as well as his personal archive in Ras al-Matn. These individuals, their stories, and the sources they provided compelled me to write *Beirut Radical* with a central, seemingly unattainable goal. With Imad as the guide, I seek to reconstruct the lives, memories, and afterlives, of those individuals who died in the war.

Even if not always, Imad's experiences are representative of a broader group of people: those young Arab men, particularly from left-wing, pro-Palestinian parties, who supported those causes before the Lebanese Civil War, took up arms for them during the war, and perished in battle. Yet, I stress the impossibility of my task because Imad's life and path are human, unique, complex, and can hardly speak to others. To acknowledge this is important, but the stakes at play here—war, violence, memory—warrant more than a mere acknowledgment. So before we get to know Imad, I ask, is it wrong for us to want to know him?

The answer to this question is both yes and no. The resounding no is based on what I alluded to above: a history of a people, an era, a war that is missing those who came to participate in it, and what brought them there, reads formulaic, cold, and sterile. Moreover, as I have been reminded by one of my colleagues, to know Imad, write about him, and tell his story to those who don't know him (i.e., almost all of my readers) honors his memory, his family, and his comrades, ensuring that none are forgotten.[14]

At the same time, over the years I have become painfully aware of the resounding yes to this question: it *can be* unethical to narrate the dead, especially those brutally killed like Imad. In her work on the stories of enslaved African women in the Americas, Saidiya Hartman argues that to tell their stories can "commit further violence," "reiterating violent speech and depicting again rituals of torture." With a history of racial discrimination, sexual violence, and trauma as the backdrop for her scholarship, Hartman asks, "Why subject the dead to new dangers and to a second order of violence?"[15]

While Imad and "Venus," Hartman's historical subject, couldn't be more different, how I met Imad is similar to Hartman's path to Venus. Venus is not one woman, but thousands of enslaved African women. Their archival fragments are found in "a ships ledger in the tally of debits; in an overseer's journal" or US court cases files of the 1700s.[16] Historians do not first meet them through their own voices or lives, but the brutal violence that was inflicted upon their bodies. Similarly in the case of Imad, I met a man through his death by gunshots. The obituary I read, whether one agrees with the Communist Party's cause or not, was used to rally other members of the party to kill other people.

Some may be suspect that the dead, as non-living, can be traumatized more in the afterlife. Yet, if their memory lives on only through the violence they experienced, and historians choose to narrate this violence, uncritically, we choose to have their blood on our hands. Equally important, to read my words on Imad can cause pain for those living—those who would rather not be subjected to the scars of Lebanon's wars, whether for the first time, tenth, or one-hundredth.

Despite these quandaries, Hartman provides two best practices for carrying on. First, to combat the violence historians find in the archive, they must "transgress the protocols of the archive" and "imagine what cannot be verified" in it.[17] For Hartman, she reads violent sources against the grain for some semblance of Venus' biography, and more importantly, moves into realms of fantasy, speculation, and novelistic writing when the archive is silent. Cercas does something similar, mixing how he came to write a book on his uncle, confessionally, with the archival story and family memories of his uncle. I build from the two, like Hartman, reading party sources against the grain, like Cercas, opening up about my journey, using oral history, and bringing in personal archival sources on Imad. I add to their meditations through the approach of this book, global microhistory—where historical speculation is not all that different from novelistic or fantasy writing—to, in Hartman's words, "paint as full a picture" possible of Imad's life and others he touched.[18]

Second, Hartman contends that any history of Venus must be geared toward a history of the present. Writing about past violence, critically, is "a way of naming our time, thinking our present, and envisioning the past which created it."[19] I take this call, dedicating much of *Beirut Radical* to an exploration of memories about Imad from those living today.[20] I strongly believe that what they tell me about him is as much, if not more, about their present—for some, nostalgic for a time when emancipatory politics were more robust among the youth in Lebanon, for others, bemoaning the loss of a stable, rich Lebanon to those radical liberation causes—as Imad's past.

With these ethical concerns of how to narrate the dead never far from my mind, I find Imad's biography, and how it is understood and mobilized, can help toward answering a number of questions central to the history of Lebanon and the world. Beyond asking who Imad, as a single person, was/is, his life and death can inform the following: who were the young Arabs that came of age in the 1960s? What were their hopes, dreams, and aspirations? What politics did they imagine? What were they willing to risk for a new, alternative future? What were the circumstances of their deaths? And, just like I asked when I first met Imad, how are they "used" first by parties, but also comrades and families, toward certain ends in the politics of memorialization?

Imad as a Window

Imad Yusuf Nuwayhid (1944–75), whose name means pillar, was born in Ras al-Matn, a village in Mount Lebanon about an hour east of Beirut. With a population of 5,000 at the time of his birth, it is a small natural refuge, lined with the iconic *snobar*, pine trees, of the mountain.[21] Imad's mother, Umm Jihad, was from the nearby village of Majdal Baana, while his father, Yusuf, was from Ras al-Matn.[22] Both were Druze, a Muslim faith and identity indigenous to this area of the Middle East.[23] Like many other Lebanese, Imad was wholly of his birth village and the city, Beirut, where he grew up. Lebanon's heritage as a separate entity rested in Mount Lebanon, its namesake after all.[24] However, Lebanon's post-independent future (1943–onward), particularly its economy, would be Beirut.[25] Imad's early life shows that even if these worlds were different (urban vs. rural, hectic vs. tranquil), they were never far apart. He was always back and forth, spending his childhood summers in Ras al-Matn, and the school term in the capital, years of which I focus on in Chapter 1.

In terms of his education, Imad also lived between multiple, connected, worlds. The village he hailed from was perhaps most well-known for a school and orphanage founded by Daniel and Emily Oliver, Scottish Quakers with financial ties to the Society of Friends chapter in Philadelphia, Pennsylvania. While Imad never attended this school, some of his closest family, comrades, and mentors did, and it held a focal role in the life of the village. Instead, Imad completed his primary schooling at the prestigious *Lycée Français De*

Beyrouth (founded in 1909). Then, in the 1960s, he enrolled in the public Raml al-Zarif high school. It was lauded for its dedicated, rigorous teachers and administrators, who also happened to be Arab nationalists and leftists.[26]

Even before the French colonized and held Lebanon as a mandate (1920–43), they set up Christian-based, liberal institutions for educating elite and middle-class Beirutis in French language and culture.[27] *Lycée Français De Beyrouth*, where Imad's father Yusuf taught for years, and his children attended, was part of this mission. However, much less is known about American educational influence in the country in the early 1900s, like that exerted through the Oliver school and orphanage. Imad's life and village provide a window into this world. As I will assert, the Olivers' vision and actions are quite similar to those detailed by scholars working on western missionaries in the Middle East.[28] They evangelized in the hope—even if less successful than they planned—to make Christians, or at least Christian educated young people, often where Muslims once were. In contrast were schools like Raml al-Zarif, set up to forge a local, civic attitude and combat foreign education. At Raml al-Zarif is where the story of Imad's politicization, as well as that of his fellow classmates, unfolds.

Imad's professional life came into form around 1966. After finishing high school in that year, he moved from Lebanon to West Germany to work as an intern at the Hotel Hanover Intercontinental, years which serves as the focus of Chapter 2. Then, after a brief period back in Lebanon working at Hotel Phoenicia Intercontinental and pursuing a degree in law, he switched course and sought hospitality management training in Lausanne, Switzerland, at the prestigious *École Hôtelière de Lausanne*. Finally, he moved to London and Dublin, the latter of which would be his last hotel position abroad.[29] Across this decade, Lebanon's service economy grew as Beirut became a banking center for Gulf oil money and a hub for European and American businessmen and tourists. As the tourism market boomed, Imad was lucky enough to have a family friend in the sector who got him his first job at Hotel Phoenicia.

Similar to how Imad can lead to an exploration of American educational influence in Lebanon, an examination of Imad's job path can illuminate how the United States sought to project power through tourism in the post-war Middle East. Conventionally, this US agenda has been characterized by academics and policy makers as benign imperialism or merely diplomacy.[30]

Taking my cue from those working in other Cold War contexts, I contend that the United States and US companies used their financial instruments, technological prowess, and marketing power to mold pro-US environments abroad with pro-US values and pro-US business practices. The tourism industry of sixties Lebanon was one site for this influence.[31] These features of a new, American empire, then, impacted the coming of age of young people in Cold War Lebanon. It also, like with Imad, shaped the careers they could choose from.

In the summer of 1969, only a few months before pursuing a hospitality degree in Switzerland, Imad translated Abram Leon's *The Jewish Question: A Marxist Interpretation*. Both choices are at the core of chapter 3 of *Beirut Radical*. For the translation, Imad's discovery of a 1940s European anti-Zionist text was shaped by the political watershed of his generation: the defeat of the Arab side in the 1967 Arab-Israeli war and the further annexation of Palestinian and Arab land to Israel. Perhaps more so than anything else in Imad's life or death, his path represents the broader trend of post-1967 youth radicalization in the Arab world. Following the defeat, he and other young people across the region began supporting guerrilla warfare to liberate Palestine.[32] Along with moving further from conventional military solutions, I will show how they turned away from the Arab nationalism that regimes like Egypt and Syria had promoted. In its place they built the pro-Palestinian Arab Left—broadly conceived as parties and movements with socialist to communist leanings dedicated to the Palestinian cause—of the late 1960s and 1970s.[33] The networks of youth leftists in the Arab world did not merely attest to the loss and change their stances. As Bardawil argues, they intervened with new interpretations of the Palestinian problem as part of "their revolutionary political practice."[34] In their search for alternative pathways, there were those like Imad inspired by historic leftist texts, including that of Marx, Mao, Lenin, and here, Leon.

Some of these Arab youth, whether by choice—education—or necessity—work—had to experience the chasm of 1967 outside their home countries. This was the case for Imad, who, at the ripe age of twenty-three, traveled abroad. Here, again, Imad's life opens up an analysis of how "foreigners" formed their identity far from and with a longing for their home. For Imad, it was in Hanover, West Germany, Lausanne, Switzerland, and London, England that Imad had to experience the disruption of 1967, training and working in countries where he was often treated like an outsider.

When Imad arrived in Hanover in the 1960s, he bought into the European dream—that a career and life in Europe would provide more stability and joy than one possible in his home country. By the 1970s, he was painfully aware of his second-class status in Europe and the countries that imposed it. He then left London in 1971 with a solidly anti-European, pro-Arab politics.

Beyond identity formation, these aspects of Imad's biography provide a window into the becoming of a young Arab leftist abroad. His experiences in Europe help to globalize the history of the Arab Left—beyond, but in relation to the Arab world—and consider single lives within the Arab Left. Of course, there is abundant literature on the impact of revolutionary leftist leaders in Lebanon, most notably Kamal Jumblatt (1917–77), the Druze, pan-Arab, and (eventually) pro-Palestinian leader of the Progressive Socialist Party and the Lebanese National Movement.[35] Moreover, scholars working on the Arab Left of the sixties have done superb work on lesser-known thinkers and movements that developed a pro-Palestinian, transnational, leftist ideology.[36] Still unclear though are those, in George's words, beyond the "professional intellectual component," like Imad.[37] Indeed, I explain how their lives, global journeys, and careers also played a central role in the creation of the Arab Left.

These experiences of Imad, global and local, macro and micro, help set up the first of the two core objectives of *Beirut Radical*: adding richness to the history of the sixties and leftist youth that came of age during this era. In his groundbreaking book *The Sixties*, Arthur Marwick sees the decade (stretching both ways) as a cohesive period, "characterized by the vast number of innovative activities taking place *simultaneously*, by unprecedented *interaction and acceleration*."[38] The developments he traces in Britain, France, Italy, and the United States include the "formation of new [anti-establishment] subcultures" and "unprecedented influence of young people," facilitated through "important advances in technology," ranging from television to international travel.[39]

However, only recently have the sixties, both as an era and idea, been considered beyond western Europe and the United States. Scholars of places as distant as Mexico and Tunisia, Tanzania and Vietnam, have created the term "Global Sixties" to make a case for a global period of "simultaneity and similarity" with local variants.[40] These writers are not merely interested in adding peoples, cases, and sources beyond the West into the study of the West's sixties. They make the argument that countries like Palestine, Algeria, Cuba, and their independence struggles, shaped youth politics in the West.[41]

Imad's story allows for intimacy into global youth connections of the sixties. This perspective is crucial, as it still remains unclear—at least in scholarship—what were the effects of this era, not for the elites, leaders, and youth society as a whole, but for singular, typical (albeit middle-class) young people like Imad. Here, Imad's politics show that for Arab youth, post-1967, coming of age in the Cold War, the choice was rarely between the ideologies of capitalism or socialism. The majority of young people favored the latter at most or at least a generic anti-imperialist self-reliance that defied pro-Western capitalism. Even so, Imad and others were left asking: What am I going to do with my life? My career?

These questions lead to one of the most important conclusions I can draw from Imad's life. Although many working on the Global Sixties take up students, they include very little on what those students were actually studying.[42] For Imad, in terms of his time and emotional dedication, his studies in hotel administration seem as, if not more, important than his politics. Put another way, even if his radical, communist, pro-Palestinian politics are more intriguing, his career training and choices equally shaped his identity. This finding complicates scholarship on the sixties, showing how young people sought out multiple paths in tandem, a true autonomy. Accordingly, I argue that Imad's beliefs and actions, crystalized over the course of two tumultuous decades of the Cold War, signal a generation of what I call "practical radicals."

My use of the term is quite simple. Without contradiction, but not without awareness, young Arabs pursued causes they believed in and careers they believed in, equally, both of which they believed had the ability to change their lives and the world. The term is indebted to writers, like Zeina Maasri and Robyn Creswell, who characterize an era, and a place, Beirut in the 1960s–70s, in which liberalism (openness) and cosmopolitanism (diversity and mixing) facilitated radicalism (emancipation and liberation) and vice versa.[43] I add to this by bringing in the "practical" components, which focus less on adaptations of liberalism or cosmopolitanism as a system of values, but global capitalism, its system of values, and the resistance it generated.

The tangible power of capitalism meant that young people like Imad strove to fulfill concerns of the status quo—getting a job, maintaining it, creating a career—at the very same time they sought to upend it. Indeed, seeking autonomy and nonalignment between the forces of global capitalism and leftist radicalism is at the core of being a practical radical. This concept can help understand why many youth across the world ended up choosing their jobs over their ideas. In fact, I strongly believe these young people should not be seen as selling out or that this choice marked the "death" of this radical decade.[44] At the same time, those like Imad, who went the other direction, dying for their radicalism, should not be seen as outliers. They grant an opportunity for a close examination on the precise moments in which some young people risked their livelihoods and careers for causes they believed in.

To return to Imad's life, and Chapter 4 of *Beirut Radical*, from 1971 until his untimely death in 1975, Imad would live in Lebanon. He got his old job back at the Hotel Phoenicia Intercontinental and returned to his law degree. He also reconnected with his friends and comrades in Beirut, first becoming a member of a smaller leftist organization, and eventually joining the ranks of the Lebanese Communist Party in 1973. Like other, more mainstream leftist parties in Lebanon since the 1967 war, the Lebanese Communist Party had begun to wholly embrace the Palestinian cause. Unlike others, it was willing to fight for it when the country became divided on support for the *fedayeen*— those who sacrifice themselves, referring to fighters of the Palestinian Liberation Organization.

Imad's rationale for joining the party was common and sheds light on leftist, Beiruti politics at this exact moment. By the mid-1970s, the Communist Party had the organization, infrastructure, and force to actually fight alongside the Palestinians, something quite appealing to Imad. From a growing interest in Palestinian liberation at Raml al-Zarif high school, through advocating for it in Europe, to entering the pro-Palestinian Communist Party, I map the circuitous journey by which one young Lebanese leftist surrendered his personal autonomy to the Palestinian cause. Even if not outliers, those who took up arms, regardless of whether they met the same fate as Imad, were no longer practical radicals. They gave up the former for the latter.

Quickly thereafter is the point at which Imad's story became known by more than his family and friends: when he died in battle in October 1975, the first phase of the Lebanese Civil War. This is the juncture of the book where the story changes, from one about life on war's eve to, the second objective of the book, considering how lives are remembered, forgotten, or misremembered thereafter. I take up this theme in Chapter 5 (during the early war years) and Chapter 6 (in the 1980s and into today). During the war, the articles, reports, and volumes dedicated to martyrs, like those to Imad, demonstrate the amount of resources parties put toward memorializing their fighters and recruiting new ones. After the war ended in the 1990s, there was no collective truth and reconciliation process in Lebanon. In its place was a general amnesty law that absolved most militia leaders of war crimes. But while some scholars have argued this context generated a form of war amnesia, my conversations with Imad's loved ones defy this assertion.[45] All are willing to talk about his choices in vivid detail, even if they have different perspectives on what those choices mean.

This leads back to why I was struck by Imad's biography in the first place. Scholars of Lebanon have written little about individuals who died in the war or, equally important, how they are remembered thereafter.[46] Regarding those fallen like Imad, the living breathing reminders of the past, my intention is to humanize their perspectives and recognize them as what they were: reasonable. Per Mohammed el-Kurd, I do not seek to "sanitize" or "subdue" them to fit into some idealized version of the civilized, rational, non-violent human.[47] Rather, those leftists, anti-Zionists, fighters, and Beirut (practical) radicals were not outside the norms of humanity, but central to it. Thus, to consider Imad's legacy today is to uncover how memory is made, remade, and reinterpreted at different times, all at the micro-level.

This leads to the second core argument of *Beirut Radical*. What unfolds following Imad's death reflects how an array of actors take individuals, and their memory, as the foundation for their competing meaning-making projects during and beyond wartime. The Lebanese Communist Party claimed Imad as theirs as they created what I refer to as his "martyr narrative:" the story on his death, its meaning, and what the living had to do to avenge Imad and other "martyrs."[48] Many of his comrades, friends, and family agreed to, and played a role in this narrative, accepting him as a communist martyr. However, others, specifically some family members, resist the narrative of Imad as a communist, and reimagine his beliefs and actions in a post-war context. The project, process, and battle over memory are something I detail at length in the final chapter of this book. But for now, in sum, what I find through this exploration of the politics of memory in Lebanon is a mix of valorization, trauma, nostalgia, and corrective storytelling, depending on who is doing the remembering and when they do it.

The Promise and Peril of a Global Microhistory

The focus, style of writing, and the main arguments I make in this book regarding practical radicals and battles over memory are largely the product of a method: global microhistory.[49] To consider Imad's life, death, and legacy as a window, as I just did, is largely possible through its assumptions. Global microhistory allows me the opportunity to bring together what may first appear to be separate, unrelated topics: tourism in the Middle East, sixties global youth, and Lebanon's wars. But why Imad in the first place? Some readers may be wondering: does he, an "ordinary" person, deserve a book? In his famous *The Cheese and the Worms*, Carlo Ginzburg provides an answer to this question:

> But if the sources offer us the possibility of reconstructing not only indistinct masses but also individual personalities, it would be absurd to ignore it. To extend the historic concept of "individual" in the direction of the lower classes is a worthwhile objective ... [.] [I]n a modest individual who is himself lacking in significance and for this very reason representative, it is still possible to trace, as in a microcosm, the characteristics of an entire social stratum in a specific historical period[.][50]

In the case of Imad, the sources are there, and thus, Ginzburg would think it absurd not to study him. While remembering Hartman's cautions (do not merely reproduce the violence of the archive and connect past and present), a microstudy such as this reconstructs a sense of who Imad was, where he is representative of larger trends, and also where his story complicates them. Imad's story, however, is not only his—it is his siblings, his coworkers, and his comrades. This microhistory, then, should also consider the people he encountered, that he touched, and that touched him, all across the globe.

This realization links to the global aspect of a global microhistory. On one level, this qualifier is simple: Imad spent time in different places across the globe, and hence, his story, even if intimate, and microscopic, must account for that realm. This is also the case in the micro-level work of John Paul Ghobrial, who came up with the term "global microhistory." The main character of his inquiry is Elias of Babylon, a priest from Iraq in the seventeenth century who traveled around Europe and Spanish America. While the context, like that of Imad, is simply global, Ghobrial's contributions to microhistory bring in the method of global history with its focus on capturing "connectedness" between the histories of multiple places and seemingly different peoples. In that task, Ghobrial reminds his reader that "the close study of global life drags us back necessarily to a deep local history."[51] In the case of Imad, his travels from Hanover to London, his engagement with colleagues and friends abroad, and his connection with global thinkers informed his life in Beirut. In sum, then, a global microhistory takes the same call to action that Ginzburg lays out, and supersizes it, in an attempt to make claims about eras and people beyond the local, but connected to that locale.

Intimate stories, connecting the unconnected, rich source work, and macro-level, global conclusions; these may be the promises of such an approach, but peril abounds. Microhistory, global or otherwise, as well as its cousin biography, assumes that the individual matters. While this may seem harmless, Jill Lepore identifies dangers in those scholars who obsess over individuals, or what she terms "Historians Who Love too Much." Lepore first distinguishes microhistory and biography. The latter is "largely founded on a belief in the singularity and significance of an individual's life and his contribution to history," while in microhistory the "individual's life serves as an allegory for broader issues affecting the culture as a whole."[52]

Both assumptions can be problematic. Regarding biography, to assume that individuals are significant cannot be separated from both Western Enlightenment thought and the age we currently live in. From the 1500s to 1700s, thinkers discovered the individual. Ranging from Martin Luther to Voltaire, European writers argued humans as the makers of history. They face trials and tribulations, but almost anything is surmountable. Biography mimics this assumption. With an individual as the subject of any book, the worst peril is to pretend that they are unbounded by context. It is not to argue that someone like Imad had no agency, but is individual agency the most effective way to represent his story? Or, rather, are Imad's life and afterlife more closely the product of decades of Arab and Palestinian dispossession, the Lebanese Civil War, and the current moment of instability in the Middle East?

Microhistory's assumptions fare no better. To believe an individual is an "allegory," as Lepore notes, is to risk instrumentalizing that individual, using them, as a tool for the sake of an argument.[53] Hence, while biography may suffer from obsession of the individual, microhistory can suffer from exploitation of an individual. But are humans, in all their beliefs, values, experiences, and contradictions, generalizable? Can all their emotions and complexities become arguments?

I have been critical of the individualism akin to biography for some time, and seek to combat it in *Beirut Radical* through contextualizing Imad's environment—sixties and seventies Lebanon, for one—and his actions. However, until I started presenting this work on Imad, I rarely considered the perils of exploitation under microhistory.[54] I also rarely questioned the authority I had to write this book, as a white, non-Arab academic with no personal connection (beyond interest) to Lebanon and the Middle East.[55] I am more cognizant of these issues today—as well as those introduced to me by Hartman and Venus—and write, not divorced from them, but with them in my mind and close to my heart. But, as I hope I have made clear, and reiterate throughout this book, Imad continues to beckon me. I find myself, like Cercas, pulled in, as a friend once said to him, "After all you didn't choose this subject: the subject chose you. And those are the best subjects."[56]

~

This is where I would often include a paragraph or two on sources under my method of global microhistory. But I don't, because beyond those I noted above (obituaries, newspaper reports of battles, translations), I would like them to come as a surprise to the reader. Instead, I choose to end this introduction with a meditation on sources, archives, and access. Bound to my sources under global microhistory, some chapters of this book will have more personal sources (e.g., Chapter 2 where I explore letters Imad wrote home from Hanover) and will accordingly read like a rich biography. On the other hand, there are some chapters where I have less personal documentation (Chapter 4,

Imad back in Lebanon in the early 1970s), leaning more into microhistory with other primary sources, interviews I have conducted, and secondary literature as my guide. I am indebted to countless archivists, librarians, and contacts who helped along the way. To write about them, beyond the acknowledgments, as I do in every chapter, is my ode to what Maya Mikdashi calls "giving up control" of the archive and making space for "the assemblage [people, processes, paper] that makes" the archive.[57]

In this vein, let me pay respect to one archive here. They are the archives and archivists of *École Hôtelière de Lausanne*, which help me reconstruct Imad's school days in Switzerland, the focus of the latter half of Chapter 3. Switzerland has strong data privacy laws, which the university is obligated to follow. This means the process by which I could examine Imad's student file was more involved than archival clearance in Lebanon or the United States. I needed a letter from Imad's family, granting me permission to see his files. One of Imad's brothers, Jawad Nuwayhid, graciously agreed, but this letter had to be mailed physically from Lebanon, along with a copy of Jawad's ID card and the Nuwayhid birth registry, which confirmed the relationship between Jawad and Imad. This took eight months, a process that the archival team at *École Hôtelière de Lausanne* and Imad's family patiently facilitated. They are the reason I am able to explore this aspect of Imad's life in the first place and make an argument about the practical, career-centric aspects of sixties youth activism.

Yet, not all can travel around the world visiting archives or have the access I do. I get summers off, I have no kids, a spouse with a flexible work schedule, and a job that has funded my research for years. Also, as a non-Lebanese Lebanon specialist (knowledgeable of, but not too close), I believe Imad's family is most willing to help me, whether in this archival request or the thousands of questions I have asked them and others. So while the subject of Imad may have chosen me, I have the background, funds, and connections to be chosen.

Mindful of this privilege, the ethical issues this specific project raises, the unattainable goals it has, I still chose to write this book. So with a continued eye toward balance and awareness, let us begin where Imad's life started, and where my research ended: Beirut in the 1940s–60s.

Figure 0.2 Map of Lebanon. Imad's village of Ras al-Matn is about 6 miles north of Bhamdoun (labeled, below Aaley) and about 17 miles east of Beirut. Courtesy of Nations Online Project, nationsonline.org.

Village, City, and American Empire in Lebanon

From Snobar to Steel Town

Ras al-Matn, June 19, 2022

"It was quite a smart and innovative engineering decision by Oliver. He imported steel high beams from U.S. Steel and used them around the edges of the first floor of the Sariyah in order to build a second floor without replacing the foundation of the building." I stand with Rifaat Nuwayhid as he points to an abandoned, 500-year-old Ottoman sariyah, a castle. He is a distant cousin of Imad Nuwayhid, the subject of this book. He is also a civil engineer and resident of Ras al-Matn, so the design details of Daniel and Emily Oliver's orphanage and school are important to him. But he has no idea how important they are to me. They connect Imad and his village to my home of Pittsburgh, Pennsylvania.

I had been visiting Ras al-Matn along with (first) Imad's cousins and (then) siblings since 2016. The drive from Beirut to the village is about an hour by car due east and leads towards Mount Lebanon (see Figure 0.2 above). As the city and its traffic disappear behind, you zigzag through the mountain and its valleys. One sign that you are getting closer to Ras al-Matn is the doubling, then tripling of the snobar trees (see Figure 1.1 below). These are tall, lush green pine trees, indigenous to Lebanon, and distinguishable by their umbrella shape. The cedar may be that adorned on the Lebanese flag, but to me, this is the tree that symbolizes Lebanon.

The main road of Ras al-Matn is just that: one, main road. Once you arrive to the center of the town, straight ahead is Sahat Nuwayhid, the Nuwayhid Square, and Bayt Nuwayhid, the house of the Nuwayhids. The Nuwayhids are one of two or three large families in Ras al-Matn. While the square has always been a

Figure 1.1 The growing snobar trees as you wind up the mountain toward Ras al-Matn (and a guard rail tagged "P.S.P.," the Progressive Socialist Party, a popular political party in the area). Picture taken by author in 2018.

gathering place, Bayt Nuwayhid was once a cinema, now a hall for village events. From there, up a large hill, stands the house of Rifaat Nuwayhid, next to the abandoned Sariyah and school.

Also with me on this visit was Jawad Nuwayhid, Imad Nuwayhid's younger brother and Nabil Khishin, Imad's friend and comrade. The night before I met Rifaat outside the Sariyah was the first time I had heard the name Daniel Oliver. That Saturday evening, Jawad, Nabil, and I went to the house of Sami Ghazali. Sami—who has since passed away, Allah yerhamo Sami—is the nephew of Najib Salha, arguably the most famous person to hail from Ras al-Matn, and Imad's boss at Hotel Phoenicia Intercontinental. Sami tells us that his uncle was an orphan, given refuge at the Daniel and Emily Oliver school and orphanage, and that Daniel Oliver took a liking to his uncle. The rest, Salha's fame, is history. I was fascinated by what I learned about Salha and Oliver. The former was a rags to riches story, the latter the story of a foreign school in Ras al-Matn. And both of them, in intimate and distant ways, were connected to Imad.

*The next day, Rifaat, de facto trustee of the Sariyah, as its neighbor, hosted us for coffee. As we sit and talk, and I tell him about my new-found interest in Oliver, Rifaat retrieves a book for me. Titled "Seeing is Believing," it is, as the first page reads, "A photographic story of some of the accomplishments of two Quaker Missionaries," Daniel and Emily Oliver. It is filled with pictures of early 1900s Ras al-Matn, the school (which was converted in 1907 and open until 1958), and its students—lined up, learning in class, playing sports, and making, whether shoes, rugs or bedding. Most eye-catching to me is a set of before and after pictures in the book. The before, a picture of a young boy, captioned as "No Father—no Mother—no home—hopeless, hungry and in rags—until the Olivers took him in." The after, a suited young man, captioned as "**Graduated**—He had no chance— now he has every chance."[1] Later, I wrote in my notes, "Almost looks like those Indian boarding schools." I was referencing those schools across North America of a similar era that claimed they solved the problems of so-called "uncivilized" indigenous children through Christian education and Western clothing.*

However, Rifaat, Jawad, and Nabil believe that the Olivers were good for the village. These Scottish Quakers with American funds never tried to convert their students, Rifaat tells me. They just wanted to give them a place to live and learn. Jawad is in agreement, informing me that Daniel and Emily Oliver are buried in Ras al-Matn. Even Nabil—one of the more radical and contrarian people I have ever met—has nothing ill to say of the Olivers. In retrospect, this conversation checked my bias. While on the outside, this school's training may look like cultural erasure, the Lebanese I was interacting with thought very differently.

Right before we leave Ras al-Matn to return to Beirut, Rifaat shows me the Sariyah up close. As we walk around, he points out the steel beams from U.S. Steel. He tells me he knows they are U.S. Steel because as a child he saw the stamp on the beams, which had since been painted over. Pittsburgh, Pennsylvania, where I was born, has been the home of U.S. Steel since 1901. Like the school and orphanage, U.S. Steel is a pillar of my community. Over 5,000 miles away from my home, I am connected to Ras al-Matn.

Back in Beirut a few days later, I have coffee with colleague Maya Mikdashi, author of the wonderful Sextarianism: Sovereignty, Secularism, and the State in Lebanon. I tell her about my project and the Ras al-Matn to Pittsburgh connection I had learned over the weekend. She suggests, the first to do so, why not write about these encounters in this book. She also, one of the first to do so, speaks of my connection to Imad as potentially fated. At the end of the meeting, I ask her to sign my copy of her book. She writes, in the inside cover, "Believe in Fate!"

***

Hotel employee. Career-driven. Leftist intellectual. Fighter. Martyr. Before considering who Imad will become, and how he is remembered, I think it is crucial to know where he came from. The where is not a single place. He came from a Mount Lebanon village, a Druze family, the capital of Beirut, a leftist high school, and Hotel Phoenicia Intercontinental. While these locales are unique to Imad's story, the context in which they existed was not: Cold War Lebanon.

Taking up the early independence period (1943–58), Carolyn Gates refers to Lebanon as the "Merchant Republic."[2] The term is a nod to the country's open, laissez-faire, free market economic system, tilted toward the West. A countermovement to these trends was the growth of anti-imperial and anti-Western Arab nationalism, popularized by Egyptian President Gamal Abel Nasser, and his Nasserism.[3] Imad's story stands at the center of both of these Cold War trends. He looked to the West economically, to the region and the East politically, and within educationally. To choose all, without contradiction, I argue, was to be a practical radical.

With Imad as the guide, this chapter reconstructs some of the major forces that I believe colored Cold War Lebanon. Along the way, I introduce Daniel and Emily Oliver, Scottish Quakers who set up a school and orphanage in Ras al-Matn with US capital investment. You will meet Najib Salha, the owner and proprietor of Hotel Phoenicia Intercontinental, a subsidiary of Pan American Airways, and Intercontinental Hotel Corporation's eighteenth property and first in the Middle East. These characters, and where and how they connect to Cold War forces, are most perceivable at the micro-level. Particularly, they bring to the surface the growth of American empire in Lebanon.[4]

The term shouldn't be controversial. America has seen itself, since its founding, as an empire.[5] Experts on American religious efforts abroad and US tourism in Latin America have extended this reality to make a seemingly more provocative claim. They consider missionaries and businessmen as builders of American empire. They argue that with the US government at their back, they had the cover to teach Christian values or shape local tourist markets, which, in turn, extended US influence beyond military intervention or annexation.[6]

Two points from Imad's early life (hailing from a village that housed a US-backed Quaker school and working at a hotel with US funds) allow me to adopt this concept of American empire, a term not often used when focusing on American interest and influence in Lebanon, or elsewhere in the Middle East for that matter.[7] No, America did not colonize the Middle East, like France or Britain. But as this chapter seeks to show, the United States used its economic and educational prowess in the twentieth century to mold Lebanon, and the Lebanese, in its image. Pan American Airways, Intercontinental Hotel Corporation, and its leaders conceived Beirut as a cosmopolitan capital with a global reach, open to Western tourists and businessmen. Similarly, missionaries like Oliver and Daniel Bliss, the founder of the Syrian Protestant College—what would become the American University of Beirut—considered Lebanon as a bastion of liberal, Christian, education, one they sought to further.

This finding confirms those who name the American empire and focus on it in previously understudied locations. Something distinct that Imad, Daniel Oliver, Najib Salha, Hotel Phoenicia, and the micro-level make clear is that this was never a one-way relationship.[8] American empire was, at every turn, contentious and negotiated. Local tourism promoters and businessmen, like Salha, leveraged US capital to promote their own interests and visions for Lebanon. Arabic-language institutions, teachers, and students, like Imad, challenged the stranglehold foreign institutions like Oliver's had in Lebanon. Thus, Imad's story, in all the ways it is exceptional and representative, provides a lived example of American empire in the Cold War.

Being a Kid in Cold War Lebanon

Imad was born August 10, 1944, in Ras al-Matn, Lebanon.[9] It was a hard year for the village. The effects of world war were still palpable. As late as November 1944, resident missionaries Daniel and Emily Oliver thanked US Quakers for their recent clothes donations, which could finally get to the village after over seven years of shipping delays.[10] A year later, only days after the war had officially ended, the Olivers commented on how another shipment left orphans and poor villagers alike "looking gay and pleased, so differently from what they had done before." They, who had been previously wearing "cotton rags," "could not believe the feel of their hands as they felt the warm wool garments, and could not believe their eyes as they saw what was sent and given to them."[11] Maybe Oliver oversold their reaction, but a similar joy would likely carry across the village and into the next year, 1946, when French troops left Lebanon for good.

The French had been there in a colonial and military capacity since the First World War. Following the Ottoman surrender in 1918, France acquired the province of *bilad al-Sham*, Greater Syria. As a part of its "divide-and-rule" strategy, it then separated it into two entities, Greater Lebanon and Syria.[12] While the French largely succeeded in this policy throughout the 1920s, popular uprisings erupted in both entities in the 1930s, with a cross-section of elite and popular forces in Lebanon suing France into treaty in 1943. Syrian independence would have to wait a few years, until French troops left in 1946, marking the final political separation between Lebanon and Syria.[13] As a baby, Imad would not remember them, but his early years were marked by limbo: technically independent, but still occupied by a wartime foreign power, cheering for the end of war and empire, but also severed from Lebanon's Arab, Syrian brethren. The legacy of these trends, unfolding in a Cold War context, would leave an impression on his youth.

Imad was one of seven children birthed by Umm Jihad. Her namesake, mother of Jihad, was her first-born child, Jihad, now deceased, who was followed by four boys and two girls: Imad, Jawad, Jinan (deceased), Iyad, Lina, and Salim.[14] Imad's loved ones describe him accordingly:

> Imad loved life
> He was a gentle man, he is different than the others, very kind, he likes to
> read
> Sociable, loving, and very intelligent
> His eyes were always shining with hope and joy
> He was very special, smart, dedicated to his studies and self-development
> He wasn't just clever, he was handsome, a nice spirit, he had a love of life,
> very democratic[15]

Joyful, charming, and intelligent. His smarts, something everyone mentions in one way or another, were a product of his father. Yusuf Salim Nuwayhid was an intellectual through and through. As I learn from a website on his life, created by two of his sons, Jawad and Iyad, Yusuf received his baccalaureate in 1930 from the prestigious *Lycée Français de Beyrouth*.[16] That same year, he traveled to France to study at the Sorbonne, and after three years of school, he received his licensure in Arabic language and literature. With these degrees, and the pedigree of the Sorbonne, Yusuf was able to land a job teaching Arabic grammar and literature at his alma mater, *Lycée Français de Beyrouth*.[17]

His training reaped tangible benefits, including a middle-class salary that allowed him and his family to live comfortably—particularly after the war—between Ras al-Matn and Beirut.[18] While he was known as a "strict teacher," and held his children to a high standard, he was also very supportive of them.[19] His coming of age abroad, a positive experience, would lead him to encourage and finance a similar path for his children, including his son Imad.

Imad and his siblings would grow up spending the school year in the Zaydaniyya neighborhood of Beirut and the summers in Ras al-Matn.[20] His current home and birth village couldn't be more different. Zaydaniyya is a diverse (albeit mostly Muslim) working-to-middle-class neighborhood in a mixed part of town.[21] It is southeast of the bustling commercial district of Hamra, and southwest of Beirut's Martyrs' Square, nominally downtown and the main thoroughfare in the city. Both were major stops on the tramline of the time, which connected commerce and entertainment to the residential neighborhoods just south of downtown. Imad likely knew this tram well, using it to get around town with friends.[22] In contrast, one would be hard-pressed to find public transport or many cars in Ras al-Matn in the 1950s and 1960s.[23] And while mixed, with some Christian families (Maronite, Greek Orthodox, and Protestant), Ras al-Matn was, and is, "a predominantly Druze village."[24]

That a smaller community, such as the Druze, would hold "concentration in mountain districts" like Ras al-Matn was no coincidence.[25] It was central to the survival of the faith. The Druze, more so than anything, believe in *tawhid*, the concept of the oneness of God.[26] For this preference of "unitarian principles" over anything else—including the five pillars of Islam—as well their belief in reincarnation, Sunni and Shia Muslims have often considered Druze as heretics. To protect their community, the Druze practice *taqiyya*, secrecy of the faith, and accept majority Muslim beliefs in public. They also historically settled in the hinterland, keeping to themselves, which shaped their community as a distinct "ethno-religious group."[27]

Imad's father, Yusuf, was a pillar of the Druze community, close with Druze businessmen—Najib Salha—politicians—like Kamal Jumblatt, founder and leader of the Progressive Socialist Party—and religious leaders—like Grand Sheikh Muhammad Abou Shakra.[28] But perhaps more so than being Druze, Yusuf was an Arab, especially politically. Imad's father was known as measured, balanced, secular, and non-affiliated, but leaning toward Arab nationalism and in the support of Gamal Abdel Nasser of Egypt in the 1950s–60s.[29] This political identity was not uncommon for Druze of the time, and perhaps, in a similar vein to *taqiyya*, a means to fit into mainstream, pan-Arabism.[30]

Imad would choose a similar orientation early in his life. As regards secularism, he believed strongly in the separation of politics from religion. He once criticized religious leaders, Druze or otherwise, writing "all of the religious men intervened in matters of the state and the courts." Following his father, he valued education and independent thinking, and hence, also chastised those who blindly follow religious figures. In the same letter to his family, he lamented "those, some of which do not know how to write or read, take to the first word they hear … [from] their big sheikh who thinks he is saving or defending the Druze people."[31] I have written elsewhere how accusations of sectarianism, even from an anti-sectarian individual like Imad, are the product of a sectarian society and institutions.[32] Beyond these contextual aspects (i.e., living in a society where sect is everywhere), I have not seen a "Druze" outlook or thinking in any of Imad's sources, unless you consider that Druze outlook to be categorically secular, pan-Arab, and open to new ideas.

Even if not particularly religious or narrowly sectarian, socially, Imad and the Nuwayhids were Druze through and through. Any free time they could get was spent in the mountain with the "closely knit people" of their community.[33] Not only did Imad spend every summer of his childhood in Ras al-Matn, but every single day of the summer.[34] In this way, city and village almost existed in different worlds; Beirut, associated with jobs, school, and commotion and Ras al-Matn linked with play, free time, and peacefulness. This points to how, like the famous historian Albert Hourani argues, there were separate "ideologies of the mountain and the city" in Lebanon.[35] But, in other ways, the distinction defies the experience of Imad. Young people like him—and there were many who had connections to village and city in other parts of the country—straddle these different worlds, as they were shaped by and integrated into both of them.[36]

In his early childhood, though, the rural hinterland seems to have had more of an effect in his becoming.[37] So what was it like? A Quaker from Swarthmore Pennsylvania who had spent time in Ras al-Matn describes it as such: "Never will be forgotten the beauty of the village situated high on the mountain side overlooking vineyards and tiny hamlets dotted here and there, the road to Damascus with its caravans coming and going, and in the distance the Blue Mediterranean."[38] Not everyone shared these sentiments, though. One student at Oliver's school wrote in 1934 that "Ras el-Metn was to me an abominable, lonely, isolated place, where, as we used to say, 'Anchorites [Christian ascetics] should find their Utopia.'"[39]

Residents today that I am in touch with sound more like the Quaker promotional material in their praise. They describe it as beautiful, easy-going, and "humble and modest."[40] This was great for children like Imad. The Nuwayhids knew all the Druze families, so the kids could play at multiple houses and locales around town. Another cousin of Imad, Iman Nuwayhid, who also grew up in Beirut with summers in Ras al-Matn, remembers these days vividly:

> Our [main] playground was definitely the square, what we call the Nuwayhid square close to our house, but practically the whole village was a playground. We can go anywhere…so things were open, things were relaxed, things always felt safe, and actually enjoyable. They were good memories. Of course, sometimes we were bored because we don't have a lot of action for kids, but mostly playing ball, playing in the fields, helping when it is time to collect apples or harvest somethings and with the cousins, it was amazing memories.[41]

To fight back any mid-day boredom, one popular hangout was the local cinema, Rivoli. The kids could see a host of films, mostly black and white, from the Arab cinema hub of Egypt.[42]

The villages of this area of Mount Lebanon were not what they used to be. They had once served as the base for a host of silk factories in the 1800s.[43]

But as European manufacturing and two world wars had sunk the industry, the region became mostly known for its tourist and educational capacities by the 1950s. Well before Imad started working in the hotel industry, Mount Lebanon was a hub for regional tourism with many hotels, including one in Ras al-Matn.[44] One foreign resident in 1925 states that "The hotel which opened this year in Ras, has had a good measure of success, and the patrons seem pleased with it. We occasionally get some of these people at our First-day meetings."[45]

The writer of this letter, American teacher William Bacon Evans, is referencing the Quaker religious meetings that were attached to the school and orphanage that Daniel and Emily Oliver ran. Theirs was one of many, predominantly English and American schools, dotting the area: the Souq al-Gharb Presbyterian School, the Quaker Brummana Friends High School, and the Middle East Center for Arab Studies in Shemlan.[46] Daniel Oliver was a Scottish Quaker who had served his community in Morocco before arriving in *bilad al-Sham* in 1890. Emily Wright was an English Quaker who was teaching at the girls school in Brummana. They married in 1895 and were then transferred by the Scottish Friends Mission to run a new Quaker school in Ras al-Matn. It would be housed in a 400-year-old Ottoman *sariyah*, which had a series of renovations funded by Scottish, British, and American Quakers throughout the early 1900s.[47] And decades later, after Emily and Daniel solidified their connections to the American Quaker community, the school and orphanage's board of directors and funding mechanisms were based in Philadelphia, Pennsylvania, the epicenter of American Quakerism.[48]

In its first years of 1907–8, the student body was comprised mostly of "day scholars," or young boys from the area that were not orphans.[49] During crises, these demographics shifted. In the aftermath of the First World War (when the orphanage took on Armenian refugees), the Second World War (locals displaced), and the Arab-Israeli war of 1948 (Palestinians), the orphan population rose.[50] 1954 marked the school's largest enrollment: 198 students, 138 of which were day scholars.[51] This was one if its last full years before local crises—the 1956 earthquake and the 1958 War—forced the school to close permanently.

Perhaps the most famous student to graduate from the Oliver school was Najib Salha, Imad's eventual boss at Hotel Phoenicia Intercontinental. Najib's background was quite tragic. His father died when he was young, leaving his widowed mother to care for the children. She was poor, the children had to work, and Najib's brother died young while carrying food home under harsh weather conditions.[52] Najib's saving grace was his enrollment at the Oliver school from 1923 to 1926.[53]

What Daniel Oliver thought of Najib is unclear through archival sources, although family tell me he took a liking to him.[54] Najib was part of what Oliver and teachers called the "Sudan Boys." In a letter home, teacher William Bacon Evans outlines the program to his family:

> D.O. (and all of us) are greatly pleased because there has come a bid for young Syrians for telegraph posts in the Sudan, and way seems to be opening for 6 to go. If all works out, they are to receive 10 Pounds (Egyptian) a month (and passage), which while it seems small to you, appears fabulous wealth to young aspirants here![55]

The plan did work out, a product of Oliver's connection with British officials in British-occupied Sudan. This relationship, in Oliver's words, meant that "The Financial and the Postal Telegraph Department of the Sudanese Government have given a standing order to take all the boys from the orphanage."[56] Najib parlayed this post into a job in Saudi Arabia working for the finance ministry. By the time he returned to Lebanon in the 1950s, he was a "successful businessman" with major investments in banking (including Intra Bank, one of Lebanon's' biggest in the 1950s–60s), industry (including Filco, a Lebanese refrigeration company), and the hospitality sector (including, before Phoenicia, as a shareholder in the St. George Hotel).[57]

An incredible story and trajectory indeed, made possible by Daniel and Emily Oliver, their school, and the funds of American Quakers. Accordingly, it is not surprising that Najib thought highly of the Olivers, the teachers, and the school. He stayed in touch, sending letters and keeping them abreast of his triumphs.[58] However, I have not found documentation on how he was treated. Did he receive direct funds from American Quakers? As a Druze at a Christian school, did anyone try to steer him toward Christianity?

Here, others student experiences are instructive, including those orphans that received direct financial investment from American Quakers. One family, for example, gave money and support to a single orphan for decades.[59] They must have been pleased to later hear from Oliver that the boy had become a "true Christian," "a member of the society of Friends."[60] And there were those day scholars that would benefit from Oliver's connections. One of these friends was Daniel Bliss, an American missionary and the founder of the Syrian Protestant College. Jointly, they created a pipeline between Ras al-Matn, Brummana Friends High School, and American University of Beirut. Some of Imad's family members followed this educational path after graduating from Oliver's school.[61]

While it is unclear if Najib had direct financial support, he succeeded because of Oliver's networks. And although Salha, who was Druze, never converted, to create Christians in the Arab, Muslim, Middle East was the end goal of the Olivers. To be clear, the Quakers did not see themselves as converting. In one update to an American Quaker family in 1945, Daniel Oliver writes, "We do not ever seek to proselytize, or to get boys to become Quakers—never: but we do try to teach them how to live, and follow Jesus Christ the only perfect, infallible Teacher and Saviour [*sic*]."[62] At its most literal, this appears a contradiction—no conversion, merely Christian teachings and principles. However, these words from Oliver reflect a belief that providing a Christian education to poor Arabs was the goal and conversion a plus.

Regardless of how strongly the Olivers wanted to convert, other sources show that they wanted regional influence. Take this sentence found in the conclusion of a 1930s informational pamphlet:

> As in the past, so in the present [Greater Syria's] geographical position gives it tremendous political importance and we want to use faithfully the advantages which this gives so that this Quaker outpost on the slopes of the Lebanon may be an effective witness to the teaching and spirit and life of Jesus Christ.[63]

The Olivers were clearly aware that this area of the world had geostrategic importance in a context where European colonialism was entrenched. They, like other Quakers, missionaries and Christian settlers across the world, then sought to leverage this imperial venture to their benefit.[64] One example of this was with the Sudan boys, using Daniel's connections, British influence in the area, and the positive experiences of those like Salha to further their mission. That mission, with US funds and British support at its back, was to mold these youth under a Christian education.

Whether Imad Nuwayhid would have thought of the school in these terms is unknown. However, he thought highly of Najib Salha and likely appreciated what the school had done for his mentor. Furthermore, even though its money was coming from the United States, Imad—or anyone else for that matter, students or villagers—likely did not consider the school as influenced directly by America. Founded under the Ottomans, transferred to the French, with British and Scottish founders, it probably appeared generically Western. Thus, the sources do not allow me to argue that any of these dynamics gave Imad a negative view of America. Nevertheless, in Imad's teen years, well before he would come to work for an American company, he would witness US influence, interests, and sway in his country.

Nine years after Lebanon's independence in 1943, a peaceful, cross-sectarian movement sacked the country's founding president, Bishara al-Khuri, who was replaced by Camille Chamoun (1952–8).[65] In an early Cold War context, Chamoun was central to positioning Lebanon as squarely pro-Western. His rise coincided with that of Gamal Abdel Nasser, but Chamoun, much to the chagrin of many involved in the 1952 revolution who endorsed his candidacy, went in the opposite direction. He considered joining the pro-West Baghdad Pact in 1955, refused to cut ties with France after the Suez Crisis of 1956 and openly opposed the unification of Syria and Egypt into the United Arab Republic in 1958. While Nasser was the symbol for an anti-imperial Arab nationalism, Chamoun became representative of an elite, pro-Western Lebanese separatism.[66]

At this age, Imad, like his father, would have been Arab nationalist and pro-Nasser, even if not politically active until his high school days in the 1960s. Most Druze, as one of Imad's cousins, Walid Nuwayhid, relays, were "pro-Abdel Nasser" and "happy for the union between Egypt and Syria." He tells me the story of when Nasser visited Damascus in March 1958 following the union. Nasser was met by Kamal Jumblatt, the face of the anti-Chamoun movement. At the time, Walid's teacher in Ras al-Matn asked if her students wanted to go to Damascus to see Nasser. They said yes, young boys and girls, cheering

Abdel Nasser ya Gamal, ya Gamal Abdel Nasser. While they never made it to see Nasser—it was too crowded to get close, with hundreds and thousands of visitors—Walid thought it was a "very nice trip, I still remember this trip."[67]

Two months later, a war began. Following the assassination of anti-Chamoun journalist Nasib al-Matni, Kamal Jumblatt launched an armed revolution from the mountain toward Beirut. It sought to occupy the airport, the Presidential Palace, and overthrow Camille Chamoun. At each turn, it clashed with his security forces and allied parties. The conflict took another dimension when, after a military coup in Iraq against the monarchy there, the United States sent marines to Lebanon to defuse the situation and ensure Lebanon remained sovereign and pro-Western. The war ended in October 1958 with 4,000 casualties and a US-brokered truce which unseated Chamoun and replaced him with the military general who never intervened in the conflict: Fuad Chihab (1958–64).[68]

Local sparks, regional tensions, and global implications, the 1958 War was an early Cold War conflict par excellence, one that shaped the young generation of Lebanese, what Khalaf calls their "initiation into militancy."[69] Imad was thirteen at the time, still in grade school. Again, unfortunately, there is no indication of exactly what he thought of this war, or whether he experienced any of the fighting. While Walid's story is helpful in demonstrating youth excitement for pan-Arab nationalism, it does not signal much more than that for Imad. Hence, I cannot claim with much authority that Imad was anti-American following 1958. At the same time, like many other youth, the image of US marines docking on the shores of Beirut likely had an effect on his politics in opposition to US policies.

As of 1958, Imad was enrolled in the same school where his father taught, the *Lycée Français de Beyrouth.* It was founded in the early 1900s as part of the *Mission Laïque Française,* the French Secular Mission, meant "to promote the use of the French language and a knowledge of its civilization amongst non-Francophone peoples as a means of furthering its foreign interests."[70] Even though secular, it was not unlike the Oliver school, which used education as a part of a broader, foreign-backed agenda. However, as the French took over Lebanon in 1920, and made French language compulsory in all schools, *Lycée Français* became a part of a state, centralized educational platform.[71]

When Imad was a student at *Lycée Français de Beyrouth*, in a post-French context, its name had distance from its imperial legacy. It was a school and an elite one at that. While it was still "one of the best French schools," it also had an impressive Arabic department, headed by Imad's father.[72] Moreover, while largely for the middle and upper classes—and there was not much mingling between these groups—it was religiously mixed with Muslim and Christian students.[73]

Lycée Français de Beyrouth's establishment in the early 1900s, and pedigree by the 1950s, was indicative of the cosmopolitan, diverse capital of Beirut. Since the late 1800s, every new school, company, bank, hospital, and café signaled Ottoman, French, and then, Lebanese investment in the city as the driver.[74] Almost all major economic developments came through the city, relegating other regions to specific functions, whether that be agriculture for the south or the mountain for vacationing. So while Imad and other youth went back and forth, their style and culture was shaped much more by their urban environment: sixties Beirut.

For lack of a more clinical description, Imad was a hipster. Take his Phoenicia badge, the earliest picture I have of him (see Figure 1.2 below). While a jacket was a formality, the turtleneck became a signature for Imad. It was a product of the creation of specific men's wear in Europe and the United States, and by the 1960s, a sign of a certain intellectual counterculture.[75] His hair matches that counterculture, long, wavy, and coiffed. "Imad was normal like others," one family member tells me. "His clothes, his hair, his life in general like the [sixties and] seventies generation."[76]

This style should not be seen as a Western import. It is a product of what Featherstone calls "glocalization," for our purposes, the interpretation and adaptation of the global and Western in a local context.[77] In sixties Beirut, to wear a turtleneck, style your hair a certain way, or drink Coca-Cola, as Imad certainly would have, was not purely Western in meaning or intention. Imad was part of an urban scene—Cold War Beirut, marked by its openness and activity—where young people were engaging global brands, styles, and ideologies on their own terms.

This local interpretation of the global is reflected in Imad's tastes at the time. For one, Imad loved music. Some of his favorites were Iraqi singer Nazem al-Ghazali, French-Armenian tenor Charles Aznavour, and Egyptian-French

Georges Moustaki.[78] Ghazali was an Arab traditionalist through and through, but the others were the product of hybrid upbrings and musical traditions, one that catered to young people who wanted to connect both with their culture and the wider world.

After spending most of his youth at *Lycée Français*, Imad moved schools and started high school at Raml al-Zarif in 1963. Like many of his family members, he could have continued at the lycée where his father still taught. But he didn't. Yusuf wouldn't have disapproved, I believe. Imad would not suffer a dip in rigor at "one of the best public schools in Beirut."[79] As Favier writes, Raml al-Zarif was "renowned for the seriousness of its teaching."[80] Imad could then receive a top-notch public education at Raml al-Zarif, one within walking distance to the Nuwayhid flat in Zaydaniyya.

Yusuf likely also appreciated that instruction at Raml al-Zarif was all in Arabic. Since the first, large, anti-French protests in 1930s Lebanon, chants of "down with foreign schools," in favor of Arabic-language schools, were an expression of an indigenous nationalism.[81] In a post-colonial context, to attend a prestigious Arab-language school, and not an American or French one, was an expression of one's politics. One of Imad's brothers, Jawad, tells me this is why Imad moved on from *Lycée Français*.[82] As noted above, children of 1958, like Imad "were swept off their feet at a very young age by the title waves of Arab nationalisms."[83] Imad's friend, Nabil Khishin, confirms that Imad would be better served elsewhere politically. "[I]n other schools, especially the schools of the public sector, the level of political consciousness was much higher than in the *Lycée Français*."[84] To have a school that would mesh and cultivate his politics would be an appeal for Imad. It would also be a stand against empire through education.

At Raml al-Zarif, Imad was in the literature track, studying philosophy and history.[85] Given the time period, the curriculum likely favored Western thinkers (from Aristotle to Voltaire), but given the school, it likely had a component on "Arab civilization."[86] What he learned does not seem as important as the environment in which he learned it. One Nuwayhid tells me that at Raml al-Zarif "most of the teachers are leftists, communists," while another contact recalls it was a starting point for student demonstrations in the sixties.[87] Other students credit the school as the beginning of their "real commitment" to leftist and pan-Arab causes.[88] Similarly for Imad, Raml al-

Zarif was where he dropped a generic, anti-imperial Arab nationalism for something more principled. Toward the end of his schooling, it appears Imad joined an organization called the Student Forces Front (*Front des Forces Étudiantes* or *Jabhat al-Quwwat al-Tulabiyya*).[89] It was formed around 1965, "oriented toward the reading and discussion of Marxist tenets," and "one of the crucibles of the new Lebanese Left."[90]

Imad would graduate in 1966, two years before he would join any political party or movement. Thus, while Imad developed leftist credentials at Raml al-Zarif, and it was a place where teachers would recruit students to their particular causes, it appears Imad left unaffiliated.[91] His graduation also came a year before the Arab-Israeli War of 1967, when, as I discuss in later chapters, the political scene in Beirut changed radically. By 1969, for example, the school housed a student union in defense of Palestinians and the Palestinian cause in Lebanon.[92] Thus, Imad's path through an Arab nationalist, anti-colonial, leftist education provides an interesting case: one where the student came before the watershed moments, but shifted in that same direction anyways. For that reason, I believe Imad was, at the very least, introduced to the Left and Palestine as a cause in high school. More speculative, but justified by his later dedication to these causes, Imad was already at the forefront of a New Left that was becoming Marxist, Pan-Arab, and pro-Palestinian, all in one.

The United States and Hotel Phoenicia Come to Beirut

In the mid-1960s, Imad was at a crossroads: would he continue his studies in philosophy or enter the job market? Jawad tells me his brother was concerned he would not be able to find a career in the former, so he chose the latter.[93] This is where Najib Salha enters Imad's story. Being from a small village, the same sect, and of similar stature in the community, the Nuwayhids and Salhas were good friends, particularly Imad and Najib's son Mazen.[94] Salha then set Imad up with an internship at Hotel Phoenicia Intercontinental in downtown Beirut. Salha had been the owner and proprietor of the hotel since 1956, the year that the project was greenlit by Beirut municipality following direct negotiations with Intercontinental Hotel Corporation, a subsidiary of Pan American Airways. The hotel then opened to much fanfare in late 1961.[95]

Imad would train in the kitchen from July to September 1965 and in room service, likely through 1966 (see Figure 1.2 below).[96]

There is no evidence that Imad considered Hotel Phoenicia as part of an American brand or franchise. There is also no evidence that Imad thought of himself as working for an American company, whether in Beirut, or later, as he would, in Hanover, West Germany. In his absence, and to explore the broader significance of this American company in Beirut, I turn away from Imad for a moment.

Intercontinental Hotel Corporation was part of the vision of Pan American Airways and its founder Juan Trippe. With support and funds from the US government, Pan Am/Intercontinental mobilized the technologies of its global fleet and the marketing savoy that created its universally-recognized brand to forge what I see as a "closed tourist loop." They sought to promote, ferry, and house Americans—whether tourists or businessmen—in its planes and its properties, in this case, to, from, and in Beirut.[97]

Pan American Airways had operated since 1927, with its first flights from Pan Am headquarters in South Florida to Havana, then South Florida across the Americas, then the United States across the Pacific.[98] All the while, Pan American had received US federal support—both verbal and financial— in their global mission. But there were terms to that investment, especially as a global war was brewing. Without hesitation and one of the first, Trippe and Pan Am offered up its airfields in Central and South America to house US bombers during the Second World War.[99]

With the growth of the US military industrial complex in the 1950s, Pan Am and then Intercontinental recruited retired military for leadership positions.

Figure 1.2 Imad Nuwayhid's work badge at Hotel Phoenicia Intercontinental *c.* 1966. Courtesy of the Nuwayhid family.

For instance, Trippe brought on Roger Lewis to serve in Pan Am's number two position, Executive Vice President, in 1956. His prior job was Assistant Secretary of the Air Force.[100] These connections sustained Pan Am's relationship with active military. Lewis would take meetings, labeled confidential, on topics such as "re IRBM [intermediate range ballistic misses]," "the Ad Hoc Study group on Manned Aircraft weapon System (Including Helicopters)," and the "AF [Air Force] large engine development program."[101]

For its service during the war years, Pan Am was rewarded with government support in whatever areas it wanted to build out, including hotels. In 1946, the Export-Import Bank granted Pan American a 25,000,000 line of credit for hotel development.[102] Capital would be funneled to a new subsidiary, Intercontinental Hotel Corporation, fully owned by Pan American. Then in 1948, following ongoing conversations between Pan Am and the US State Department, funds were approved for hotel projects in Latin America. This agenda mimicked its air fleet, from the Americas (with its first hotels in Brazil, Mexico, and Uruguay in the late 1940s to early 1950s) to a global arena.[103] It was also an extension of then Secretary of State George Marshall's plan for US-led development and security in Latin America, Europe, and Japan.[104]

Of course, Intercontinental's main objective was to make profits and extend its reach. Nonetheless, it is essential to recall the context in which the company's goals were envisioned: the Cold War. In this era, à la Marshall, tourism was seen as a tool to extend American economic values of liberty, combat the economic forces of the Soviets, and thereby win the Cold War.[105] US big shots in the global hotel industry, ranging from Hilton to Marriott, were quite open about this goal.[106] For its part, first in a 1948 internal memo, titled "For our information," Intercontinental listed its Cold War objectives:

1. The widespread development of tourism in foreign countries—as a means of creating additional sources of dollar exchange;
2. Increased travel abroad by US businessmen—an instrument for extending further the influence of US commercial enterprise;
3. The promotion of international travel—a medium through which greater international good-will and understanding is created.[107]

Here, Intercontinental focused on tourism writ large, for the sake of what it called "the public interest."[108] But how would its hotels fit into this policy? The company wanted to be a part of the movement of dollars around the world, and in its hotels, through American tourists. It sought to extend US economic interests by housing American businessmen. And lastly, perhaps most important, it would promote US values—coded as "good-will"—through encouraging borderless travel and accommodations.

Intercontinental then took this corporate culture into the public domain, justifying its existence on similar grounds to interested parties. In 1954, newly appointed Intercontinental President, Bryon Calhoun, spoke to members of Congress at a House of Representatives hearing, titled "to promote the foreign policy of the United States by fostering international travel." Calhoun, who was not ex-armed forces, but had been in the hotel business for thirty-plus years, argued that as international travel expanded, airplane seats were not all that mattered. He says, "There are other points along the international air routes such as the Middle East, Istanbul, Turkey is one, Beirut, Bangkok … where travel can't go because there isn't a place for the people to go when they arrive there."[109] In the jet age, Calhoun was trying to convince US lawmakers that hotels were just as important as the planes, beds equal to engines, in the goal of opening up new locales and markets.

Calhoun may be right on the importance of hotels, but his point on the lack of existing accommodations was erroneous, something he knew. Istanbul, Beirut, and Bangkok had vibrant hotel sectors for some time, and they were not alone.[110] As Skwoit argues in the case of Latin America, US tourism advocates would often claim infrastructure was poor, at the hands of a less than modern and civilized government and people, to convince those with money and power that the tourist site was "ripe for exploitation."[111] If this seems a stretch, Calhoun's comments on hotels and the promotion of American values may be more convincing: "Everything starts and stops in [our] hotel, and it generates spending and new habits and leads to a complete changing of their [local] viewpoints, and way of life."[112] To build an American hotel in Beirut, then, would foster positive views of America in Beirut, solidly placing Lebanon in the orbit of an American empire through tourism.

Intercontinental's next president, Peter Grimm, continued this agenda. Like Calhoun, he came from a hotel background, but communicated a Cold War security argument that sounds like it could have come from a member of the armed services. In 1957, he spoke to a full house of students at Cornell University's School of Hotel Administration—akin to the Director of the CIA visiting Georgetown. In what reads as a scoff, Grimm says, "We do this [support hospitality efforts around the globe] not out of some fuzzy philanthropic sense but in the clear knowledge that our economic strength and security depend upon peace and prosperity in the rest of the world."[113] Grimm talked the Cold War talk, indeed. But to ensure economically and militarily secure environments, the company needed voices that were well trained and connected. This may be one reason why Pan Am's second-in-command, ex-Air Force Roger Lewis, oversaw both the company's defense projects and its global hotel portfolio.

In sum, American influence in the Cold War, or American empire abroad, hinged, in part, on a local environment that was pro-American—economically, militarily, politically—allowing American planes, hotels, and businesses to flourish. Wowing American tourists in those locales was an added bonus, as Grimm confirms, "[he] will have his impressions formed by what he experiences in the lobby, the public rooms, and in his hotel room."[114] But before Intercontinental could get a hotel in the Middle East, that American tourists would visit, and Lebanese like Imad Nuwayhid would work in, it had to get flights there.

When Intercontinental in Beirut was still an idea, Pan Am sought a base of operations in and through *bilad al-Sham*. As early as 1945, Pan Am investigated the "potential of importance of the cities of Beirut and Damascus as intermediate points on the P.A.A. route [from the U.S.] through the Middle East—to Calcutta."[115] The first Pan Am survey flight took off a year later, and on July 1, 1950, "At 0820 a Pan American World Airways constellation [plane] landed on schedule to inaugurate the new semi-weekly New York-Beirut service."[116]

Integral to the advent of international air travel through Beirut was William Campbell. He was a Princeton grad and Orientalist professor of archaeology, turned leader in the US Army Middle East command during the Second World War, turned head of a shipping and distribution company in post-war Lebanon and Syria called the American Levant Company with a consultancy role at Pan American Airways.[117] While it is unclear exactly what his company shipped, it is likely tied to another main reason Pan Am became more interested in Beirut by the late 1940s. This was Beirut's proximity to the Trans-Arabian Pipeline, or TAPLINE, pumping oil between 1950 and 1976. Beirut was the largest city at the end of the economic line that would run from south Lebanon through Jordan, Iraq, and Saudi Arabia. Many American companies followed Campbell's lead, bringing their businesses to Beirut in the 1950s. They included Dow Chemical, Caterpillar Tractor, International Telephone and Telegraph (ITT), Chase Bank, Bank of America, and First National Bank.[118] The latter companies signal that Lebanon was no longer just a Merchant Republic; it was a Banking Republic, recycling petrodollars and the wealth associated to the oil industry.[119]

Campbell, who eventually became vice-president of TAPLINE, was not the only one interested in Beirut's central role in the global oil economy. Amos Hiatt, Middle East Regional Director for Pan Am, wrote in the early 1950s, "There are few places in the world as attractive as Beirut, the Paris of the Middle East. It is growing rapidly, it is the terminal of the thirty-inch pipeline across Saudi Arabia, and is the headquarters for many of the big oil companies."[120] Beyond their promotion of Beirut to Pan Am, Campbell and Hiatt jointly advocated for a new airport to realize this potential. To much fanfare, and with local buy-in, Beirut International Airport opened in 1954. Beirut was thus inaugurated as an "aerocity" with the capacity to connect "a regional network of destinations" to a "global network of air routes."[121] A world-class hotel, owned and operated by Pan Am, would then be another dot along Pan Am's growing, global empire.

But as Hiatt insinuated, Beirut had become a destination in and of itself, "the Paris of the Middle East." While this phrase has its own history, so does the hotel industry, a space that Intercontinental was not the first occupy.[122] The Italians built the first hotels in Beirut's central business district in the 1840s–50s.[123] And since the mandate period, the French had, as Santer argues, "considered tourism as an ideal means to propagate the colonial empire," and, per Daam, used tourism to "raise awareness and acceptance of the overseas empire among the French and an international audience."[124] They sold Lebanon as a place for French tourists to sojourn, and constructed and managed places for them to stay through the *Société Des Grands Hotels Du Levant,* the Society of Grand Hotels in Lebanon. Ranging from the St. George (1934) to the Normandy Hotel (1940), the number of hotels built throughout the city tripled throughout the mandate period.[125] This pre-Phoenicia context, I argue, demonstrates that "Pan Am and Intercontinental did not forge an empire of its choosing nor controlled the tourism market in Lebanon."[126] In other words, their attempt at building a tourism empire through Beirut and Lebanon was not predestined. It was contentious, negotiated, and multi-directional, all at the hands of local tourism promoters.

Although Intercontinental was entering a crowded field, it was the first American company on the ground in the Beirut hotel sector. It did not, however, reinvent the wheel when it came to marketing Beirut as a strange, but familiar, destination. In a Phoenicia brochure of the 1960s, Intercontinental sold Beirut as "the city of glorious contrasts" alongside pictures of ancient ruins and modern skyscrapers.[127] These phrases and visuals were a part of the Western branding of Beirut as the West of—and in—the East. They weren't the only players in this image creation. Local promoters had a central role to play in branding Beirut and bringing foreign tourists to their country, city, and hotel.

Najib Salha, a graduate of Oliver's school, a leader of Ras al-Matn, and Imad's future boss, was one of these promoters. Before he was even approached by Intercontinental regarding their interest in building a Beirut hotel, he already had a plan.[128] The project was initially called either "Hotel Beirut" or "Hotel Plaza-Savoy."[129] Mock-ups were drawn and the interiors set *c.* 1954–6.[130] The team would include Edward Durell Stone, a successful US architect most known for the Museum of Modern Art (MOMA-1937) in New York and the Kennedy Center for Performing Arts in Washington, DC (1959).[131] For Salha's hotel, Stone would work with local architects (by way of Egypt) Ferdinand Dagher and Radolphe Elias.[132] This East-meet-West pairing mirrored their design plans, structured with arabesques and porticos in the Italian and Mughal style. The interior was eventually overseen by Intercontinental's Neil Prince. Per a recent exhibit dedicated to him, he thrived at the Phoenicia, the first time he "applied his philosophy of design tied to location."[133] As a whole, then, the hotel would stand as "an icon of modern design in the International Style adapted to the local climate."[134]

Not only was Salha ahead of the Americans in vision, design, and team members, he had shown in an earlier instance that he would push them. Before returning to Beirut in the 1950s, Salha worked, as reported proudly by Daniel Oliver, for the "Finance Minister [Sheikh Abdullah Suleiman] with King Ibn Saud of Arabia."[135] In his advisory rule to Sheikh Suleiman, Salha was the negotiator on a hotel deal with Intercontinental. His path crossed with Amos Hiatt, Regional Director for Pan Am and Intercontinental, attempting to close a deal on a hotel in Dammam. It failed, Hiatt claimed, because "neither one of them is interested in the contribution a hotel can make to Arabia nor in the benefits it would bring to other parts of the economy, and hence profit them. They look for ways to draw off money now."[136] It appears that the incentive fee that Salha demanded, a charge of 15 percent of total profits that would go to the Salha-Suleiman team, was unacceptable to Intercontinental.[137] Whether this amounts to a get-rich-quick scheme, per Hiatt, is not important. It shows that Salha would not back down in negotiations.

Later, back in Beirut in 1956, Salha would not be working with Hiatt, but M. Lee Dayton, his replacement. He was brought on not for his hotel experience but for his knowledge of US interest in the area. Dayton worked on the Marshall Plan and the US Aid Mission, both of which rebuilt Europe and its allies, like Turkey, in the US image.[138] It is not clear if Dayton knew of Salha or of the botched negotiations in Saudi Arabia, although he met similar roadblocks. They started discussing the prospective hotel in January 1956, but it stalled because both parties could not find an agreeable incentive fee structure. Salha did not want to give Intercontinental more than 20 percent of the hotel's profits, while Dayton told Salha "25 percent was the absolute bottom."[139] In a March 1956 letter to his boss, Dayton's first line reads, "in the absence of any communication from Najib Salha I have continued to explore other possibilities here."[140]

After almost a year of negotiations, Salha and Dayton came to a deal. Intercontinental would complete all "professional architectural[,] engineering[,] decorative[,] and hotel equipment services."[141] In return, Salha's local financing team, represented by the *Société Des Grands Hotels Du Levant*—now a fully autonomous, Lebanese body—would have to pay the payroll of all Intercontinental personnel and "reasonable expenses paid or incurred" (traveling, per diem, long distance phone calls, etc.) as their work was completed.[142] Finally, once in operation, the hotel would only have to furnish Intercontinental 20 percent of its annual earnings, not 25 percent.[143] Salha held strong and got his way this time.

All of this seems fairly standard. Also, likely common in these agreements was to not name "the Hotel" in question.[144] But since January 1956, Salha and his team were referring to this hotel as "the Phoenicia."[145] I can only assume that Dayton's team liked the name. It was a nod to Lebanon's—largely imagined— westward facing ancient past, inflected in the modern age.[146]

To return to the deal, equally consequential was something only outlined in a private letter from Dayton to Salha. Intercontinental would "purchase from you, 15,000 shares [or 20 percent] of the capital stock of La Societe Des Grands Hotels du Liban," which Salha served as its chair.[147] Hence, Intercontinental was buying in to have leverage, not just in the Phoenicia and Salha, but hotel development in Lebanon more broadly. But as always, this was not one-sided. For Salha and the hotel industry, this meant that one of the largest hotel corporations in the world was investing in Lebanon, long-term.

~

It took five long years to build the hotel, but Imad Nuwayhid did not have to wait for that. By the time he started work in 1965, the hotel had been open for four years and was a well-oiled machine. Its occupancy rate for the second half of 1966 was 91.5 percent, ranking it in the top three of Intercontinental's global holdings.[148] Those bookings were made through the most advanced hotel reservations and billings system in all of Lebanon.[149] Foreigners and locals alike could meet in one of the hotel's three largest spaces—the grand ballroom, the banquet hall, and entertainment auditorium—holding over 2,200 people combined.[150] In between a show or a business meeting, they could enjoy a cocktail at one of the Phoenicia's three lounges, the most for any Intercontinental hotel in the world.[151]

Of course, Imad's job was part of a family friend's doing. But it was also a part of Lebanon's push to make Beirut a cosmopolitan capital with the tourism industry as its anchor. In other words, to work at Phoenicia in the sixties was to be on the forefront of something exciting. The boom of the era was generated by tourism advocates, like Salha, the Lebanese government, and its newly created National Council for Tourism. With an already established Western interest, and particularly US funds, the council worked to shift Lebanon—like Intercontinental and Pan Am, through advertising and marketing—from a largely regional tourism hub, with the mountain as its selling point, to a global one on the pristine beaches of Beirut.[152] Imad's style, hair, and music choices also reflected this rebranding choice: Arab, but looking outward.

In addition to selling Beirut to foreigners, the vision had to be sold to the Lebanese. It is no coincidence that in the midst of the boom, *al-Siyaha*, a journal dedicated to tourism, was launched. While its ads for the new casino, and pictures of the new Beirut crop of hotels demonstrated the move, so did its features. A 1965 article, titled "Crisis in Mount Lebanon," discusses how "every year was going from bad to worse." People did not want to stay in mountain hotels anymore, the writer comments. "If the situation continues with these rates the owners of these hotels will have to lock up the doors of their hotels."[153] This was in contrast to Beirut hotels, which were thriving. An article in the same edition provides statistical evidence for such. By 1965, there had been a 25–30 percent increase in Beirut hotel revenue over the last five years, a jump "that hasn't been seen before." Guests from all over the world were "looking to be close to the sea and beaches and its locale in the middle point allowing for ruins trips and tourism destinations all over Lebanon."[154]

Imad never worked in any of the other 300+ hotels in sixties Beirut, just Phoenicia.[155] It was the crown jewel, at the core of the boom. His first posting was in the kitchen, where he would serve in one of three concepts. *L'Amerique* was a coffee shop that a Phoenicia brochure referred to as "Yankee-a-la Orient." The *Tea Room* served as a lunch spot with "tempting salads, exquisite pastries and complete beverage service." Last was the *L'Age D'or*, the main dining that mixed "international cuisine and Lebanese specialties."[156] Like everything the Phoenicia did, it mixed a global, modern, and American brand with local touches. But the guests Imad would encounter were mostly European and Americans. Circa 1966, 43 percent of guests were from the United States and Canada and 22 percent were from Europe.[157] While in the kitchen, his encounters with guests may have been limited, he eventually worked as a room clerk, where his duties would likely range from assigning rooms and greeting guests.[158]

Once checked in, foreign tourists were treated to world-class accommodations at Phoenicia, sipping on arak cocktails at the underwater

Sous la Mer bar or watching belly-dancing icon Nadia Gamal at the hotel's *La Paon Rouge* nightclub.[159] But how did they get there in the first place? Yes, Americans likely arrived on a Pan Am jet, direct from New York, but how did they find out about Lebanon as a tourist attraction? Beyond company brochures and magazines, the Lebanese Ministry of Tourism held an information office in New York at 527 Madison Ave, only blocks from Rockefeller Center.[160] By the 1970s, they held nine tourism offices globally, including in London, Stockholm, and Cairo.[161] As I have written elsewhere, "This reality, especially that there was only one office in the U.S., but five in Europe and three in the Middle East, demonstrates how Lebanon, Beirut, and Phoenicia by extension, leveraged American attempts at empire and U.S. capital interest to build its own [global] brand."[162]

Lebanese tourism advocates engineered these trends. Yes, they had US funds, but they used those funds to craft indigenous modernity and development. Sometimes the promoters leaned into Western stereotypes of "the Orient" to fuel that development. Brochures selling "the crossroads of Occident and Orient," promoting "Oriental dance," and allowing film crews to set action thrillers with mustachioed, fez-clad villains in and beyond the capital were part of this strategy.[163] Imad may have taken issue with these representations, at least the Imad we will come to know in later years and chapters. For their worth, however, it appears promoters did not care how their land and people were depicted, as long as they could do the depicting.

Modernization and Dependency

I don't know whether Imad actually liked his job at the Phoenicia. While his family seem to think he did, one of his closest friends didn't even know he worked there, something I touch on in a later chapter. More importantly though, I have no documentary evidence from Imad—letters at the time or letters later commenting specifically on his time at Phoenicia—either positive or negative as to this question.[164] It is clear, as I outline in Chapter 2, that he continues down the hospitality path. A month after receiving his diploma in August 1966, he left Lebanon for an internship in Hanover, West Germany, working at the Hotel Hanover Intercontinental.[165] Moreover, as I detail in Chapter 3, he left Lebanon again to seek advanced training in hotel administration at *École Hôtelière de Lausanne*. Perhaps whether he loved his job or not is beyond the point. It was his career, the practical, financial foundations for his life.

Although speculative, it is possible that Imad saw himself, and his job, as contributing to the development of his home country. While the tourism industry netted a reasonable 87 million lira in 1961, by the end of 1964, the winter before Imad started his job at Phoenicia, sector revenue equaled 145 million.[166] That income would amount to about 10 percent of the country's GDP in the 1960s and 1970s, rivaling Beirut and Lebanon with any tourist locale in the world, then or now.[167] Hotel Phoenicia, Imad's employer, "an international recognizable [hotel] … a center piece of post card views of the city," was a large part of this growth, in economics and image, a modern hotel in an outward-looking county.[168]

Beyond the numbers were tangible effects in the labor economy, something Lebanon tourism advocates, at home and abroad, were keen to document. A 1966 Intercontinental Hotel Corporation press release on the successes of the company and its benefits to the world include some information on Phoenicia's role, as well as a paragraph on the "origin of an Arab Furniture Factory." With Intercontinental's modern-meets-ancient, global-meets-local design aesthetic as the guide, the hotel would need local furniture and local furniture makers. The press release describes how an "Arab father-and-son [duo], owners of a small, back alley wood shop," had to "enlarge their work force from 30 to 125 craftsmen and build a modern factory." The investment paid dividends—$500,000 a year of revenue to be exact. It also allowed the furniture makers to build their business and export their furniture abroad. In another instance, the press release continues, "authentic Lebanese fabric" for draperies was needed, creating a "thriving cottage industry" for hand-weaving, staffed by "women and girls of a mountain village near Beirut."[169] As was the case with Najib Salha, an American hotel empire could not exist without local agents. In some small way then, these furniture makers and weavers also held leverage in this contentious network of influences.

This was the modernization linked to Imad's job, something that maybe made him proud. But there was a huge cost: dependence on US companies and their patrons. In 1946, well before the tourism boom of Imad's time at Phoenicia, Naim Amiuni from the Ministry of Economy foretold that a tourism-based economy, one that always produced more revenue in services than industry, would turn Lebanon into a "class of servants."[170] In a similar vein, Palestinian-American intellectual Edward Said opined in the 1970s, "Don't you wish you could wake up one day and read that plans were afoot to build a great Arab library instead of a new hotel?"[171]

Intercontinental would argue, convincingly, that these new hotels created new jobs for the likes of Imad and others in connected industries. But as Sara Fregonese finds, luxury hotels like Phoenicia were "sites where the socioeconomic inequalities surrounding the city … were emphasized and reproduced."[172] In other words, they were symbols for a certain development strategy—per Said toward the capitalist economy, away from the knowledge economy—the "lopsidedness of the Lebanese economy"—toward one industry, away from others—and the displacement of low- and middle-income peoples in the neighborhoods where these hotels were built in the first place.[173]

1960s Lebanon, Beirut, Hotel Phoenicia, and other hotels like it served the business interests, way of life, and influence of the West. While not unlike the educational influence of the West, with agents ranging from the *Mission Laïque Française*, Daniel and Emily Oliver, and Daniel Bliss, tourism influences from abroad held much more sway in the national imagination. Indeed, dependence on it would not go unnoticed by Lebanese officials or Arab thinkers, as Amiuni and Said's words demonstrate. But did Imad notice it?

At this stage, it is unclear. It could be he was too young, not yet jaded in the way those like Amiuni or Said were. Or maybe it is because he was coming of age in it. Imad grew up in Cold War Lebanon, between city and village, his Druze community and secular Arab nationalism. Wholly unique, his generation was forced to favor the West, and particularly the United States, economically, something that made the city he lived in feel modern, hip, cool, and global, all perks for a young person. This was, at the same time, his politics and thinking developed in a different direction: away from the United States, capitalism, and the West.

For Imad to benefit from US development, but come to despise the United States, would in no way be hypocritical. Rather, these sentiments were balanced and mediated by a generation of young men and women, what I describe in later chapters as practical radicals. In the context of the Arab world, they came of age under a growing American empire, fueled in some small part by hotels like Phoenicia, that spurred economic growth in Lebanon and dependence on the vision of that growth: capitalist, pro-United States, and later, in service of a country that fully supported Zionism and the state of Israel. Imad stood against the latter, even as a high school student, as the Palestinian cause was on his mind. This was as he helped build his country with US financial support. While working at Phoenicia may have given Imad a first-hand look at what US-backed, indigenous modernity looked like, he was not unique in his cultivation of a pro-US development, anti-US politics outlook.

These trends drove this generation's dedication toward being equally practical and radical—fulfilling societal and familial expectations on becoming a gainfully employed adult and striving for systemic change. Indeed, American empire, Pan Am, Intercontinental, and Hotel Phoenicia were a set of symbols that would both sustain dreams of modernity and calls for total revolution. Again, I can't conclude that Imad saw it exactly this way at the time, but in the end, that is inconsequential. This is because he became very aware of the place both his career and his radical politics would have, equally, in the shaping of his life, away from home.

2

Coming of Age Abroad

The Family Archive

Beirut, June 5, 2018

Iyad Nuwayhid and I sit for lunch at a luxury hotel downtown. He slides me an 8 × 11 envelope across the table with my name on it. I didn't open it then, but I could hardly wait. Its contents included copies of Imad Nuwayhid's work badges from his time at Hotel Phoenicia, educational certificates from secondary school in Beirut, as well as letters of recommendation from his supervisors and teachers in Europe. It also included a number of letters that Imad wrote home to his family, the majority of which were sent while he interned at a hotel in Hanover, West Germany (1966–7). I still remember delicately opening the envelope Iyad gave me and immediately taking a photo (see Figure 2.1). It was the point I knew I had the makings of what you are reading: a book on Imad Nuwayhid, in part, through his own words.

Iyad Nuwayhid is one of Imad's younger brothers. He is an international salesperson working for Hatcon, a Saudi-owned company specializing in industrial oil and gas equipment. I met Iyad for the first time the weekend prior at his home in Ras al-Matn. The gathering was arranged by his older brother, Jawad Nuwayhid, who I also had just met a matter of days before. Jawad and Iyad had either declined or were unavailable during a prior visit to Lebanon. I later learned that Jawad in particular was initially suspect of me and my interest in his deceased brother Imad. But after a good word from some of his cousins who I had been working with since 2016, Jawad agreed to meet.

Jawad is a retired architect who, like many of the Nuwayhids, splits his time between Beirut and Ras al-Matn. At our first meeting in Beirut, Jawad informed me that in a chest at his brother Iyad's house laid his father Yusuf's

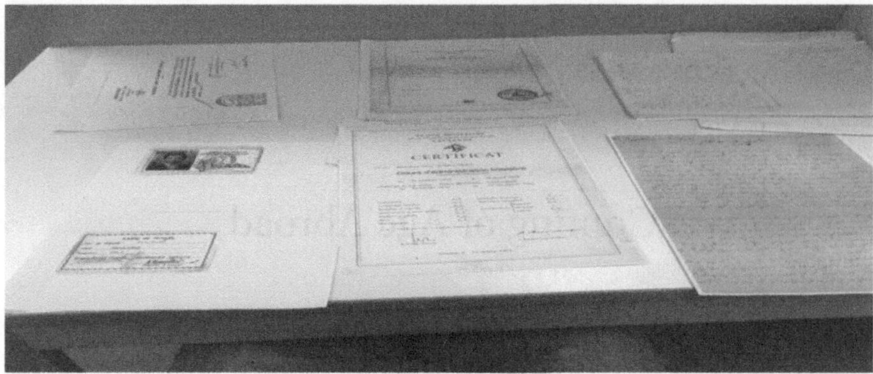

Figure 2.1 A panorama of the documents acquired from Iyad Nuwayhid and the Nuwayhid family. Picture taken by author, June 5, 2018.

papers, including Imad's files and letters. Jawad drove me up to Ras al-Matn that weekend to visit Iyad and their sister Lina.

Part of this visit was nerve racking. Was I pushing too hard? Talking too much about their brother's death? What led to it? The war? The other part was joyful. Imad's siblings and I shared food, laughter, and conversations on their brother, his personality, and his love life. I must have made a decent impression. Iyad agreed to photocopy Imad's files and deliver them to me in Beirut. The location of our second meeting on June 5, 2018 was, to say the very least, fitting: Hotel Phoenicia Intercontinental where his brother Imad once worked.

***

After finishing high school and interning at Hotel Phoenicia Intercontinental, Imad Nuwayhid embarked on his first of several sojourns in Europe. As detailed in the previous chapter, Najib Salha, Hotel Phoenicia owner and friend of the family, cut Imad a break with this Beirut internship. Salha came through for Imad again, this time on the international stage. He secured Imad a paid internship at the newly opened Intercontinental Hotel in Hanover. At age twenty-two, this was Imad's moment; a young Lebanese man in Europe, resolute to experience new things, meet new people, and discover who he was. Unlike in Chapter 1, others' words and descriptions do not have to stand in for Imad. In fifteen letters home, he narrates his time in Europe. As a whole, I find they can provide a window into "coming of age" in the sixties.

The year was 1966. The locale Hanover, West Germany, placing Imad's becoming in Cold War Europe and the "West's" 1960s, an era of political, cultural, social, economic, and sexual upheaval and change, predominately for and by young people.[1] In Chapter 1, I took up the swinging sixties and growing up in the Cold War outside the West, touching on how young people in Beirut made sense of the West, engaged in global capitalism, and started to shape their politics in distinction to American empire. In this chapter, I return to what I referred to as Imad's glocalization (i.e., his global outlook in a certain locale), but in a new context. In Hendrickson's words, I explore "how the Third World may have received the First," particularly while living in it.[2] As an Arab "foreigner" in a European city, Imad provides an answer to this inquiry, but one we may not expect.

In his earliest letters home, Imad laments how the Lebanese and Arabs were less disciplined and ordered than Germans, and more superficial and corrupt. Moreover, one does not find Imad participating in West Germany's sixties, especially politically. Yes, he talked to people about Palestine, which was steadily becoming his cause. But as West German youth of similar political persuasions and international outlooks revolted against their government, Imad was working.[3]

While his radical credentials may not be as obvious during his early days in West Germany, they crystalized the longer he stayed in Europe, a combination of his experiences as a foreign worker and unfolding events back home. In this way, I argue that Imad illuminates a different sixties, not a Western sixties or a Lebanese sixties, but that occupied by foreigners like him in Europe. These sixties were punctuated by a different type of insecurity, one that included discrimination and desperation in the European labor market.[4]

At the same time, his engagement with sixties culture and consumption are undeniable, picking up where he left off in sixties Beirut. Talk of cowboy shirts, Coca-Cola, and collecting records litters the pages of his letters. Between long working hours, he used whatever spare time and cash he had to find leisure and travel, both within the country and elsewhere in Europe. In this way, he was not unlike other middle-class European youth, explorative, mobile, and outward looking.[5]

Until recently, culture, in its own right, was often missing from investigations of the Global Sixties.[6] Imad's letters thus help fill some gaps from a unique vantage point. Nevertheless, an aspect that I find is also absent in Global Sixties Studies is revealed through Imad: the struggle for autonomy during the Cold War. Now in sixties West Germany, Imad balanced pursuing a job and advocating for a liberation cause. Imad, like others of his generation—albeit in a different place and position as a foreigner—chose his own path. I find that these practical radicals sought non-alignment, with goals that would fulfill *both* their political concerns and career aspirations.

This absence of a radical politics, replaced by an alternative vision for autonomy, is most tangible at the micro-level through a series of personal letters Imad wrote home. As Gerber explains, "the personal letter is an intimate artifact of the letter writer."[7] Similarly, Makepeace argues that letters offer a "tenderness, rawness and humility" not often found in memoirs or oral history.[8] In the case of Imad, these letters have the potential to demonstrate his hopes and fears, trials and tribulations, while in sixties Europe.

In consulting such sources, seeking to make broader claims about coming of age abroad, the researcher must proceed with caution. Like many other cases, letters from Imad's family to him are missing, as well as any letters he wrote to friends. Also missing is what Imad chose not to write about, ranging from his political activities to sexual exploits.[9] These omissions could be driven by taboo, but also, in a Cold War context, self-censorship and fear of his letters being read by West German authorities for so-called communist leanings.

I embrace these challenges and speculate—within bounds and alongside secondary scholarship—on what Imad saw, thought, and did, beyond these pages. I also consider where his experience would mesh, or not, with that of young West Germans or other foreigners abroad. Yet, beyond serving as a foggy window into one's life, letters can show how humans build their life through reflection.[10] Whether it was envisioning a career or spelling out his feelings on politics back home, I find that the act of writing was formative in shaping Imad's identity.

Thus, through a close and critical reading of these letters, alongside descriptions of sixties, Cold War West Germany, Imad's becoming away from home comes to life. It starts with his first observations on Europe and Europeans and ends with his commentary on the loss of the Arab side in the 1967 Arab-Israeli war. Alongside a life altering trip to Paris, this particular event transformed Imad and many young Arabs like him. It marked *the* political watershed of his generation.

First Impressions of Sixties Europe

Since I left Beirut I felt strange. Or rather, say it is a new feeling. The plane had left and behind it the ground and with it my thoughts and feelings of determination were unchanged. All that there is that I started thinking of the future.. The past no longer cares but rather it becomes a memory.

—Imad, letter home, September 6, 1966

The above comes from the first lines of Imad's first letter home to his family. He wrote it in Vienna after arriving by plane from Istanbul. It was a comparatively short letter and a bit sloppy, as he wrote fast while waiting for a train to Geneva.[11] In it, Imad waxes poetically, fully aware that this is his coming of age. He conveys to his family what he is experiencing. In a word, excitement—for the future that lays ahead of him in Hanover. But what would Imad find once he arrived?

Hanover's population has hovered around 500,000–600,000 since the 1960s, making it a medium-sized city of West Germany.[12] Quaint, modest, and green, it must have felt much smaller than Beirut. But according to family, Imad liked the place.[13] Known as a connectivity hub in the northern sector of the country—by rail and plane—it was squarely West German.[14] Like other regions of the Federal Republic of Germany, including the walled and divided Berlin, Hanover was molded in the image of the United States in a Cold War context. Isolated and torn immediately following the Nazi era, the Holocaust, and the Second World War, by the 1960s, West Germany had come in from the cold, joining the club—in the eyes of the United States, UK, and France at least—of Western democracies in a "bulwark against Communism" from the east.[15] Economically, West Germany was becoming more integrated, and young West Germans traveled around Europe at unprecedented rates.[16]

So Imad arrived at a transition point: West Germany seeking to move away from its Nazi past and toward a united, westward-looking Europe. While perhaps not as radical or widespread as France or the UK, West Germany had its own '68 moment. Activists sought a reckoning with the past—and the conservative government's inability to reckon with it—criticized a present dominated by consumer culture, and crafted a vision for the future with young, leftist West Germans at the forefront.[17] Ties to the United States cut into the field of activists too, as West German youth looked to American icons in sixties protests, ranging from Abbie Hoffman and the Diggers to Martin Luther King Jr. and the Black Power movement.[18] They took their inspiration from other sources, ranging from Third World causes in spite of the West (like the Algerian War of Independence) to West Germany's some 10,000 foreign students who "served as models of the politically active student."[19]

However, in most respects, Imad Nuwayhid would not be a model. For one, it does not appear he participated in any political movements while in West Germany. In its place, he writes glowingly about what he called *nafsiyat al-Urubiyya*, "the European psyche."[20] His first, most detailed observations were based on his brief stay in Switzerland enroute to West Germany. Imad writes in his second letter home, "and the people here as it appears to me, are modest, naturally socialist, there is no difference between the rich and the poor … And everyone treats you with great respect and appreciation and never chase you for thanks or money."[21]

Imad would come to revise this outlook slightly, or at least see difference in the more politically conservative, West German context. Yet, from the beginning of his travels, Imad, as a budding leftist himself, was excited to be in Europe, a place where socialism seemed mainstream, not just practiced in small student circles like in Beirut. As indicated in the above quote, Imad thought this socialist outlook seeped into European hospitality. "It is possible to get to know anyone you want [by] knock[ing] on their door … They respect those who respect them and respect their system."[22] Imad clearly respected their way and wanted to learn about it from as many people as possible. By his own count in one letter, he once spoke with twenty people in a single day.[23]

One thing Imad had a lot to say about was the status of women in Europe, especially women at work. While writing home from Geneva, he expands on women's labor:

> the women work in every field, nice beautiful women, school aged pupils, university students, all of them work, you see them in the restaurants, they serve the customers, they sell newspapers, they sell tickets in the bus, they sweep the roads … I have been pleased by this activity, that spirit, this exuberance, and women from our country are submissive, who do not know [anything] but new hairstyles and shoes.[24]

In what reads as perhaps his most absorbing observation—in a letter addressed to his father alone—Imad reveals several things about himself, the culture he came from, and the one he is watching. First, he is extremely impressed by what he sees in Europe. Ranging from ticket takers to students, women work in all sectors. They are active, not merely equal to men, but they are almost like men. In the same letter he writes, "What caught my attention are the old women in their hats and their elegance … they spend time in the coffee shops, they sit in the public parks, like men, as they lack [nothing] but the loss of time."[25]

The way Imad describes women also provides a window into his worldview coming into form. His stance on women's equality was similar to that of socialist, communist, or even secular nationalist opinions on the topic across the globe at the time.[26] For one, consider post-revolutionary China, where "the official view of women has continued to stress heavily, and often exclusively, the economic determinants of women's status, with the major concern being to mobilize women into social production."[27] At least at the age of twenty-two, and as it related to young women, to work was to be a good woman. This, for Imad, is in contrast to the Lebanese woman, who was, in a word, superficial. Here, Imad offers an anti-capitalist critique: humans consumed by styles and products is detrimental. What is perhaps more noticeable though is the comparisons themselves, between progress in Europe and decadence in Lebanon.

These distinctions followed Imad to West Germany. Three months into his internship, he praised the West German work ethic. "In Germany," he writes, "the man is like a machine [as] he works without fatigue or complaint, serving, striving for the sake of his future and his nation's future." This was unlike the Lebanese, who "do not work except to receive the public pension [*al-maʿash*] at the end of the month, and where are you sons of my nation?"[28]

As many young, leftist West Germans criticized their society, their past, and their government, Imad praised the people and their system. This is most clear when considering his comparisons to Lebanon, where people work solely for money, not national development. Imad's words amount to an indictment on capitalism in Lebanon, where he comments on how the state and private companies alike imposed conditions similar to *al-sukhra*, "forced labor."[29] That Imad uses this term shows that he, as a young student of the Left, was aware of the history of low wage or no wage labor—often for infrastructural projects—under the Ottoman and French colonial systems.[30] To Imad, the main difference in 1960s *laissez-faire* Lebanon was that the Lebanese were doing this work for a meager salary in an equally unfulfilling, unregulated, and exploitative system.[31]

These favorable characterizations toward Europe and away from Lebanon extended beyond work and into culture, temperament, and "civilization," *al-hadara*, a term Imad frequently uses when describing the differences between the Lebanese and Germans.[32] Take these comparisons:

> You look at them [the Germans] and you see gentleheartedness on their eyes, you see calmness on their faces, for things upset them, for things disturb their lives, they work, and they do not argue a thing, never.

> [In Lebanon] I recall those weak faces, those scary eyes, the peculiarity, those pale faces, which you see confusion and a lack of tranquility, you see unhappiness and fear for the future and they hide in holes and trenches.. sigh..sigh with a growing heartbreak and sigh with a pain for the sons of my nation.[33]

Ethical workers vs. profit seekers; sacrifice vs. superficialness; poised vs. scared; strong vs. weak; vivaciousness vs. paleness; at this juncture, Imad saw West Germany as extraordinary in many respects, and thought that he, his country, and his people could learn something from these people.

In his celebration of Germanness, however, he rarely mentions the Nazi Party, Hitler, or the Holocaust. Only once, and much later in his stay, did Imad address "Nazi thinking," still in the air in West Germany. He witnessed white supremacy, as "many of the people … consider other people lesser than them," especially foreigners. He prefaces this by saying that German "intolerance," toward other German citizens at least, "is not driven by hate, malice, or aversion as is the case in our country," an apparent reference to sectarian, inter-personal othering in Lebanon.[34] Here, Imad turns a genuine critique of Germany, based on his growing experience as a foreigner, toward Lebanon. It demonstrates what was the focus of his scorn. Imad targeted his own society and culture.

Imad's writing on loss, inferiority, and self-denigration is what scholars refer to loosely as post-colonialism or the feelings tied to being colonized by the West that extend well beyond those periods.[35] More specifically, Imad was trying to escape those feelings by becoming a part of Europe and saw it as central to his coming of age. He writes that now, living in West Germany he had left, "the life of lavishness which I uprooted" and moved toward "the principles of progress and advancement, principles of the [German] civilization represented in discipline and patience."[36] Hence, much like other Arab foreigners in the West across the twentieth century, Imad, even if subtly, distinguished himself from his homeland to gain access to the West.[37]

Just because Imad criticized his home and people does not mean he enjoyed it. In the same letter where he compared the Lebanese and Germans, ostensibly favoring the latter, he starts with, "My heart is truly weak when describing what pervades with a sense of my feelings towards my new life."[38] Being torn meant his new revelations on Europe were not fixed, unwavering, or unidirectional.

In fact, by the early 1970s, whether living in Europe or Lebanon, Imad changed, proud of his heritage. In one letter home from London, he speaks critically of European society, history, and racism:

> They [the British] get the Pakistani, Hindi, and African people to work under their direction cheaply and within social conditions, to say the least, that are filthy, not appropriate for "civilized people." Is it civilization that the people lie in division and pitting them against each other and dividing them[?][39]

By 1971, his answer to this question was a firm no; European society is not civilized. But this first trip, the first few months, and 1966, was a liminal period. Imad did not speak ill of Europe, nor seemed to be involved in their political upheavals. In the end, as will be shown, it appears Imad was consumed with work and interpersonal relations. But beyond these personal and economic considerations, Imad was pursuing autonomy. He chose to call out issues of his home where he saw them, and his new environs as he came to know them more.

Imad also wrote home about what he did, listened to, and wore. Imad still sported his turtleneck (see Figure 1.1), also a sign of being lefty and young in West Germany.[40] In what appears as a new style direction, he mentions that he wore *libas al-kawbui,* "cowboy clothes."[41] Besides that he did this for four days while traveling, without a change of clothes, he does not describe what he means by this dress. The choice could be a part of the growing Beat and rock scene. It was most inspired by Beatlemania and most active in Hamburg, where Imad once visited.[42] But as Imad never writes on rock music, his new look was more likely tied to hippie counter-culture.[43] Equally importantly though is Imad's reference to European acceptance of this style. "No one looked in disdain or wonder," he claims.[44] Beyond articulating European openness, these words on his style, in a personal letter home, demonstrate that Imad is willing to show his parents who he is becoming.

Yet, there are aspects of Imad's life that he chose to omit. Writing to his whole family after his trip to Hamburg, Imad leaves his description of the infamous Red-Light district of St. Pauli Street at this: "It is not possible to write or describe the views of striptease which you see at every step."[45] Among the bright lights, which he imagined were like "Las Vegas," he reassures his family that he and his male friends did not visit the cabarets, clubs, or bars. "The time did not allow for us to stay up late," due to the supposed early closure of their youth hostel.[46]

Regarding his sex life, Imad was also silent. This shouldn't be a surprise, but this exclusion is paired with an openness to discuss the sex lives of German women. Take this bit from a late 1966 letter, specifically addressed to his father:

> Imagine that the girl here she sleeps with her boyfriend and in the same bed and this is what disgusts me when I think—God forbid—that one of those [girls] will be a part of my future, this with strong respect for their experience in life and their intricate knowledge unbeknownst to the eastern men.[47]

Working through his sexual identity, during West Germany's sexual revolution, Imad was fascinated by European openness and freedom, even in matters that shocked him.[48] But beyond this general commentary, Imad had opportunities to talk about himself, particularly a "German girl" he references often.[49] Jawad Nuwayhid, Imad's brother, confirms this was his girlfriend and that she later visited him in Beirut.[50] Instead of introducing her in his letters as such, he describes her family, written in shorthand as "the Germany family," more than her, almost as if she is not there.[51] In sum, Imad was an open book on the culture he encountered, but he sometimes self-censored when communicating his personal engagement with this culture.

What Imad was always candid on were his daily costs, a place where Lebanon was not actually the target of his criticism. He writes, "Life in Hanover is contradictory, and here essential things are expensive and there [Lebanon] essential things are cheap." This included transportation to work (6 Deutsche marks, or roughly 45 Lebanese lira by Imad's calculations) and food and drink.[52] It was too expensive to eat out, so he often cooked at home (50 marks a week) at his rented apartment (90 marks a month). He also had to foot the bill on household items, as the hotel did not provide bedsheets and a blanket (90 marks) nor an iron (15 marks). If he had the chance to go out with friends and co-workers, he would get a beer (1.5 marks) or a Coca-Cola (1 mark).[53]

We already know that Imad loved music (as described in Chapter 1, mostly pop or classical singers of mixed Arab-European background), but his taste for classical music—not the Beatles—grew in West Germany. On several occasions, he attended concerts with his "female friend" and her family.[54] He reports back:

> Her family loves art, even worships it, and I saw a Concert [capitalized, Latin script] with them the day before yesterday and they were humming when hearing the piano or the violin as Arabs [do] when hearing [famous Egyptian singer] Umm Kulthum … and you all cannot imagine how happy I am :.. and this thing is necessary for culture and the broadening the horizons of life.[55]

Like meeting European people, Imad believed experiencing European culture was enriching him.[56] To this end, he "decided to purchase a classical record" for his apartment. He would do so after "receiving the money [from work] and … the record costs 60 Lebanese lira or 9 marks …"[57]

Through these purchases—as well as travel, including trips around Germany and later to Paris—Imad engaged in the consumptive practices of middle-class European youth in the post-war period. As Schildt and Siegfried argue, "Because the economic circumstances had by and large been stabilized, contemporaries had additional means at their disposal, which could be utilized for interests that were not essential for the assurance of one's existence."[58] Buying Coca-Cola, beer, records, and traveling is both indicative of Imad's life abroad in Europe and shaped—even if in some small way—its mass consumer culture.

At the same time, Imad communicated frustration with the cost of these material goods. In particular, the expense to go out to a café or enjoy a fine meal was a sticking point.[59] This early criticism of Europe's consumer culture, not its politics, was perhaps the main way Imad connected with sixties European protest.[60] But unlike his European counterparts, Imad, a foreigner from the Arab world, experienced a wider gap between the aspiration of an ideal sixties society and the money it took to join it. As Hobsbawm argues, "general affluence never came within sight of the majority of the world's population" during the so-called "Golden Age" of the 1960s.[61] Indeed, this gulf would come to color the political becoming of Imad and many other practical radicals like him.

Foreigners and West Germany

Shortly after arriving in Hanover in September 1966, Imad started his job at the Intercontinental Hotel (see Figure 2.2).[62] The 9-story, 300-room hotel had opened a year earlier downtown, across the street from the iconic city hall.[63] Like Imad's prior place of employment, Beirut's Hotel Phoenicia, it was, according to an Intercontinental press release titled the "Showplace of Hannover," an attempt "to combine the old with the new."[64] Also like the Phoenicia, it was part of the corporation's late Cold War era expansion. As I argued in Chapter 1, the objective was to build an American empire through tourism and win the Cold War by inculcating pro-US business practices across these regions.

Imad's first posting was in room service, a new section for him in the industry, followed by rotations in the bar and kitchen.[65] Imad often worked two six-hour shifts, regardless of section, with a break in between those shifts, six days a week. This amounted to a seventy-two-hour work week.[66] A typical day, as he explains to his family in an October 1966 letter home, looked something like this:

> I begin work either at five or six in the morning … and when I return to
> my residence I retire to bed at eight as work is somewhat burdensome and

I got used to this a little ... With all this fatigue, I am in much pleasure
and diligence and after two days I will obtain more profits in the section
which I work [room service] ... estimated at 20–40 marks, [which] will help
me a lot.[67]

Early mornings, no late nights, joy, hard work, and a learning curve in a new
position. Imad may have been determined, but he was also tired, and driven
by profits.

Imad was one of some 425,000 foreigners who started work in West
Germany in 1966, what the government, citizenry, and workers themselves
referred to loosely as *gastarbeiter*, guest worker(s). For that year, the number

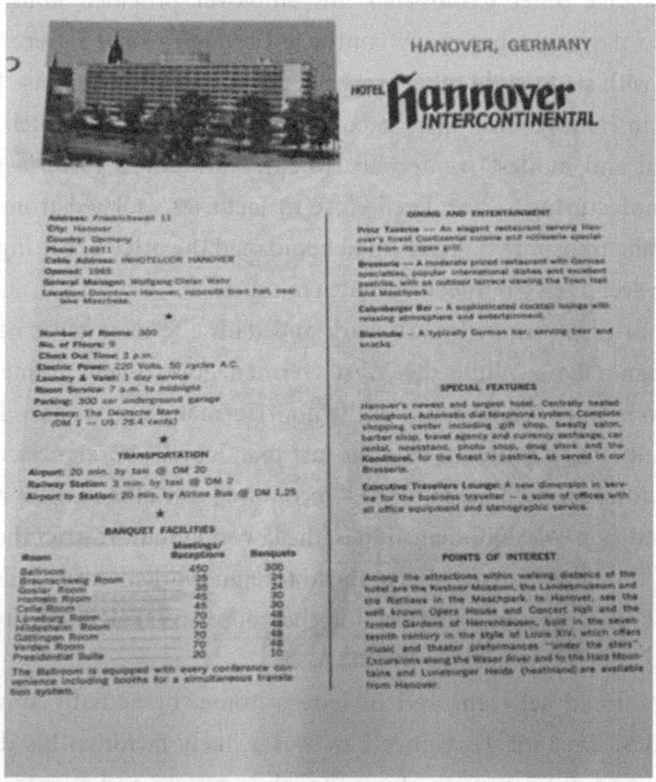

Figure 2.2 An Intercontinental fact sheet for its hotel in Hanover. The "newest and
largest" hotel in the city at the time is pictured top left in addition to information on its
"special features" and "points of interest" in the area. "Hotel Hannover Intercontinental,"
1966, Intercontinental Hotel Corporation, Box 1, in Pan American World Airways,
Inc. records. Courtesy of Special Collections, University of Miami Libraries, Coral
Gables, Florida.

of foreign workers in West Germany was almost 300,000 more than any other country in Europe.[68] This was part of West Germany's post-war development plan, responding to a shrinking western European workforce and the "redomestication" of women in the 1950s.[69] Starting in 1955, the West Germany government began recruiting Italians to fill these labor shortages, and by the 1960s, Turks and Yugoslavians constituted the two largest foreign workforces.[70]

However, Imad was not a contracted *gastarbeiter*, but an intern. While there is an abundance of research on the plight of the *gastarbeiter*, Imad's experiences provide a window into the much less known situation of foreign interns in sixties Europe—more comfortable in some ways, more insecure in others.[71] Like other *gastarbeiter*, his employer provided housing (even if he had to pay rent), but many contracted foreign workers were forced to cohabitate with six to eight other workers.[72] This was never the case for Imad, who while in Hanover lived in a "nice room," arranged by the hotel, and then a "beautiful and modest" rented apartment.[73] Moreover, *gastarbeiter*, often in the manufacturing sector, lived close to factories, isolated from cities or reliable public transport.[74] While Imad bemoaned the price of getting to work, it was only ever a ten- to fifteen-minute commute.[75]

Similar to *gastarbeiter*, Imad's work and daily life were governed by the 1965 Foreigner Law. While the West German government framed it as a necessity to legalize the presence of the non-German, non-western European workforce, it codified foreign labor as just that: labor.[76] Foreigners were seen as commodities and evaluated for their economic role alone unless it entailed potential sedition. As Slobodian argues, the law sought to "restrict the political activity of foreigners," particularly those foreign workers and students who protested West Germany support for the repressive rulers of their home countries.[77]

Whether Imad self-censored in letters home, or actually stayed away from politics, the 1965 Foreigner Law was a likely factor in his decision.[78] However, Imad did complain about the labor system and stigmas faced by foreign workers. He discusses days and events where he had to work those two shifts, but back to back, without a break—"we don't go to our house except to sleep even without food after more than 12 hours of work."[79] And while not speaking of his employers or co-workers, Imad comments that for all their positive traits and love for their country, many Germans "hate foreigners and try to enslave them."[80]

What Imad did not share with other *gastarbeiter*, the main source of his complaints, but also his uniqueness, was a contract or residential permit.[81] Per the 1965 Foreigner Law, the duration of a foreign worker's stay was always meant to be temporary, two years, although many stayed longer. The mechanism by which individuals were official and outstayed their contracts was "bilateral recruitment treaties."[82] West Germany had such agreements with several non-neighboring countries, including Turkey, Yugoslavia, Portugal, and Morocco, but not Lebanon.[83] In fact, Imad appears to be the only Lebanese worker at his hotel. When the money was good, or funds were coming in from his family, he did experience something like a European middle-class lifestyle, going out with friends and traveling around the continent. This did not change the fact that his position at Hanover Intercontinental did not come with immediate protection of residence, making his work situation less formalized and his pay unreliable.

Imad was informed by his employer that he could apply for residency and receive a worker's permit. He kept his family abreast of these developments, which caused much frustration. "From the side of the work permit," he writes in December 1966, "the answer was always negative and I have learned that it is impossible now to receive it."[84] Perhaps Imad was a bit dramatic here, because in January he follows up, "I did not lose hope in it [the permit] never but I have to wait around a month or two months to claim it. That is after I have been [here] for six months."[85] As of spring 1967, it appears he still did not have one, but it is unclear if the issue was ever resolved.[86]

This meant that at least through the first half of his internship, Imad did not have a formal salary. He was paid on a job-by-job basis, tips, overtime work, or an informal increase to pay, like a holiday bonus. One day Imad reported back, "I work daily more than 12 hours without pay," which pushed him to find a night job working at a gas station.[87] Exasperated with his situation, struggling to survive, he ends the above quoted letter to his family with a notice that "I await my monthly money from you all."[88]

This last line became a fixture of Imad's letters. Given his tenuous work status, high daily costs in West Germany, and the want for some kind of leisure, Imad often asked for money. Take these examples:

> Please also increase the amount which you all will send to me this month
> which is to 200 marks because of expenses at the beginning of the year.[89]
>
> and truly you have been late [in sending money] recently … and this
> delay caused an imbalance in my budget and my payments and I am still
> in this imbalance today … please expedite this so that it arrives around 200
> marks.[90]
>
> I plead of you to send [100] marks as well and more because of the
> transportations [to get home to Lebanon] and some [dental] payments cost
> a lot.[91]

While letters sent from Imad's family are absent for consultation, it appears his family always came through, even if they were late by Imad's standards. As I noted in Chapter 1, Imad's family was fairly well off. His father Yusuf's modest teacher salary meant they could fund Imad's situation.[92] This did not flatten his hardships, but likely made them more manageable. At the same time, this was not a one-way relationship. Imad added money to his thanks, sometimes sending home a portion of what he owed his parents for their investment in him.[93]

The long workdays, uncertainty around receiving a permit, and the insecurity of this position pressed on Imad. This resulted in homesickness, one of the most palpable emotions exhibited throughout Imad's letters. A month into his internship, Imad writes the following:

> You all went for a week and did not receive a letter from me and I troubled
> you all and concerned you all and anxiety took you over, and how am I, and
> I am alone with strange people around me and how am I as long as I do not
> know your news for three weeks … and I bring you all into my loneliness..I
> was lying to myself when I thought that I am not affected, as your letter came
> as clear evidence on my feelings towards you all, and I shed tears, tears of
> pleasure and joy when I read the first word.[94]

Imad's words carry regret and sadness—regret for not having time to write a letter, presumably because of the grueling days, sadness that he had not heard from his parents in several weeks. Yet, his family always responded to his letters, quite promptly. This is marked by the word "answered," inscribed by Imad's father on the majority of letters I investigated.[95] And although I do not know what they said to their son, it is clear that Imad cared for his family.

This to his sister in one letter: "Lina, so what is her news, and did she pass her school exams." To his brother, "Jawad, how is he. I hope for his success and passing."[96] And to his father, I "ask from you to be very patient in this time of hardship with the beginning of the new school year."[97]

While Imad depended on the love of his family and their financial investment, this does not mean he had no support network while in Europe nor that he hated his job. For one, he reports warmly on a blowout of a Christmas party, hosted by the hotel, attended by some 300 people, workers, guests, and city residents alike.[98] In another letter, Imad commends his colleagues and "the mutual love between the comrades."[99] The use of the word *al-rifaq*, comrades, in a brotherly and Marxist sense, is instructive; some of his colleagues were more than just co-workers and perhaps shared some of his political views about the world.

Imad describes several new friends in letters home to his family. One was an unnamed Irish colleague, who lent him a bike to get to work.[100] In another letter Imad makes passing reference to a Turkish friend, but most important was an Egyptian.[101] He "works in the hotel," Imad describes. "He is like a brother to me living in the neighboring room to me[,] he always advises me and guides me down the right path and he is very experienced."[102] Imad later clarifies that his friend is twenty-seven, five years older than him, and that he is a Coptic Christian who taught English in Syria and enjoyed his travels to Lebanon. It appears he had come to Germany to teach, but Imad laments, "luck did not help him here," likely a reference to similar issues that his friend faced getting a worker's permit. After a long day of work, Imad would wait up for him "so we could stay up later together, a day does not go by without us sitting, reporting, and discussing."[103]

Having an older mentor who could help navigate labor informality would be crucial for a young Arab in Europe. Imad had other Arab contacts along the way to his job, including Dr. Ali Ghaith, who studied medicine and lived in Geneva.[104] The Ghaiths and Nuwayhids were neighbors in Beirut, so Dr. Ali was happy to help him get situated in Europe.[105] Although coming of age may have been distinct for an Arab in sixties West Germany, to lean on migrant networks is an inter-generational and transnational phenomenon.[106] While Imad had some European friends—including the family and young woman he spent many weekends and holidays with—these forms of support were a lifeline and likely made Europe feel a bit more like home.

Even though it is unclear whether Imad ever received a worker's permit, he was eventually provided insurance of sorts for a major dental procedure. He details this in a letter to his family alongside a complex diagram on the work to be done. "I do not know how much this will cost me," Imad states bluntly.[107] But later during his stay, after apparently enrolling for "social security," he was able to get most of that operation paid off.[108] Thus, even as the system as a whole eluded foreigners who hoped to create more long-term careers in Europe, Imad was able to reap some of its benefits.

While homesickness, tooth pain, and inferiority plagued Imad, he believed his life in Europe, at least at this juncture, was part of a greater and necessary good. Late in his internship, he writes "Truly that I am tired at work, but this is for my benefit and my future."[109] That future included multiple hopes and dreams that he outlines in his letters: attending hotel administration school in Switzerland at *École Hôtelière de Lausanne*, taking an internship in London, and working in Ireland. Essential to all of this, Imad believed, was language training. He practiced English with his Irish friend and loved working in room service, because "I am able to speak with many of the workers and the guests in the rooms and my knowledge in the German language has become not too bad."[110] He considered German a difficult language. To supplement this onsite training, Imad enrolled in German-language classes for a six-month period. It cost him 45 marks, or 300 lira, something his parents likely helped fund.[111]

These people, whether friends, teachers, or family, were guiding Imad toward the career he imagined for himself. Still hardships abound. After expressing interest in applying to *École Hôtelière de Lausanne* in an October 1966 letter, he writes the following in December:

> My kind father: The topic of my rejection in Lausanne may concern you and this a natural thing for every father who watches over his son and helps in crystalizing his affairs and I was also surprised [by the rejection] but the situation fluctuated and I decided to remain in Germany [for the] year to learn German then after that move to England for a period of nine months to train in its hotel in Reception [capitalized, in Latin script] and the Front Office [same] and this has been advised to me by Mazen Salha in Beirut..and this will help me to learn English well.[112]

Imad's surprise was warranted. He met the degree and French-language qualifications for admittance at *École Hôtelière de Lausanne*.[113] It appears that his lack of experience in reception, the course he applied for, and limited knowledge of other European languages, dashed his hopes.

Regardless of the why, notice the detail in which Imad spells out these decisions for his father. One reading of this is practical. Imad needed his father's buy-in (emotional and financial) to take this alternative path, one that he was pushed into after failing to get into *École Hôtelière de Lausanne*. This is likely the reason that Imad mentions Mazen Salha, the son of Najib Salha, his former boss and a well-respected family friend.

But there is another reading here, a more optimistic one, even given what befalls Imad in the wake of the 1967 War, the 1973 Lebanese army-Palestinian *fedayeen* clashes, and the 1975 Civil War. Imad hoped to build upon his internship—instead of seeing it as a one-time, botched experiment—seeking out other work experiences and cultivating skills in Europe. The assumption for Imad, his parents, and other foreigners abroad was that these experiences would benefit their career and life. However, they needed capital to create that path. These are the practical components of youth like Imad, working within the system, even as they critiqued it, and mobilizing their parents' hope in them to sustain their dreams.

The Shock of '67

The crisis and what we have been through is nothing but a blow to the head, we lost our nerves, we lost our confidence, we got scared, we trembled.[114]

The crisis that Imad is referring to in this June 26, 1967, letter is the Arab-Israeli War of 1967. This is the first, and chief, political issue or contemporary event that concerned Imad while abroad. He is silent on war in Vietnam. He does not comment on recent elections in France. Closer to his current residence, there is no mention in his letters of the Shah of Iran's infamous June 1967 visit to West Germany.[115] Again, the omissions may be due to self-censorship. Equally plausible is that Imad assumed his parents did not know about these events or they would not care. Regarding events in West Germany, perhaps, as I have suggested above, Imad was working, striving toward a career, largely isolated from local politics. But the war of 1967, one he would write extensively on, a war that occurred thousands of miles away, would leave the strongest imprint on his personal becoming and those Arabs of his generation.

In several letters home leading up to the June war, Imad mentions Palestine. Unfolding events were a point of conversation with friends and acquaintances alike. In these discussions, it reads as if Imad took every opportunity to let Germans know what he thought about the issue. For example, in January 1967, while at his German family's house, a TV report came up on "exercises of the Palestinian [Liberation] Army and its maneuvers in the Sinai," part of what would become the escalation leading to the 1967 war. He writes "and the information of the political people [read politicians, maybe analysts] here is very weak and slim … and it is easy for you to convince [friends and family] of your view and this is what I always do especially regarding our Arab issue …"[116]

These Germans were likely more sympathetic than some of their brethren, given that they had spent time in Turkey and Syria.[117] 'Arif Hajjaj, a Palestinian studying in West Germany at the University of Heidelberg at the same time, had a very different experience when discussing Palestine. According to Prestel, 'Arif could never convince German students of the Palestinian perspective as they, in 'Arif's own words, "suffer[ed] feelings of guilt towards the Jews." Still much like Imad, to advocate for Palestine provided 'Arif with a "feeling of responsivity towards [his] homeland."[118]

Beyond passing references to Palestine, Imad gives a more detailed account in a May 1967 letter. He provides his commentary on Arab politics, Gamal Abdel Nasser, Israel, and German media coverage, and in some small way, it shows the worldview of an Arab youth, abroad, in the very moment before the loss. First, Imad conveys the plot points common in most histories of the 1967 war, especially regarding Egypt's role in the leadup. They include Nasser's demand for UN troops to evacuate Egyptian-administered Gaza and the Gulf of Aqaba; Nasser's decision to increase troops in the Sinai following that demand to the UN; and that Nasser's calculations were part of a defensive posturing not an act of war.[119] What is more unique is Imad's focus on the "Israeli Jewish propaganda" on the war and how it shaped

West German perspectives.[120] That coverage, in Imad's estimation, was categorically anti-Nasser.

He describes West German characterizations in newspapers, television, and on the street as such:

> You hear the German opinion all of it against Nasser because he is the initiator and because he wants the war and wants the destruction and this is inhumane from him and uncivilized and that he wants the expulsion of the Jew or to displace them.[121]

Imad does not critique any of these positions, likely because he knows his parents, like him, would see them as biased toward Israel. Instead, he stresses the following to his family: "What is absent is the facts and truths which have befallen the Palestinian people since the Nakba [disaster, the 1948 Arab-Israeli war]."[122]

Imad appreciated the German spirit, but not their impartiality on the issue of Palestine. In this media, Jews of Israel were painted as tragic victims alone with no discussion of the displacement and depopulation of Arab Palestine. This did not make Imad angry, I believe. He came to expect this denial, so he writes about it, simply as a matter of *al-waqa'i' wa al-haqa'iq*, "facts and truths."[123] In other words, akin to the intellectuals he would later come to admire, he states firmly what Germans miss (a Palestinian or Arab perspective), and why they miss it (unconditional support for Israel), both as a means to expose the perspective as propaganda.

At the end of this portion of this May 1967 letter, Imad asks, "Is it possible for you all to explain to me the issue and its developments in detail and far from the twisting and feelings, but coupled with evidence"?[124] While this is a place where letters from Imad's family to their son would be illuminating, it is unlikely Imad ever got that context before the June war.[125] In their absence, what is most intriguing is the question itself. It indicates that Imad trusted his parents' perspectives on these dynamics and relied on them.

Note Imad's engagement with the German press in this letter, but not that of the Arabic press. In fact, it does not appear Imad was reading Lebanese newspapers while in West Germany. In 1967 at least, none were in circulation.[126] His family could have been sending him papers along with money, but Imad never mentions this in his letters. In its place, he thanks his father for sending him a book titled *al-Wasit fi al-Qanun al-Dusturi, The Broker in Constitutional Law*. In the wake of Imad's rejection at Lausanne, this is perhaps a subtle suggestion that he considered a change in career path.[127] Regardless, this absence of discussion—or reading—of the leftist press in Beirut strengthens my conviction that Imad kept his head down in Europe, focusing on his job, not European or Arab politics, until the events in his home country no longer afforded him that luxury.

His next letter, weeks after the six-day defeat of Egyptian, Syrian, and Jordanian forces by Israel, begins with "Wow, and one thousand wows" regarding "the days of the crisis around the tenth of the present month ... I have been in great pain."[128] It is not strange that Imad conveys surprise and agony with the loss. They mirror popular sentiment in the Arab world following the loss.[129] Walid Nuwayhid, Imad's cousin, tells me, in Lebanon, "Our feelings in that time were disaster, all of us, because we believed that Egypt and Abdel Nasser are very strong, and they will protect us, and they are strong enough to defeat [Israel]. We think that we lost everything. It's a very sad story."[130] Imad's friend, Nabil Khishin, who like Walid was in Lebanon at the time, concurs: "It was a catastrophe for us. We believed [in] all the years of [military] buildup ... [that] Abdel Nasser will liberate Palestine ... And to be honest until now I cannot understand what happened in 1967 ... Everyone couldn't believe what happened."[131]

Nevertheless, it may be odd to Arabic speakers that Imad uses the word *azma*, crisis, and not *hazima* (defeat) or *naksa* (setback), the latter of which Nasser used immediately to downplay the loss.[132] *Azma* reads more generic, and in some contexts, a neutral or conservative take on a conflict.[133] Imad was neither. His use reflects his shock, but also hope that this is merely a smaller crisis and not a life altering event. The trauma of the defeat, alas, would continue to overwhelm Imad, Walid, Nabil, and millions of other Arabs.

Beyond shock and sadness, Imad felt despair that an event like this could happen so close to home. Imad was too young for the 1948 Nakba, or the 1958 war in Lebanon, but this war, in his youth, made him worry about his family. Imad "pained for [their] pain," he admits, "because waiting [was] difficult, and in waiting was agony. My heart trembled, I was saddened, I did not know what to do, did you receive my letter or not."[134] At the same time, Imad's young compatriots in Lebanon prepared for a fight. In his memoir, leftist activist Fawwaz Traboulsi claims that from the first day of the war, Arab students at the American University of Beirut "volunteered" to go defend Damascus and Amman.[135] Not quite university age yet, Walid Nuwayhid, pleaded to his father, unsuccessfully, to "join the fighting."[136] Yet, a foreigner abroad, all Imad could do was fret. He was first and foremost concerned about his loved ones, not merely the state of Arab politics.

In June, Imad actually commented more on the role of the United States in the war than anything specific going on in Lebanon, Egypt, Jordan, or Syria. He writes, "Today we knew America intervened, today we knew that America conspired against us."[137] This admission is not striking in form. Imad is echoing a claim Nasser made since the loss: the US Air Force had participated in airstrikes with Israel against Egypt. Most historians of the war and US foreign policy refute this.[138] While the United States had given Israel offensive helicopters in 1966, that was a onetime sale meant to counterbalance their pre-existing military support for Jordan.[139]

Imad's admission is, however, striking in its presence alone and marks his political transformation in motion. As I detailed in Chapter 1, in his engagements with an American corporation—Intercontinental—and his contact with American-funded missionaries in his home village—Daniel Oliver and the school and orphanage in Ras al-Matn—Imad never criticized the United States or its role in the Middle East. Before this June 1967 letter, Imad only once mentioned America, noting a conversation he had with his German-speaking colleagues and guests on the "American control over the German economy."[140] But, in the summer of 1967, the ire of many young Arabs with America grew. This was as the United States moved much closer to Israel, the birth of the so-called "special relationship."[141] These militaristic aspects of American empire, not its earliest influence through tourism or education, would lead Imad to refashion his views of the United States.

The year 1967 also shook Imad's outlook on the path toward Arab and Palestinian liberation. He writes, "We became spineless ourselves, emotion terrified us and overcame us ..."[142] The "we" here, I do not think, is the Lebanese, or Arab civilization more broadly, like observed in Imad's earlier letters. Rather it is Arab states, and Arab heads of state more precisely. Imad began to lose faith in the offered plans of the 1960s to beat Zionism. He was not alone. His friend Nabil says, "Like every war … ['67] generated some positive results. Like the rise of the Palestinian resistance."[143]

Historian Yoav Di-Capua believes June '67 to be the May '68 of the Arab world. I agree with this sentiment, and like him, I describe in the following chapters how the shock it generated turned Arab nationalists into Marxists, and signaled the Arab Left's full investment in the Palestinian cause.[144] To be clear, before 1967, some Arab nationalist and leftists forces in Lebanon were already centering Palestinian liberation in their agendas, forces that Imad was connected to.[145] But, the magnitude of the loss marks the turning point away from a state-centric, Nasser-led approach to Palestinian liberation. Post-'67 almost all leftist parties and movements in Lebanon inched closer and closer to the ideology of armed struggle and working directly with the newly formed Palestinian Liberation Organization.

More broadly, Imad's growing support for unconventional warfare and guerrilla tactics, apparent in subsequent years, was not unlike others across the globe. From Uruguay to Vietnam, through Palestine, young people in the Global Sixties were engaging in "conversations about 'paths to revolution' … [,] emphasizing a need for armed struggle and discussing the role of younger generations in these political processes."[146] Connected regionally and globally, Imad was part of an Arab generation demanding to be more involved and searching for new answers.

~

Equally contributing to Imad's changing views was a trip to Paris in September 1967. Its timing was significant, in the wake of the war, and by his own estimation, it was "the trip of a lifetime."[147] He strolled the city, one day taking a long trek from the Louvre to the Arc de Triomphe to the Eiffel Tower. He also connected with his father—who trained at the Sorbonne on his way to teaching at the prestigious *Lycée Français de Beyrouth*—by walking by its campus and going to museums and historical sites like Yusuf would have.[148]

Most important, the trip made him see West Germany differently. Speaking to his family on Paris as a global, diverse city, Imad relays, "The pleasure from this [is] that you are not asked what is your nationality as is the case in Germany. The foreigner in Germany is known in its form and color … and somewhat despised …" Moreover, he saw the French "closer to the revolution, to liberation" than the ordered Germans, the former of which reminded him of the "psychology" of the Lebanese: "short patience [, the Frenchman and Lebanon] acts immediately."[149]

Imad was still self-critical, discussing in his Paris letter that the rebellious spirit that connected France to Lebanon could spawn indifference.[150] Nevertheless, these are new opinions, ones Imad had not expressed before. Following a long, trying stay in West Germany and the trauma of a war loss, his trip to Paris provided an alternative West. Hence, I find that the radicalism of the sixties, at least in Imad's case as a working foreigner, did not come like a wave. It was gradual, contextual, and personal. Following this period in his life, Imad believed that the way to rebuild Arab civilization, and counter the self-denigration he felt in Germany, was to forge a revolution against the reactive forces, locally and globally, that held Arabs, Palestinians, and Lebanese down. As I explain in the subsequent chapters, after Europe Imad began to invest more in this logic, little by little, ceding the autonomy he had as a practical radical.

Coming Home

The last day of Imad's internship was October 15, 1967. He left the country four days later.[151] It appears the pay, tasks, and mere status as an intern had run its course. His boss, Wolfgang-Dieter Wehr, wrote a glowing recommendation. "We are happy to certify that Mr. Nouaihed made use of the opportunities available to him to expand his knowledge of the hotel business … [. He] is a polite and friendly employee who always reliably and correctly carried out the tasks assigned to him."[152]

Imad's last days in Hanover coincided with a recession in West Germany and a subsequent flight of foreign workers, including 98,000 more leaving when compared with the year before.[153] The economic downturn of 1966–7, felt from the United States to Lebanon, could be why it was so hard for Imad to secure more permanent residence in West Germany or employment elsewhere Europe.[154] While Imad had earlier expressed his hope to train with Intercontinental in England or Ireland, he admits in his second to last letter home that "after waiting four months[,] my travel and work license … arrived, but I will not travel today … and this is my final decision …"[155] In his last letter, perhaps feeling the need to clarify, he writes, "The decision to return to Beirut is more important than travel to Ireland, a new field of culture, learning, and mastering English, but life is expensive and [I have] very little money."[156] The former could have been true, but would have not been an issue if the latter was not more true. Imad knew his family would understand his financial hardships, and that one could only dream up a career if they could afford it. For this reason, Imad "temporarily postponed" his plans and came home to Beirut.[157]

Mu'aqataan, temporarily, is the key word here. Perhaps what is most fascinating in his letters, which include many fascinations—from commentary on German and Lebanese women to diagrams of dental work—is that everything Imad set out to do and be he did later in his life. Rejected at *École Hôtelière de Lausanne* in 1966, he would be accepted and attend in 1969. Unable to travel to England or Ireland in 1967, these were places he would work in 1971–2. And in his final letter home, he requests, "As to my affairs for my affiliation to the Lebanese University Law division, I plead you all do not forget or delay in any way from [sending] the forms."[158] This last ask to his parents, among many asks, was so he could attend the upcoming winter term, which he did, starting November 1967.

These were all steps along Imad's job trajectory, those which he built in his letter writing. To adapt Charles Sabel's words for our purposes, Imad was imagining "a career at work." Coming of age abroad in the West's sixties and internalizing inferiority, Imad also progressed into what he thought he would become in the workforce. At the same time, as Imad's relationship to Europe was changing, becoming more complicated by current events and experiences as a foreign worker, he imagined a world where Palestinians and Arabs were truly liberated. Like Sabel's worker interviewees from the United States and Europe, Imad could hold contradictory views on work and politics, but became "obligated by the nature of [this] dilemma to determine the relation of his political beliefs to his economic world view."[159] Imad would continue to shape his politics, almost in spite of his job. Yet, at least for the time being, his vision of a career at work, and the importance of that work, was unwavering.

To be a practical radical, I argue, was to navigate, mediate, and negotiate these forces of capitalism and total revolution. To this end, it is important to remember where Imad came from to draw conclusions on coming of age as a foreigner abroad in the Global Sixties. His first letter home reads, "I felt a new personality changed above the clouds and I began a milestone of personal determination. Perhaps a personality of determination was attracted to me, the new personality began to enter my being."[160] Simply put, star-gazing young people are not just determined for the sake of a job. For Imad, perhaps he did not know it when he left West Germany in 1967, but the determination to solidify his position as an Arab leftist in a changing world would only grow.

3

Radical Translations, Practical Decisions

Meeting the Comrades

Ras al-Matn, May 16, 2016

The first time I visit Imad Nuwayhid's village was with his cousin Iman Nuwayhid. After a meeting in Beirut, Iman is kind enough to invite me for a day trip to Ras al-Matn. On the trip, I am introduced to Iman's brother, Walid Nuwayhid. I had already met him though, in the archives at least. December 9, 1975, the Lebanese Communist Party's newspaper al-Nida' reported that Walid had spoken on behalf of Imad's family and friends at a rally in honor of Imad that took place in Ras al-Matn following Imad's death. From the article, I wasn't sure if Walid was affiliated to the Communist Party, as he was referred to as a "comrade" without a party position. But I got the sense that Walid was close to Imad—his cousin, friend, and brother in arms in the Left.

Walid confirms my gut feeling when we meet in Ras al-Matn. He and Imad were close, or close enough that he knew the following: while Imad was living in Paris in the late 1960s, he was compelled by a French intellectual to translate Abram Leon's book La Conception Matérialiste de la Question Juive, The Jewish Question: A Marxist Interpretation. Per one Communist Party remembrance, I was already aware Imad had translated this book. Yet, hearing this story about a young Lebanese idealist, living in Paris, perhaps in the midst of Paris' 1968 moment, urged to translate, was a milestone along the way of turning a section of my dissertation on a largely anonymous "martyr" into this book on Imad Nuwayhid.

Walid was not a member of the Communist Party with Imad, but part of the Lebanese Communist Action Organization, a group formed in the 1970s within

Lebanon's constellation of leftist parties and movements. Walid is a journalist, starting his career with his organizational newspaper, al-Muharir, and continuing in Lebanon and beyond (Cyprus, London, Bahrain) well after the war. As Walid and I talk about Imad and my project, he encourages me to get in touch with one of Imad's closest comrades, Nabil Khishin, who, Walid says, would likely know more about Imad's days in France.

Beirut, June 16, 2022

I sit in a restaurant on West Beirut's iconic Hamra Street as I watch the man I just met, Nabil, shout the following at Jawad Nuwayhid's son: "If you love America so much why don't you go live there." Imad's siblings, Jawad and Iyad, had kindly invited me out for a family lunch at their younger brother Salim's restaurant called Little Beirut, and I asked them if Nabil (who I had yet to meet) could come. Jawad knew Nabil from their school days in the 1960s and he agreed to my invitation. He may have regretted this decision—I did—as he watched his 22-year-old son get yelled at by Nabil.

Since I met Walid Nuwayhid in 2016, he had tried to coordinate a get together between Nabil Khishin and myself. Once we finally connected via email in 2018, Nabil informed me that he didn't see Imad when he was living in France. Instead, while in Lebanon, Nabil helped his friend translate The Jewish Question: A Marxist Interpretation. The two were a part of a leftist group in the late 1960s called the Union of Lebanese Communists. Like Walid, Nabil eventually moved outside Lebanon, first studying in Lyon and then working as a translator in Dubai. Although I was interested in meeting any of Imad's comrades, that Nabil could speak to Imad's translation pushed me to set up a meeting with him next time I was in Lebanon.

At Little Beirut on Hamra Street, Nabil asks me what I thought about American foreign policy in the Middle East and elsewhere, and I gave him my opinion on its indiscretions. Jawad's son interjects with his own view, largely in support of the United States, and the argument ensued. While I do not recall the points either made, I later wrote in my notes, "really awkward but [Nabil] does appear stuck in ways even if right." After the contention subsided, and the meal was over, I walk Nabil to his car and he explains his worldview. He sees Marxism as scientific, not ideological. If someone were to show him another appealing way, he'd be open, but he hasn't seen anything better. I learn over our next few meetings that he bemoans those who were with him and Imad in the sixties and seventies, but have since taken a step away from the causes of the Lebanese Left. One of those men, who Nabil and Walid urge me to meet as well, is Rida Ismael.

Beirut, June 22, 2022

This is one of my more thrilling meetings, or at least the ride to get to my destination of Rida Ismael's office. Like Walid, I had seen Rida in the archives before meeting him in person. He is quoted at length in the first al-Nida' article I ever saw on Imad's death in the battle of Qantari. In the report, I learned that Rida was the head of the nearby Communist Party office in the Zaydaniyya neighborhood of Beirut as well as the brother of one of those killed in the battle: Diyab Ismael. I later learn from Walid and Nabil that he was also a close friend of Imad.

Today, Rida Ismael is on the executive board for Tahseen Khayat Group, a broadcasting, media, and publishing company, the latter of which Rida oversees. While no longer politically active, he is willing to talk about Imad. As I head toward Rida's office I get a call from him. He insists that someone comes pick me up to bring me from where I am (about twenty minutes by foot) to his office. I politely decline, informing him I can walk there before a car would get there in traffic. He assures me a car will not be picking me up. What felt like seconds later, a motorbike arrives at my location. The driver signals me to hop on the back. It was my first experience riding in Lebanon, as we dart through major thoroughfares and side streets. I am so glad I got to experience that slice of Beirut transport, but I won't, willingly at least, sign up any time soon!

Once face to face with Rida, I learn how close he and Imad were. "Imad is not only a friend and comrade," Rida tells me, "he had a great impact on my life personally." Imad and Rida were both from Zaydaniyya, went to Raml al-Zarif high school a few years apart, and had the exact same political trajectory: from Union of Lebanese Communists, to the Lebanese Communist Action Organization, to the Lebanese Communist Party. Throughout the late 1960s to mid-1970s, when Imad was in the country at least, Rida and Imad spent almost every day together. It thus makes perfect sense when Rida tells me he lost a part of himself on October 28, 1975, the day his best friend and comrade Imad died.

***

Advanced training in the hotel industry and a future for a liberated Palestine were equally pressing concerns for Imad. Neither, however, would be immediately realized. As described in the previous chapter, Imad was denied acceptance at *École Hôtelière de Lausanne* in late 1966. And while the Arab loss of Palestine in 1967 jumpstarted the idea that the armed masses, not Arab states, were the only ones who could defeat Israel, Israel continued to expand. Growing up in Cold War Lebanon and coming of age in Cold War Europe meant Imad was already adept at navigating the forces of global capitalism and left-wing ideologies, striving for his version of autonomy. But as indicated in Imad's letters following June '67, this became much harder as the United States supported, both political and economically, the state, Israel, that was causing Arab suffering. Still, as I seek to make clear in this chapter, even as Imad's politics became more radical, his dedication to a future in the hotel industry remained steadfast.

During this period, the late 1960s to early 1970s, Imad succeeded in what was his greatest intellectual feat: translating Abram Leon's *La Conception Matérialiste de la Question Juive, The Jewish Question: A Marxist Interpretation*, from French to Arabic under the title *al-Mafhum al-Madi lil-Mas'ala al-Yahudiyya* (direct translation of the French title) with the "radical publishing house," *Dar al-Tali'a lil-Taba'a wa al-Nashr*, the Vanguard House for Publishing and Printing (see Figure 3.1) in November 1969.[1] Leon or the title are not likely household names today, regardless of one's politics. But in the 1970s, as Elmaliach argues, the book was "the 'bible' of anti-Zionism," and a "best seller in terms of theoretical Marxist literature and necessary item on the bookshelves of many radicals across the world."[2]

This achievement, however, did not outshine an another, immediate accomplishment: gaining acceptance and attending *École Hôtelière de Lausanne* for a course in hotel administration from October 1969 to March 1970, and then completing onsite training at a local hotel from July to December 1970.[3] *École Hôtelière de Lausanne* was the first school dedicated to hospitality training in the world and remains one of the top schools today.[4] Without Imad's words on the subject, which do not exist, I can't say which accomplishment he found more impressive. In its place, I propose their dual import in his life. Succeeding intellectually, academically, politically, and in job training, this period in

Figure 3.1 The cover page of Imad's 1969 translation of Abram Leon's *The Jewish Question: A Marxist Interpretation*. The author's name is at the top center, above the title, and the translator's name is below. Published by Dar al-Tali'a lil-Taba'a wa al-Nashr, Beirut. Picture taken at Jafet Library, American University of Beirut.

Imad's life allows a window into the hopes and dreams of an Arab leftist and a practical radical, fully invested in their politics and career path.

These two triumphs serve as the basis for two of the most central claims of *Beirut Radical*.[5] Regarding the intellectual, through investigating Imad's translation of Leon's book, particularly the introduction for the Arabic volume that he wrote, I find that he saw himself as a creator of leftist, anti-Zionist thought. He and other young Arab leftists like him that took up translation in the sixties and seventies were not merely reproducing Western ideas in Arabic.[6] They Arabized the ideas themselves, circulating them to new audiences—young leftist Arabs—and focusing on the text's significance for the contemporary Palestinian struggle. With Imad's work as the focus, I seek to forge a new perspective on the Global Sixties with Arab leftist youth, beyond the leadership, elite, and intellectual classes, not on the fringes, but at the core of a transnational cause and transnational knowledge production.[7]

The second part of the chapter moves with Imad to Switzerland. His student files from *École Hôtelière de Lausanne* show that he did well in school and immediately took on a job in London. Building off his days in Hanover, and my argument from the prior chapter, I believe Imad was dedicated to this technical training, no more no less than the scientific Marxism he was translating. I concede, Imad's politics may be more interesting to readers. I also believe that Imad found parts of his job training quite dull. But in exploring Imad's identity, his political worldview cannot be separated from his career aspirations. And some of the best literature on student politics, both in the Arab World and beyond, miss the latter.[8] Indeed, Imad's dealings in this period give insight into what students were actually studying in the midst of student, and broader societal, upheavals of the 1960s and 1970s. I do not see this dual dedication as hypocritical, selling out, or the death of sixties activism. Rather, it is at the core of a generation of practical radicals, forced into capitalism, envisioning a life within and beyond it.

At the same time, the rubber started to meet the road for Imad. In his eyes, regardless of his prior training or good grades in Lausanne, he continued to get passed over for top jobs in Europe simply because he was a foreigner. In this context, he became more critical of the West, its policies, its cities, and its people. His letters from London in the early 1970s are useful here, reading very differently from those from Hanover. No longer did Imad look up to Europe, but his own people, articulating an unwavering support for them. This shift, I argue, signals a practical radical beginning to cede the former in service of the latter.

Imad Meets the New Left and Abram Leon

Imad wasted little time. His internship in Hanover ended in mid-October 1967, and he was back at school and work by November. For studies, he would attend Lebanese University and study law.[9] As per one of Imad's letters, in Hanover he was reading a book called *The Broker in Constitutional Law*, which "absorbed" him. Next on his reading list, when he got some spare cash, would be Montesquieu's De *l'Esprit des Loix*, *The Spirit of Law*, which he believed would be "beautiful … due to the boldness of its author and its unparalleled information."[10] Lebanese University was a fairly new university, and the only public one in Lebanon, known more for other things than its academics. As I detail in the next chapter, the university was the site of massive student protests in the 1970s. Like Raml al-Zarif high school, where Imad attended, Lebanese University was also a bastion for the New Left. For example, *Itihad al-Shuyu'iyyin al-Lubnaniyyin*, the Union of Lebanese Communists, which Imad would eventually join, would pull its ranks from the student body of Lebanese University.[11]

This era did not mark a turn away from hospitality work, however, as Imad continued his training in that sector. While taking classes at Lebanese University, he had an internship with his old employer, Hotel Phoenicia Intercontinental. After training in the kitchen, room service, and the bar in Hanover, he was ready—and likely excited—for other departments. First until March of 1968, he worked in the reception, and then until August of 1968, he staged in accounting, receiving, stores, and refrigeration.[12] Both internships were in the field of what would be his chosen track at *École Hôtelière de Lausanne* within hotel administration: *réception* and *main courante*, reception and record keeping.

Returning to Beirut in this period, Imad would have found things seemingly familiar and radically different. Developments in the tourism and hotel industry continued to look up, as the late 1960s represent an apex of sorts. The National Council for Tourism became the Ministry of Tourism with more infrastructure and funds at its disposal.[13] Pan American Airways ran eleven direct flights a week from New York to the now well-established Beirut International Airport and had a counter at Hotel Phoenicia.[14] Part out of necessity, part opportunity, Phoenicia owner Najib Salha decided to build a second tower.[15] It was finished in 1968.[16] Around the same time, Salha and Intercontinental announced plans for another property in Beirut, this one at the economy-class level.[17]

Regarding what had changed since Imad had left, he would now feel the loss of the Arab-Israeli war of 1967 at home, which had several radicalizing effects. First and foremost was the transformation of the Palestinian struggle itself, away from state-led efforts and geared toward the masses. The movement Fatah, the Opening, and its leader Yasser Arafat were at the center of the shift and at the Palestinian Liberation Organization. Among many other things, Arafat and Fatah were pivotal to the making of what Yezid Sayigh calls a "Palestine First" agenda, based on "the absolute independence of Palestinian organization and decision-making from the Arab governments and the primacy of armed struggle as the sole means of liberating Palestine."[18] Indeed, Fatah advocated for surprise raids into Israel, terror as a tactic, and guerrilla warfare. This strategy was first showcased in March 1968, when the Palestinian Liberation Army, *fedayeen* associated with Fatah, and the Jordanian army held out against Israeli forces at the Battle of Karameh.[19] As Sfeir argues, "if 1967 symbolized the Arab defeat to Israel ... [Karameh] sanctified and legitimized the Palestinian struggle."[20]

Second, as I noted in the previous chapter, the defeat of 1967 spurred the growth of the Lebanese New Left in a new direction. "We crossed a political border," one of Imad's contemporaries tells me, as youth disavowed the Nasserist-brand of pan-Arabism and moved closer to Marxism.[21] They found inspiration in, and connection to, the Palestinian liberation movement. Imad was already politically active and drawn to the Palestinian cause when he was in high school, likely part of the Marxist-oriented Student Forces Front. While back in Lebanon, it appears Imad re-engaged with those from school and the neighborhood, like his friend Rida Ismael, and met new likeminded comrades, including Nabil Khishin. Nabil was already a part of the Lebanese Communist Party, and he, along with his friend and comrade, Ghassan Fawaz, and other students of the Lebanese Communist Party, had been discussing creating a new, offshoot group, eventually named the Union of Lebanese Communists.[22] Imad was likely recruited next and he then encouraged his old friend Rida to join.[23]

Early documents from the Union of Lebanese Communists are instructive in introducing the changes afoot in the Beiruti leftist political scene. For one, its December 1968 charter bashes the Lebanese Communist Party, arguing it is "incapable of performing its pioneering role."[24] Originally called the Lebanese People's Party and formed in 1924, the Lebanese Communist Party was the oldest, most established leftist party in the country. This does not mean it could operate openly. French colonial officials banned the party and jailed its leaders in the 1920s and 1930s, and during the Cold War, Western powers kept an eye on it. The party fared no better regionally, as popular leaders like Nasser deemed communism an enemy of pan-Arabism.[25] With this prevailing hostility, and in need of an international backer, the Communist Party moved closer to the Soviet Union in the 1950s.[26]

But by the late 1960s, many young people in the Communist Party would argue that it "had sclerosis."[27] Gilbert Achcar, an academic and once member of the Union of Lebanese Communists, was one of these youths. He tells me that in this period the Lebanese Communist Party "was a corpse, a zombie," and their leader, Nicola al-Shawi, a "Stalinist" authoritarian who allowed "zero democracy."[28] Nabil clarifies the absurdity of party politics under Shawi at that point:

> I was shocked by things [the Communist Party was teaching]. For example, one whole session they were talking about Secretary General Nicola al-Shawi and how he had an eye problem and how the great doctors of the Soviet Union saved his eyes, and we started laughing about it "The eyes of Nicola al-Shawi, the eyes of Nicola al-Shawi!" Fuck Nicola al-Shawi and fuck his eyes, I am not interested in this.[29]

Not only had the Lebanese Communist Party, allow me a pun, lost its vision. It had become entirely dependent on the Soviet Union.

That dependence was becoming more controversial as the Soviet Union and rising Chinese Communist Party began to split. By the 1960s, many leftist parties across the world favored the latter, perceiving Maoism as a more genuinely Marxist, populist, and less elitist version of Marx, Lenin, and Trotsky's original idea.[30] This appealed to many leftists in Lebanon, including those who would establish the Union of Lebanese Communists and other similar groups.[31] As Walid Nuwayhid, one of Imad's cousins, tells me, "Some of them [leftist leaders] would go to China start to learn Chinese and ask for weapons."[32] While Imad never visited China, he was interested in their communist experiment. Immediately before his death, Imad was apparently writing a book titled *al-Sin ba'd 30 'Amaan, China after 30 Years.*[33]

The Lebanese Communist Party of the mid-1960s struck back against members who had these sympathies, accusing them of "being Maoists, deviationists, revisionists, or personality cultists."[34] The student faction that helped found the Union of Lebanese Communists split for these very reasons.[35] In another of its earliest documents, titled "Around the Union of Lebanese Communists," it chastised the party's dependance on the USSR and "its complete adherence to Stalinism without any analysis or changes." What was needed was a "revolutionary spirit" that followed Marxist principles regardless of who was sponsoring them.[36]

Beyond being against the Communist Party and other so-called "Old Left" parties (including the Progressive Socialist Party as well), the Union was for "the Palestinian cause."[37] In the opening paragraph of its charter, the Union frames Palestine at the core of "battle for Arab destiny," and in the specter of the "acceleration of U.S. and all other western sponsors for Israel."[38] This section of the charter was perhaps most important for Imad in the late 1960s. As seen in his last letters from Hanover, Imad was starting to become critical of the United States and how it intervened in the 1967 war to dash the hopes of a liberated Palestine and Arab world. In addition to its strong adherence to Marxist principles, not that of the Soviet Union, this dedication to Palestine may be the main reason Imad joined the group. Furthermore, those peers he respected—Ghassan Fawaz, Gilbert Achcar, and Nabil Khishin—were leading it.

The revival of the Lebanese Communist Party in the 1970s, the Left's move even closer to the Palestinian cause (beyond rhetoric), and Imad's eventual embrace of the Lebanese Communist Party will be the focus of the subsequent chapter. For now, *c.* 1968, what is most important to stress is how a shift away from the Soviet Union, toward China, and most importantly, Palestine were becoming a central part of being in the youth ranks of the New Left in Lebanon.

~

Around the time Imad joined the Union of Lebanese Communists his documentation ceases. There is a gap between August 1968 and September 1969, ending with his admittance into *École Hôtelière de Lausanne* (October '69) and the publication of *al-Mafhum al-Madi lil-Mas'ala al-Yahudiyya*, Imad's translation of Abram Leon's *La Conception Matérialiste de la Question Juive* (November '69). One of Imad's brothers, Iyad Nuwayhid, provided me a written timeline—one of the more important, if not flawed, pieces of information from Imad's family—which indicates Imad was working in more and "different departments" at Hotel Phoenicia through the end of 1969.[39] It is also plausible he was taking a break from his job and school, submitting application materials, working on his translation, and waiting to hear back on both while actively participating in the Union.

Regardless of what he was—or was not—doing, this gap creates some speculation on how he came to Leon's book in the first place. According to Walid Nuwayhid, as outlined in the introduction of this chapter, the story starts in Paris in the late 1960s. Imad "went to Paris to study," he tells me. "His financial situation was difficult, so he would make oil paintings, and he would display them on Sundays."[40] When he had free time, Imad would visit the Parisian cafes frequented by famous intellectuals, like Jean Paul Sartre.[41] One of those close to Sartre was Maxime Rodinson. Walid continues:

> Sometimes he would see Maxime Rodinson and different friends and [they would] take tea and coffee together. Then Maxime Rodinson looked at Imad and asked him "Imad why don't you translate this book, Leon's *The Jewish Question*, it is very important for the Arab readers and for the Lebanese. If you can translate it its very good."[42]

Walid is emphatic on this last point: "I think Rodinson is responsible or he urged Imad to translate this book. He asked him to do it and [Imad] did it."[43]

Maxime Rodinson was a leftist, Jewish, anti-Zionist Orientalist.[44] In the days leading up to the 1967 war, Rodinson wrote a lengthy article in Simon de Beauvoir and Jean Paul Sartre's journal *Les Temps Modernes*, titled "*Israel: Fait Colonial?*"[45] The article and successive English-language booklet represent one of the early works, in the European academy at least, to conceptualize Zionism as settler colonialism. In the words of the booklet's introduction, Rodinson proves that Israel was "the result of colonial conquest justified by an ethnocentric and racially exclusive ideology."[46] Rodinson also wrote the preface for the 1968 French edition of Abram Leon's *La Conception Matérialiste de la Question Juive.*[47]

There is, however, another story for how Imad came to meet Leon. It was first told to me by Jawad Nuwayhid and unfolds in the late 1960s Beirut political and intellectual scene I described above. While studying, working, and getting involved with the Union of Lebanese Communists, Jawad believes Imad encountered the work of Leon, likely as a part of a union-affiliated reading group.[48] "He loved reading," Jawad says, "and he might have … took it from one of his friends."[49] Gilbert Achcar fills in the dots here, informing me that "at the time [I] probably [had] a role" in Imad's decision to translate the book.[50]

The origin story from France is incredible, but plausible. Rodinson and Sartre were not only public intellectuals, but publicly available. Furthermore, they had interest in the Middle East and leftist intellectuals from the region.[51] The lack of documentation for more than a year means that Imad could be studying in the wake of the May 1968 demonstrations, which made Paris a pilgrimage for young Arab leftists like him.[52] The Beirut story is equally believable, simply because it follows the documentation I already have. Imad stayed in Beirut, working, reading, and studying. He never left for Paris to study or paint during this time. If he did, Jawad tells me, it would have been brief and "just for fun."[53] But even if more believable than the Paris story, I have no source work to confirm or deny the Beirut story. To assume Imad could not have been in France and could not have met Rodinson before translating the book is purely speculative.[54]

Without certainty, I find it fruitful to consider how both retellings can coexist. In short, Imad could have met Rodinson in France, tasked by the intellectual himself, and then gained access to Leon's *La Conception Matérialiste de la Question Juive* vis-à-vis a Beirut reading group. Instead of favoring one over the other—that is a story of a leftist foreigner in the Global North or a leftist Lebanese in the Global South—this composite acknowledges Imad's constant border crossing, and connects him to other young leftists of the Global Sixties. This includes those activists in the United States who, like and following Imad, read Leon's book and introduced it to the New American Left in 1970 with its first proper English-language publication.[55]

Writing on this era of Arab intellectual production, Bardawil sees "the practice of translation" not as a reproduction of the old, but the translator's "interventions" to make sense of their current context. These interventions were not fixed to one place or tradition, but "transgressed national, class, linguistic, ethnic, generational and disciplinary boundaries."[56] Browers adds that translations by young Arab leftists of the time were "undertaken as a part of a revolutionary praxis."[57] I agree with these assessments and adapt them to evaluate Imad's translation.[58] That is, any consideration of *al-Mafhum al-Madi lil-Mas'ala al-Yahudiyya* must conceive Imad as a part of a global cohort, birthed from hybrid scenes—from the United States through France, to Lebanon and beyond—that were forging new radical ideas.

Translating European Anti-Zionism

While mystery abounds on how Imad Nuwayhid discovered Abram Leon, the why is clear. This is because Imad writes a five-page *muqadama*, introduction, for *al-Mafhum al-Madi lil-Mas'ala al-Yahudiyya*. Before detailing what Imad found compelling in Leon's analysis, it is necessary to describe who Abram Leon was. Born into a Jewish family in Warsaw, Abram Leon (1918–44) lived in Palestine during grade school, and, perhaps most notably, joined the ranks of a group called Hashomer Hatzair, the Youth Guard, in his home of Brussels, Belgium in 1926.[59] Hashomer Hatzair was a labor Zionist organization that sought "workers' immigration and settlement on kibbutzim [in Palestine] as the nuclei of the future Jewish socialist commonwealth in Palestine."[60] By the late 1930s, however, Leon began to question Zionism writ large and Hashomer Hatzair's particular brand.

As Leon separated from Hashomer Hatzair, he started writing what would become *La Conception Matérialiste de la Question Juive*. It began as a series of articles in *La Lutte Ouvrière*, The Workers Struggle, a Belgian Trotskyist weekly newspaper, and was then compiled under the title "Theses on the Jewish Question" in May 1940. All the while, Leon deepened his Trotskyist, internationalist connections, founding the Revolutionary Communist Party that same year.[61] This was almost an impossible venture in the context of the German occupation of Belgium. Leon and his party were forced underground in the early 1940s, he was arrested in June 1944, and, within weeks, Leon was sent to the gas chambers at Auschwitz.

Following Leon's death, and the end of the Second World War, it took about a year for his contemporaries to recover his writings with a French-language edition published in 1946. Four more years were spent "locating and identifying [more of] Leon's source material and quotations," followed by an English translation in Mexico in 1950.[62] The edition that most likely served as Imad's basis was the reprinted French version in 1968, introduced by Maxime Rodinson.

Building off of Marx and others who had written on the "Jewish question" in the 1800s, Leon conceptualizes Jews as a "people class" tied to a "specific economic function" in both pre-capitalist and capitalist Europe: the merchant.[63] He argues that Jews suffered under capitalism, past and present, because of their predominant societal role as bankers, money leaders, and usurers. He writes, "The case of ancient anti-Semitism is the same as for medieval anti-Semitism; The antagonism towards the merchant in every society based principally on the production of use values."[64] This discrimination was thus not eternal or linked to specific traits of Christianity or Judaism. Instead, "in different historical periods Judaism made up part of the [capital] possessing classes and was treated as such."[65]

Leon was later criticized, including by Rodinson, for this simplistic view—Jews performed one labor role in society—and some even refer to his argument as a form of "economic antisemitism."[66] Yet, this critique is also reductive. It obscures that Leon addressed something quite tangible: the negative stereotype connecting Jews with money, as Marx put it, perceived as "huckstering" across time.[67] These criticisms also miss the point that capitalism, not Judaism as a religion or culture, was the focus of Leon's scorn.

Anyways, Leon's main contribution was not this claim, which Marx already made. It was his sweeping analysis, what he called a "scientific study of Jewish history."[68] He charts the shifts in perceptions of Jews under capitalism, from prosperity in an ancient, communal, socialist society through the ninth century to demonization culminating in fascist anti-capitalist and anti-Semitic propaganda in Nazi Germany. He then takes up political Zionism in twentieth-century Europe and what he calls the "Zionist colonization" of Palestine. He argues it would fail, categorically, because Zionism "wishes to resolve the Jewish question without destroying capitalism."[69] He goes on:

Even admitting that Anglo-American imperialism will create some kind of abortive Jewish state, we have seen that the situation of world Judaism will hardly be affected. A great Jewish immigration into Palestine after this war will confront the same difficulties as previously [resistance from the indigenous Palestinian population and Arab nationalism]. Under conditions of capitalist decay [and anti-capitalist, anti-Semitic perceptions of Jews] it is impossible to transplant millions of Jews. Only a worldwide socialist planned economy would be capable of such a miracle. Naturally this presupposes the proletarian revolution.

But Zionism wishes precisely to resolve the Jewish question independently of world revolution. By misconstruing the real sources of the Jewish question in our period, by lulling itself with puerile dreams and silly hopes, Zionism proves that it is an ideological excrescence and not a scientific doctrine.[70]

Leon's disdain for Zionism and capitalism was unequivocal. Yet, his predictions of the challenges of mass Jewish immigration to Palestine were proven false. It appears Leon, so focused on socialism as the only "resolution of the Jewish problem with a minimum suffering," was unable to conceive the import of the Holocaust, the event that ended his life, in raising global support for Jewish, Zionist settlement under nationalism and capitalism.[71]

In sum, Leon's work was an anti-capitalist, anti-nationalist, anti-imperialist Marxist analysis that marked "a very different route to emancipation for Jews and Arabs alike."[72] While Imad appears consumed by all of it, he was first drawn toward the method itself; at least it is what he mentions first in his translator's introduction. After quoting Leon, who wrote "Marxism is above all a method of analysis, but not for the sake of a textual analysis, but for the sake of the analysis of social relations," Imad notes that the book is "the first scientific attempt to analyze the economic and social role of the Jew across history."[73] This scope and ease by which Leon moved, from antiquity to political Zionism, in roughly 200 pages, impressed Imad.

Imad also argues that this translation was needed to address the "emptiness in the Arabic library of any scientific study of 'the Jewish question.'"[74] He mentions two recent studies which revolve around the topic, but appear to fall short. First is Sadiq Jallal al-Azm's (1934–2016) August 1969 article, which Imad provides the full citation: *Nahwa Fahim Afdal lil-Fikra al-Sahyuniyya*, "Towards a Better Understanding of Zionist Thought," published in *Mawaqif*,

Positions, a Beirut-based leftist journal. Second is Naji Alush (1935–2012) and his book *al-Marksiyya wa al-Mas'ala al-Yahudiyya*, *Marxism and the Jewish Question*. The former may have identified flaws in "Arab thinking" on Zionism, grounded in its supposed "hidden, polemical, and mythological" powers. But Imad insinuates Azm did not actually engage in a "scientific study" of Zionism. Imad was more direct with Alush's work, claiming it was "the first of its kind" in the Arabic canon. Still, he stresses Alush's "limits [by way] of aggregating the opinions of Marxist intellectual leaders [from Marx to Stalin], without himself engaging in an analysis of Jewish history under dialectical materialism."[75]

Remarkably, a 24-year-old places himself at the center of intellectual debates of those ten years his senior. While Alush may be unknown to many contemporary readers, Azm's 1968 book al-*Nakd al-Thati ba'd al-Hazima*, *Self-Criticism after the Defeat* is one of the most famous works of Arab thought following the '67 defeat. But Imad does not seem to care about their pedigree. This was not an isolated incident. Iman Nuwayhid, Imad's cousin, remembers "high pitched disputes" between Imad and Iman's father, Adl, who was twenty years older than Imad. There was "lots of shouting," on topics ranging from nationalism vs. internationalism to support for the Palestinian cause, which was all "disturbing" for the child Iman.[76] Whether famous or familial, Imad did not cower in the shadows of his elders. As it relates to Azm and Alush, Imad saw himself among them, a thinker.[77] His contribution, then, was to correct what he perceived as a gap in the literature, that gap being a Marxist, historical analysis, in Arabic, of the Jewish question.

Even though Imad starts his introduction with the intellectual plane, the activist one appears more pressing. Imad informs his reader that he translated Leon's work "to enrich the Arab revolutionary movement in a scientific study, as to help it understand clearly the nature of the enemy," so the Arab and Palestinian "popular crowds" could realize "the destruction of the Zionist entity."[78] In this way, Imad found Leon's work more than a guidebook for understanding the connection between Zionism, imperialism, and global capitalism. Even though it was written in the 1940s, before the creation of the state of Israel, Imad believed Leon could provide the Arab and Palestinian masses with the tools to dismantle Zionism.

Thus, Imad was not merely translating anti-Zionist Marxist thought, but contemporizing and Arabizing it.

To this end, Imad's introduction then shifts toward contemporary Arab events since Leon's passing: the disaster of '48 and the shock of '67. Here, Imad is not merely providing reasons for why the book is necessary in a post-48 and 67 world, but providing his own interpretation of that world. In one section of the introduction, he focuses on what "the defeat of June 5, 1967 did to confirm the following facts."[79] The fact that Imad dedicates the most text to is:

> The beginning of the awareness of the Arab masses of the official paradox today in the region, the paradox between it [the Arab masses] and between imperialism and its tool Israel. And the beginning of this awareness of the masses, from the Israeli occupation, and the Israeli expansive ambitions, that Israel is its direct inevitable enemy. From here, the Palestinian issue returned to the popular Arab dimension, after the Palestinian revolution was removed from the hands of the Arab governments, and it was placed in the hands of the masses.[80]

In this writing, Imad links imperialism to the state of Israel, describes Israel as the villain of the Arab masses, and lays blame on the Arab regimes for the loss of 1967. While Leon did not make these points, they had been a part of the intellectual Arab canon for some time.

The first was Constantine Zurayk, a teacher at the American University of Beirut who wrote *Ma'na al-Nakba, The Meaning of Disaster* (1948). In it, he characterizes the "Seven Arab states" as "impotent" to Zionism and "turn[ed] on their heels" by "Zionist imperialism" whose goal "is to annihilate one people to replace it with another people."[81] Hence, Zurayk identified Zionism as a settler ideology, but to theorize it as such came later—albeit in English— in Fayez Sayegh's *Zionist Colonization in Palestine* (1965). Sayegh, a diasporic Palestinian working in the United States, argues that nineteenth-century European settler colonialism gave Zionists the justification to "send [their] own *colonists* into a piece of Afro-Asian territory, establish a *settler-community,* and, in due course, set up its own state."[82] Its distinction, Sayegh finds, is that Zionism's nation-state existed not thousands of miles away, like in Britain or France, but in the place that was to be settled. **"Unlike European colonization elsewhere, therefore, Zionist colonization of Palestine was essentially**

incompatible with the continued existence of the 'native population' in the coveted country."[83]

From an anti-elite, anti-imperialism grounded in the 1940s to one of the 1960s grounded in anti-settler colonial language and ethnic cleansing, not as a perspective, but fact; all is to say by 1969, Imad Nuwayhid's claims were not new. Imad's introduction then reflects an inter-generational, anti-Zionist solidarity that runs from Europe, Leon and Rodinson, through the Arab world and the United States, Zurayk and Sayegh, to him.

In his attempt to Arabize Leon's analysis, then, why didn't Imad mention these Arab thinkers? It could be that their work had more traction in international arenas—Imad may not have known or read Sayegh, for example—or they were not explicitly Marxist—definitely the case with Zurayk. At the same time, more so than Zurayk and Sayegh, or Azm and Alush, Imad's words, like the translation, were meant more for the Palestinian and Arab masses, not an intellectual vanguard.

This is shown through the most important focus of his introduction: Imad's solution. He writes that the recent "Palestinian revolution" has led "the people," *al-sha'b*, a "vengeful people … inspired by armed struggle," to wrestle the fight from the grip of Arab regimes, which were "not radical," and hence why they met a "series of defeats" in the face of Israel. This "people's war," would, Imad believed, "transform the Arab people from an inactive kind to an active one avenging the defeat by the enemy."[84] Imad is optimistic that the "'Jewish' revolutionary element" could help in this task.[85] He prognosticates how Arab resistant to Zionism within Israel would instill "a wide awareness of the 'Jewish' popular sector of the true enemy" who would, instead, fully invest in "the Marxist solution for the Jewish question."[86]

First of note in this pivot toward a solution is Imad's use of scare quotes around the word "Jewish." He does this several times in the introduction, specifically when discussing the Jewish Left. To bracket Jewish, I believe, was not a questioning of Jewish identity, but to separate Judaism and Jews, writ large, from "Zionist Jews," something Zurayk and Sayegh also did.[87] Second, notwithstanding his return to Leon's Marxist method, it almost appears as if Imad has lost Leon in this introduction. He shifts to a sixties argument on how Arab armed struggle will reveal the woes of Zionism for Jews. Again, the translation itself was important, but this was also Imad's opportunity to be a part of the tradition he was building from, here by discussing Jews not as enemies, but potential comrades in arms. This was an opportunity he relished.

The conclusion of Imad's introduction also reveals the most obvious, but unmentioned reason that Imad translated Leon: Leon's background, transformation, thinking, and death at Auschwitz uncovered that not all Jews were, or had to be, Zionists. From one angle, why Imad does not mention this reason is perplexing, given how it could strengthen the respect of the Arab reader to anti-Zionist, Marxist Jews, like Leon or Rodinson. However, as Imad started the introduction, Leon's was a scientific study, one in which subjective biography was secondary.

Similarly, there is no biographical information on the translator, Imad Yusuf Nuwayhid, in the Arabic version of Leon's French book. While Imad knew French and Arabic, he was not a professional translator. So did he have help in his endeavor? His French grammarian father may have had something to give here, but most integral in the translation, it appears, was his friend, Nabil Khishin.[88] Nabil and Imad knew each other from the Union of Lebanese Communists, acquainting over the past year or so. It was the summer of 1969. Imad was preparing for study in Lausanne, Nabil was readying for the same (a masters in Philosophy) in Lyon.[89] While both Imad and Nabil went to French schools in their childhood, Nabil continued on to high school at *Lycée Français de Beyrouth* where Imad's father taught. Thus, Nabil was likely more proficient in French. He also claims, "my Arabic was better than his," perhaps one reason Imad elicited Nabil's help.[90]

Their lack of professional credentials does not show. A friend of mine, who is a professional translator working in Cairo, read long passages of the 1970 English version of *The Jewish Question: A Marxist Interpretation* alongside the same passages in Imad and Nabil's Arabic version. He was quite impressed, commenting, "100% they [Imad and Nabil] know what they are doing. The translation seems as professional as they come."[91]

Nabil explains the translation process to me as such. In a given session they were "sitting on a balcony … [and Imad] was reading sentences for me and I was [translating] this in Arabic or I was reviewing what he did."[92] Nabil stresses Leon's study was "not a voluminous book," and hence, "it was easy to finish it in a month," over the course of four to five sessions.[93] On this schedule, they worked tirelessly, translating thirty to forty pages of the original text per day.

Imad likely wrote his introduction thereafter, both went to Europe, and then the book was published only a few months later in November 1969.

With all its achievements, there are some aspects of the translation that are, for lack of a better word, amateur. For example, there is no standardization of references. When compared with the 1968 French version they were working from, page numbers are missing from all citations in their Arabic translation, the format of citations change from page to page, and many notes are missing.[94] In one example, Chapter 5, where Leon takes up "the development of the Jewish Question in the nineteenth century," they do not translate an explanatory footnote on the traveling nature of the non-Jewish weaver, but do translate one on Jewish demographics by profession in Ukraine.[95] On top of all of this, Nabil admits to me today there are a lot of mistakes in the translation, ones, given his profession today as a translator, he is keen to correct.[96]

What is perhaps most interesting in their decision making is which front and end matter to include or exclude. The 1968 French version that they used as their basis consisted of the following: a preface for the current version by Maxime Rodinson, the original preface by Ernest Germain (pseudonym for Ernest Mandel, a Belgium Marxist and contemporary of Leon), and an appendix including an interview with Leon Trotsky from the 1930s and a lecture from Issac Duestscher (a Polish Marxist) from the 1960s.[97] But the Arabic version translated by Imad and Nabil only includes the Germain preface, not that of Rodinson, or what was presumably his added appendix. Nabil tells me he does not remember Rodinson's introduction:

> We were working on the text of Abram Leon only … I do not remember … any introduction by Maxime Rodinson. No no, what I remember is we were working on the text itself. Why? The logical explanation is that on the copy which Imad had those things were not existing yet … or that he ignored them I do not know.[98]

The non-existent explanation is only plausible if Imad and Nabil were working from a version that does not currently exist. The only other French-language edition in their time in circulation was from 1946, and Imad's translation of notes and styles more so follows the 1968 edition.[99] While the non-existent explanation cannot be ruled out, I find Nabil's last line—"that he ignored them"—more likely.

It is not that Imad did not respect Rodinson or his preface. If we take Walid's story on how Imad came to Leon, he was indebted entirely to Rodinson. Instead, as Bardawil argues in a different context, Imad's decisions represent an "emphasis on establishing a direct link to the main texts of the tradition."[100] Accordingly, Imad was playing the role of Rodinson here, introducing the text and choosing what to take out or provide for the reader. Regarding the latter, Imad and Nabil added fifteen or so of their own translator notes. The citations, marked by the phrase *al-mutarjim*, the translator, were likely added for Arabic readers who would have little prior knowledge of ancient Jewish or medieval European history.[101] What came out, then, was the 1969 Arabic version of Leon's original work.

After a 200-page tour de force, Imad made what looks to be his last editorial choice: a list of "newly released" Arabic texts.[102] This would be useful for the Arabic readers in their further research on Israel, Zionism, and the Arab world. Of the fourteen works listed, half were original texts penned by Arab thinkers and half were translated works. Of the former, two were by Naji Alush—*al-Marksiyya wa al-Mas'ala al-Yahudiyya*, referenced by Imad in his introduction, and *al-Masira ila Filasteen, March to Palestine*, 1964—and one co-authored by the Syrians al-Haytham al-Ayubi and Akram Diri—*Nuha Istratijiyya 'Arabiyya Jadida, Towards a New Arab Strategy*, 1969. All three of these authors served as translators for multiple titles included in the list. This may point to Imad's thesis: there was a lack of original Arabic-language work on the Jewish question. A second interpretation is that these Arab authors were engaging in another type of intellectual work, translation.

For one, Naji Alush translated the work of Võ Nguyên Giáp, general of the Vietnam's People's Army and minister of Defense for the Republic of Vietnam until 1980. He was one of the key architects of multiple Viet Minh wins, as well as implementing the '68 Tet offensive.[103] These victories paved the way for the now Arabic translation of *Nasr Kabir wa Muhima 'Athima*, The *Big Victory, The Great Task*. Moreover, al-Ayubi translated the work of B. H. Liddle Hart, a British First World War soldier and military historian.[104] Not only were other Arab intellectuals engaged in translating political treatises, but texts of military strategy, including those by First World victors and Third World insurgents. Imad—or at least his publisher—was aware of this, making sure that the most relevant works were known by their reading audiences.

Other titles included *al-Thawra al-'Arabiyya wa Isra'il*, *The Arab Revolution and Israel* (1968), an original work authored by Fuad Qazan, and *American Zionism and American Foreign Policy* (1962), written by Richard Stephens and translated into Arabic as *al-Sahyuniyya al-Amrikiyya wa Siyasat Amrika al-Kharijiyya* by George Wakim. Collectively, they symbolize an attempt to write Palestine into global armed conflicts of different shades and conceive of it as a case in point in global decolonization. Linked to this, Imad wrote the following about where he believed Leon's *La Conception Matérialiste de la Question Juive* fell short:

> The historical study which Leon wrote—for its academic importance—is not enough to understand the real paradox that exists in the Arab region today, which is a reflection of the main paradox in the world, between the national liberation movement in the Third World, on one hand, and between imperialism, on the other. And Israel, as an embodiment of the Zionist Movement, does not only play the role of the protector of imperial interests in the Arab East, but the hideous exploitation of the Palestinian people. Israeli imperialism is settler colonialism in its objectivity reality—economically and socially—for the Jewish colonizers Colons [in French] are—**consciously or unconsciously**—the true exploiter of the Palestinian and Arab masses.[105]

This quote confirms Imad's understanding of Palestine as one of many Third World struggles. Indeed, Imad, like many other Arab intellectuals in the making, believed that "armed struggle was the central and most productive mode of Palestinian anti-colonial resistance" and placed that struggle "within the milieu of Third World armed revolutionary movements."[106] Those movements included Vietnam, Cuba, and China.[107] While other Arab youth engaged Vietnam and Cuba as "symbols of armed struggle and radical liberation," Imad was interested in China, later in life supposedly writing on the question of *China after 30 Years*.[108] As a whole, this demonstrates that translation across borders was not merely an intellectual exercise. Its translators, like Imad, sought to connect decolonization activists around the world, movements that appear national, separate, and distinct in hindsight.

Equally important, this final quote from Imad's introduction solidifies that he was part of an intellectual tradition, since Leon, that conceived of Zionism as settler colonialism. It included Leon, Zurayk, Sayigh, and Rodinson. Imad was a student of these scholars, even if he didn't cite all of them or know all of them. He was their torchbearer, forged through transnational, intergenerational translation, exchange, and solidarity.

While the 1969 introduction for *al-Mafhum al-Madi lil-Mas'ala al-Yahudiyya* points to the growing militancy of Imad, and other young Arab leftists like him, there is another, more mundane story here: Imad hoped to create a career for himself. The decision to go back to school and away from his translation may indicate the so-called "death of the sixties." However, Imad died for causes he came to in the sixties, so this is not the case for him. But even more broadly, this generation's professional and political credentials developed side by side. Indeed, they may lean one way or another in a given period, but that is the point, or at least my point. They sought the freedom to be practical and radical.

Back to Studies, Back to Europe

Imad did not get to see his book in print, with his name on the title page, at least not immediately. In October 1969, a month before *Dar al-Tali'a lil-Taba'a wa al-Nashr* released *al-Mafhum al-Madi lil-Mas'ala al-Yahudiyya*, Imad, again, left Lebanon for Europe to attend the *École Hôtelière* in Lausanne, Switzerland. Recall, he had once before applied to this prestigious institution but was rejected. If, as I speculated in Chapter 2, a lack of reception experience was the reason he was denied admittance, it must have looked nice that now part of his application file could read *"Réception- compatibilité Intercontinental Beyrouth,"* reception and accounting at Intercontinental Beirut, from November 1967 to August 1968.[109] A strong letter of recommendation from his internship in Hanover couldn't have hurt either.[110]

While this was not Imad's first stint in Europe, Lausanne was much different than Hanover; different language, his more familiar French; different geography, Lake Geneva and alpine views; and different transportation. In Hanover, Imad had to ride a bike or taxi to get to and from work. Lausanne was connected through its extensive public transport system, which Imad could have taken advantage of to get to his classes–his first address was only a few miles by bus or streetcar to campus—or even more likely the metro around town.[111]

Lausanne was more international than Hanover as well. The headquarters of the International Olympic Committee had been there since the late 1800s, which has made it a hub for many international sports federations.[112] Coupling this with Lausanne's place as the seat of international companies, like Nestlé, would mean Imad would likely encounter more peoples of the world than any other time of his life, particularly beyond the confines of the hotels he worked at in Beirut and Hanover.[113]

As Imad did not write—or they no longer exist—letters from Lausanne, it is unclear what his first impressions of the city were as he moved there in 1969. However, his brother Jawad says he liked it there.[114] Imad had been once before on his way to Hanover in 1966. He writes:

I have been in Lausanne for about six hours and this city is very amazing, romantic, quiet [and] peaceful like the rocks of our mountains [in Lebanon]. You do not hear any sound or movement, and everything in [the city] moves slowly and smoothly, in regularity and steadfastness.[115]

Of course, visiting somewhere for fun versus for school may have changed his perspective. Moreover, even if international, Lausanne was not as populated or bustling as Beirut. Tied to this, the political scene was less than ideal for Imad. Lausanne was not outside the movements of the Global Sixties, but beyond hippie clothing, counterculture, and perhaps some student protests, Imad's activism may have been underserved in this smaller town.[116] However, similar to Hanover, this may have been just fine for Imad. As I argued in Chapter 2, perhaps he would keep his head down, no longer a foreigner coming of age, but a foreigner creating a career.

At the center of the town, educationally, socially, and economically, were hotels. This was baked into Swiss national identity, which, not unlike Lebanon, had been centered on connectivity, tourism, and hospitality. Lausanne's lakeside alpine views were a big part of this, which a tourist ad of the 1900s boasted was only "9 hours from Paris, centre for all excursions by motor, rail, or boat on Lake Geneva, golf[,] education."[117] At that time, there was already 1,695 hotels across the country, a sizeable amount for a country of only 3 million people.[118] In addition to having a large market for receiving hotel guests, Lausanne would come to export hotels and hoteliers all around the world through its prestigious university.

École Hôtelière de Lausanne was founded in the late 1800s by Jacques Tschumi, a hotelier himself and member on the Swiss brain trust for the industry, *HotellerieSuisse*. Simply put, the infrastructure was there and the government support was there, but it was not paired with top-tier hospitality training.[119] *École Hôtelière de Lausanne* served as this educational center for the first half of the twentieth century, and after recovering from the Second World War, it was at the peak of its powers.[120] In 1948, administration created a new three-course system in *service* (restaurant and bar), *cuisine* (kitchen), and *secrétariat* (including management and administration), which by the time Imad graduated was renamed as *gestion and administration* (management and administration).[121] Per a 1960s promotion video, the point of Imad's particular course was "to prepare the students to an administrative career in the hospitality industry, and take over for the actual executives."[122] With that tall order, the hotel administration course had the reputation of being the most difficult class.[123] In the three terms prior to Imad's admittance, only 75 percent of students passed the equivalent to the hotel administration course he took. This was compared to the near 90–95 percent pass rate in service and cuisine.[124]

When Imad arrived to campus, the university had just hired a new president, Erich Gerber. His mentality reflected a changing time; the Global Sixties inflected not through student politics, but student administration. By the late 1960s in Switzerland, "the tie, which people such as students had still routinely worn at university …, was increasingly shunned as a symbol of the 'establishment.'"[125] Gerber was the first to "exempt students from wearing a tie during lessons."[126] Furthermore, he got rid of the more infantilizing terminology for students, like *elèves*, pupils, supplanting it with *étudiantes*, students.[127] These changes are ones Imad likely appreciated and benefited from. In his class photo, not only is he not wearing a tie. He is one of very few students not wearing a jacket (see Figure 3.2).

The school touted its diversity since the beginning. As of 1924, half of its students were "foreigners" and that held through Imad's time there. Today, the global institution, rebranded as "EHL Hospitality Business School," represents

Figure 3.2 The class of Winter 1969/1970, Hotel Administration course, Reception section, at *École Hôtelière de Lausanne* (above). The picture has been cropped to zoom in on Imad, top right, with three other similarly dressed students: the least formal and most hip (no jackets, sunglasses, striped shirts). Courtesy of EHL archives.

over 115 different nationalities.[128] However, the statistics, at least in the past, are a bit misleading. Anyone outside of Switzerland, but from Western Europe (France, England, Belgium), was considered a foreigner, and students from other parts of Europe (Sweden, Denmark, Italy) were often counted as from "other countries."[129] Individuals from those countries were closer to home, physically and culturally, than Imad. For lack of a better word, he was more foreign, and part of a smaller minority. By my tally, of the some 264 students who received degrees from *École Hôtelière de Lausanne* with Imad in 1970, only 20 students, or 8 percent, were foreigners beyond Europe.[130] Within his specific class, he was one of six non-European foreigners: three Greeks, one Mexican, one Uruguayan.

This made him the only Arab in his class. There were three Arabs across the student body—two Lebanese and one Jordanian—and one Turkish student, but they would not share any classes. Given a busy schedule (see below), and no course connection to these other students, it is unclear if or how well he knew them. Yes, his class picture signals some comradery—note in Figure 3.2 the man to Imad's right has his arm around him—and Jawad Nuwayhid mentions that after their course ended in the summer of 1970, "he [Imad] came by train to Lebanon with two of his [European] friends."[131] Yet, even if there were more Lebanese at school than his job in Hanover, the Arab support network he had in West Germany, most notably his Egyptian friend, was stronger and deeper than Lausanne. For that reason, he later relays the following from London:

> Life here, naturally, is better than in Switzerland and this is for multiple reasons the most important being presence of England's special history, and from this the presence of large numbers of communities that are from commonwealth countries and the colonies which are controlled by England through the past centuries.[132]

As I describe in the next section, Imad took issue with England's "special" imperial history. Still, it embedded a certain diversity, specifically of people from his home in the Arab world, one that wasn't present in Lausanne.

As compiled through program descriptions and catalogs for the 1969–70 school year, Imad's weekly schedule looked something like this:

Monday	Tuesday	Wednesday	Thursday	Friday	Saturday
Accounting & Math	Accounting & Math	Record Keeping & Mécanographie	French Cor-respondence,	Record Keeping & Mécanographie	Tourism Geography
8–10 am	8–10 am	8–10 am	8–10 am	8–10 am	8–9 am
English Cor-respondence	Tourism marketing	Accounting & Math	Accounting & Math	Accounting & Math	Typing
10–12 pm	10–11 am	11–12 pm	11–12 pm	10–12 pm	9–10 am
Receptions & Controls	Law			Receptions & Controls	Record Keeping & Mécanographie
2–4 pm	2–4pm			2–4 pm	10–12 am[133]
Machines & Calculations			Accounting & Math		
4–6 pm			4–6 pm		

Imad would have seven different instructors across these nine classes. His schedule amounted to 31 hours a week and 4.5 hours a day. With only one day off, Imad had a packed week. But unlike his internship in Hanover, he was a fulltime student. He would not have to, or be able to work any other jobs, like the gas station position he had to take to get by in Germany.[134] Hence, while perhaps his support network was weaker here, his financial situation and quality of life were better.

Perhaps what sticks out the most in this schedule is the amount of technical training Imad received. Most of his week—twenty-two hours—was spent learning the *mécanographie* machine (specifically for hotel recording keeping), general accounting, and hotel math and calculations. This was compared with only six hours of week on tourist matters and how to speak to English and French-language tourists. Within this vocational training, the coursework reads quite stiff. His reception and controls class (four hours a week) focused as much on the "regulation of service taxes" as "room reservation" while his record keeping and *mécanographie* class (six hours a week) started with learning how to do "addition, multiplication and division, percentages and inverses" on the machine.[135]

One question from a *mécanographie* exam of the time reads as such: "In the final operation, I typed 95.00 instead of [the correct] 0.95." The options for how to correct this error are hardly intelligible for a lay person like myself. However, the student whose exam I reviewed got it incorrect. They circled (D) type 95.00 first, then delete it with the red totalizer button, then type 0.95, then hit the red totalizer button. The correct answer was (B), hit the enter button, then delete 95.00 with the red totalizer button, then type 0.95, then hit the red totalizer button.[136] While D may have been a second-best choice (the only difference being the initial typing of 95.00 plus enter), there was only one way of using this machine, one way of entering a room reservation, one way of calculating room tax.

This type of work had to feel very different for Imad—different from his past work in the bar, kitchen, room, and reception in Hanover and Beirut, but most radically different from his translation work just a few months earlier. While he may have seen Marxism as a science, he could have his own interpretations; there were gaps in the literature on the Jewish question in Arabic, why Arabs needed to read Leon, and what 1948 and 1967 meant to Arabs. These would largely be missing from the coursework that was moving Imad toward his ultimate career in the hospitality management field. This may be one reason the literature on the Global Sixties misses educational training in the field of student politics. For many historical subjects, their training may have been boring, not something they commented on or recognizable to the researcher.

But beyond his family and politics, this work was the largest part of Imad's life. Either he tolerated the monotony or at least was content with other outlets for his creativity.

Imad's course in hotel administration lasted five months. He finished well but started slow. Per his report card for the first half of the course, he struggled in reception and controls (a 3.8 out of 6), record keeping and *mécanographie* (a 3.6), and hotel math (4).[137] If he had ended with those scores, that would place his grade in core courses somewhere between sufficient and insufficient, the former barely a pass, the latter "not responding to what is required to that of a beginner."[138] To be fair, these were all courses that would have been new for Imad, a technical training that may need some time to develop. Courses that he had some foundation in came more natural with the results to show (Law a 5, to start at least, and Tourism marketing, a 5.2).

His early troubles may have also been a result of how much time he missed. In the first ten-week period he missed forty-two hours.[139] That is almost two weeks, or 20 percent of that first term. His dossier does not record the reason why he missed so much time, signaling that it did not lead to disciplinary action. He did not leave the country during that period, at least according to the Lausanne city archives.[140] Perhaps, to speculate, he was partying. We know he was a social creature, both in Hanover—recall the work parties he attended, including one that "lasted until the morning"—and Beirut, even if Lausanne may appear a sleepier town.[141] Given his politics and the time, perhaps he was agitating. Yes, in Hannover, Imad kept his head down, but this was before his affiliation to the Union of Lebanese Communists and his translation of Leon's work. His politics were more developed by his Lausanne days, something he may have wanted to explore in and around the area.

One of his friend's paths may be useful in considering the politics of a practical radical. Nabil Khishin, Imad's co-translator, was at the University of Lyon at the same time. Nabil also did not go to class much, by his own admission, less than Imad. This was because "from the first year I was in Lyon I was trying to look for people who were doing political activities, especially among the Arab students."[142] He became president of the Arab Student Federation. His activities included meeting with Arab workers—mostly of North African origin—starting a branch for Palestinian solidarity, and at one point, blocking the visit of the mayor of Jerusalem to Lyon.[143] By his own measure, their network became the "strongest leftist faction" in Lyon. Then in the same interview, Nabil tells me the story of how he helped kidnap two Israeli Mossad operatives that were trying to infiltrate their cell:

> We decided to take them to Paris. We called Mahmoud al-Hamshari [Fatah operative in Paris] because he was in charge of the PLO. I told him we are bringing two prisoners. We went by car to Paris with these two guys with us. It was incredible. We could have been arrested at any time. But anyhow we managed to get them to Mahmoud al-Hamshari. I heard from him that they were sent to Jordan and executed.[144]

Somehow, Nabil passed and received his masters from the University of Lyon, even if he admits having to escape assassination several times. He then moved to Dubai to pursue the career of a translator. Emirati authorities knew of his activity in Lyon, which, he tells me, had to stop thereafter.[145]

Nabil serves as an alternative reality of a practical radical. He was fully engaged in radical politics, willing to put his life on the line for causes he believed in, but ended up pursuing a career because the former was blocked. This is slightly different for Imad, as both pathways were open for him until the very moment he ceded his autonomy to his politics, a story for the next chapter.

Interestingly enough, Nabil does not remember Imad talking about his career in the hotel industry or his job at Hotel Phoenicia.[146] He once told me, they were "completely polarized by politics ... our daily life was not a matter of discussion between us."[147] This may be true, and Imad did not feel the need to describe his life outside of Leon and the Left. I acknowledge, as I did in the last chapter, perhaps jobs were secondary to star gazing youth like Imad and Nabil. As their translation and political activity show, they were working to build a future where they and their people were truly liberated. At the same time, Imad's training was a central part of his life and largely how his family remembers him today. They invested years of time and energy toward it. So while I understand why career building is disregarded, both in the scholarship and my interviews with Imad's comrades, I find it essential to highlight the place it held in the identity formation of practical radicals.

To return to why Imad may have missed forty-two hours of school, I doubt he was as politically engaged as Nabil. He could have been trying to connect with Arabs in the city, or organize with the few Arabs at school, but Lausanne was not Lyon.[148] Perhaps it had its own sixties moment, but not the level of student and worker demonstrations and sit-ins on campus (particularly on Palestine) that Nabil would have experienced.[149] In sum, I cannot rule out that Imad missed time for politics, but unlike Nabil, if he did it likely was as a part of, not leading the cause.

After finishing the coursework at *École Hôtelière de Lausanne*, Imad started an internship at the nearby Hotel Mirabeau. In this five-month period, he would be able to practice the recording keeping, *mécanographie*, controls, and front of house, customer facing interactions he learned in school. He was paid roughly 350 francs a month, including housing and meals at Mirabeau.[150] He made up for lost time, a poor start, and did well on his final exams, receiving a composite score of 4.69.[151] This would put him at "good enough," "satisfactory, although with notable flaws and slight shortcomings."[152] While at first glance, this may not seem too impressive, he finished in the top 25 of the most difficult course at the most prestigious university in his field. "During his stay with us," writes P Barakat, executive secretary of *École Hôtelière de Lausanne*, "he gave every satisfaction from the point of view of conduct, punctuality and good behaviour."[153] Why he missed all of that time is still unknown, but he succeeded in the professional training that he saw as necessary to build his career.

Changing Beliefs in a Similar Profession

After finishing his internship and graduating in late 1970, Imad left Lausanne on March 10, 1971.[154] It appears it took him a few months, but he found a job in London, which started three days after his arrival.[155] By this point, Imad had already rethought his earlier, less critical stances on Europe. Nevertheless, his experiences of British empire in the imperial metropole marked a new stage of his critiques. Take, for example, these words in an April 1971 letter home, only a month after arrival:

> How is it possible to describe this Anglo-Saxon people as high-class when it
> swallows up the bounties of the people and their strength and it still considers
> the foreigner "the savage," practicing social, political, and economic racism
> in its ugliest and fiercest form. And the people which come to this country,

> it is not enough [for the English] to take advantage of them … its pension
> is not equal to English pension money, but rather is under [English] control
> and every day is a kind of psychological terror and sometimes the holding
> [of pensions] is practiced by the locals (the high-class)!! [In English] This
> humiliation. How is this civilization![156]

This criticism of British treatment of foreigners, with a focus on labor
exploitation, was specific to London at this time in history. As Britain shifted
from an "empire of rule to an empire of influence" in the early 1970s, the capital
continued to grow as a city of (formerly) colonized peoples.[157] In transition, the
functioning of London hinged on labor informality, one that foreign workers
like Imad experienced in and beyond their workplaces.[158] Particularly startling
to him was how, under tenuous work and infrequent pay, the British were
"pitting them against each other and dividing them: the Arabs, Pakistanis,
Indians, Liberians, Africans, Southerners [read: South Africans], the Chinese,
the Irish."[159] Imad chose his words deliberately, elsewhere writing that this was
a legacy of Britain's colonial "policy of divide and rule."[160] Here then, Imad
both links the treatment of Arabs to other oppressed people, in the Global
North and South, and critiques contemporary social and economic relations
as birthed from British imperial history.

The status of Imad's job was also affecting his views on the English and
the West. In 1966–7 from Hanover, Imad imagined climbing the corporate
latter within Intercontinental. In 1967–8, he tried to realize that, taking an
internship in Beirut as a means to set him up for that career. And even on
the other side of translating a critique of global capitalism, Zionism, and
Arab suffering under it, he sought out degree training away from his home
and his people. This is because, I think, Imad assumed that given all this
experience, he would be able to work, freely, as a foreigner in Europe. But,
by 1971, that dream was shattered. He arrived under the assumption that he
would be a salaried employee, but as he writes in his first letter home from
London:

> I work as an intern [and] thus I do not have the opportunity to become more
> powerful [at] my job or work towards anything else … the days challenge me
> from this predicament which I am in. And my situation is not possible to
> continue in any form. I have designed a job that would not last.[161]

Imad had to come home then. He believed his secondary status as a foreigner would always get in the way of his career dreams. However, was this actually the case?

The path toward upper management in the field of hospitality was long and circuitous, even for those who were Europeans working in Europe. Take a Swiss student from *École Hôtelière de Lausanne*. According to a Curriculum Vitae I examined, the student graduated in 1964, and following their internships (unlike Imad they came in to the school with no prior hotel experience) had to take another internship in a hotel in Bern. It was not until 1967 that they would become the head receptionist, at the same hotel they interned at, with two positions in between at two other hotels in two other European regions.[162]

From this perspective, Imad should not have been surprised by his internship status in London. He had just graduated with no connections in England. Perhaps he did not hold on long enough in Europe, disenchanted before he could rise the career ladder. But his status as a foreigner made him more aware that the path toward success was extremely narrow. This fueled his comments on British treatment of foreigners and his hope for a system where discrimination would disappear.

From another perspective, yes, Imad appears a bit misguided. Take another one of his fellow students, Selim El Zyr, one of three Lebanese students at *École Hôtelière de Lausanne*. Before gaining salaried positions across Europe, he received two advanced degrees, one that appears to be in hospitality management from the prestigious Cornell University. He then returned to Lebanon and the region to start his own regional hotel brand, Rotana.[163] Perhaps he was a better student, or perhaps he was less politically driven, but Zyr shows an alternative route.[164] Get more degrees, get experience in Europe, and make it back home. Imad did a truncated version of this, but one that ended in despair in Europe and a forced return home.

So Imad represents the real, tangible, career concerns and trajectory for students in the Global Sixties. But, for all that imagining, would Imad realize his career objectives? This was the crossroads for Imad, and the point at which the concept of a practical radical fades and becomes less relevant for our purposes. Within two years, as I detail in the next chapter, Imad would join the Communist Party, the same year in which he would train with *fedayeen* in south Lebanon. Then, another two years later, he would take up arms for this cause. Yes, he continued working at Phoenicia, but at that point, working at a hotel, even as a head receptionist, was more of a job than a career. Imad then is a case study of when, how, and why someone cedes their autonomy to a radical cause greater than themselves. As outlined in this chapter, this unfolded gradually through the mix of hanging out with likeminded people, engaging radical works, and experiencing hopelessness in the career that allowed for a semblance of self-sufficiency in the first place. In the specter of Europe's claims to civilization, Imad conceived a different future by the early 1970s, one he would seek to build from: "I do not mean to say that we are more civilized than the English. But I am sure that our future is favored."[165]

Looking and Fighting for a Home in the Lebanese Left

Subject: About Imad Nuwayhed

Nashville, Tennessee 2020–1

The Covid-19 pandemic was terrible. But for those like me, lucky enough to be healthy and safe, there were some silver linings. I took the time to reconnect on Zoom with old friends and leveraged the tech for new opportunities. For example, in October 2020, I gave a Zoom talk on this project, Imad Nuwayhid, and the global microhistory I was starting to write. Two days after the talk, I received the following email with the above noted subject line:

> *Dear Professor Baun,*
>
> *I have just found by coincidence your event announcement about the martyr Imad Nuwayhed, and I find it very interesting that you chose this fellow as a topic for your research. In fact, there is a song by a Lebanese communist artist called Khaled El Habre about the martyrdom of Imad and two comrades just after they died in 1976. I hope that you already had it or listened to it, as part of your project.*
>
> *Best regards*
>
> *Omar El Deeb*

I had not heard of the song Omar mentioned, or Habre. And like Omar, I was curious about his curiosity. So I replied with an explanation of my project and an inquiry on his interest in Imad. Omar responded, "I am interested in this history in particular since I am politically active in the Lebanese Communist Party."

After some back and forth, Omar and I arranged a WhatsApp call for March 2021 where we spoke for almost an hour. Among many other things, I learned that Omar occasionally googles "Lebanese Communist Party," in English, to see if there is any new English-language research out beyond Lebanon on his party. When he did that in late 2020, he saw my talk. To review, a member of the Lebanese Communist Party with information on my work found me, thousands of miles away, during a deadly pandemic no less, and reached out. This felt, in a word, fated.

Omar is a physicist and commentator on Lebanese politics. He came from a family of communists, joined the youth wing of the party when he was sixteen, then the Communist Party at age nineteen, and he currently serves as the foreign minister for the party. He was too young to know Imad, but he learned about him from Khalid al-Habre's song, as well as his father, who knew Imad before his death. We promised to stay in touch and meet next time I came to Lebanon.

Beirut, June 15, 2022

It's been over four years since the last time I was in Lebanon. In my first arranged meeting, on my first morning in Beirut, I meet Omar at the Lebanese Communist Party headquarters. We are joined by Marwan Rai (Youth Affairs), Hassan Zeitouny (Education), and Maurice Nahra (the head of party affairs for the mountain district during the war). Like others in this story, I saw Maurice in the archives before meeting him in person. Maurice spoke at Imad Nuwayhid's funeral, as reported in the party's al-Nida' newspaper the day after Imad's death. During our meeting, I learned Maurice knew Imad, both as a college student at Lebanese University and as a member of the party. Maurice met Imad at two party festivals in the early 1970s at Lebanese University. I began to think: were these the encounters when Imad decided to move from the Union of Lebanese Communists to the Lebanese Communist Party? If so, what was it about this party? At this moment in the 1970s?

***

Imad returned to Lebanon circa 1971, and so will we. He re-enrolled in Lebanese University, continuing his studies in law and—from high school— history.[1] He reconnected with old friends, like Rida Ismael, and joined new leftist groups, like *al-Munazima al-'Amal al-Shuyu'i*, the Lebanese Communist Action Organization. And, according to the party, in 1973 he found his home and joined the ranks of the Lebanese Communist Party.[2]

Imad's shift from leftist intellectual to leftist mainstream is perhaps surprising. As I outlined in the previous chapter, the state of the Lebanese Communist Party, *c.* 1968, was not good. Many young leftists found it ossified, controlled by the Soviet Union, and irrelevant. Yet, Imad's path to the party was not unique. It reflected other leftist young men and women who were at a crossroads *c.* 1973: between theoretical and realized revolution. Some of them held out in smaller cadres, but many ended up joining the Old Left parties, like the Lebanese Communist Party and Progressive Socialist Party. Imad's actions, then, provide a window into the state of the Lebanese Left, from student movements, to labor unions, to parties, in the years immediately preceding the war.

With Imad silent from 1972 to his untimely death in 1975—I have no letters from him nor, beyond reference, any published writings—perhaps it is best to summarize the previous chapter and his last written words. His dedication to armed struggle for Palestine intensified as he translated and introduced Abram Leon's anti-Zionist text in 1969. Per his letters from London in 1971, Imad's career path began to crumble, what he saw as the product of Western racism. These experiences provided a backdrop for him to connect the plight of Palestinians and Arabs to those of other oppressed people, whether in the Global South or North. At this very same time, the Lebanese Communist Party moved closer and closer to the Palestinian cause.

Equally important in analyzing the move to the Communist Party, though, is what youth leftists like Imad would be turning away from: the more intellectually driven, middle-class, fringe movements. This included groups that Imad was previously part of, including the Union of Lebanese Communists and the Lebanese Communist Action Organization. While the former was defunct by 1971, the latter was thriving. From interviewing his friends and comrades today, it appears that while the Lebanese Communist Action Organization was with the workers and Palestinians—one reason Imad joined it in the first place—it was not from either. Then, I argue, *c.* 1973, Imad and many other young leftists embraced a larger, working-class, more established fighting force that had a recent history of fighting directly with the Palestinian Liberation Movement and for the Palestinian cause.

This chapter takes up Imad's decisions and reconstructs the broader context in which he made them, what I refer to as the "early Lebanese civil war era" (1968–76).[3] Particularly important are a set of local incursions between the Lebanese state, populous, and the Palestinian liberation movement in 1972–3. Scholars of the Lebanese Civil War often reference the Saida demonstrations of February 1975 and Ain al-Rummaneh massacre of April 1975 as the sparks for the war, something I do not seek to challenge.[4] Yet a focus on the Left, and toward young people like Imad that came, quite circuitously, to the front lines, shifts our attention to a set of different, earlier, and lesser known events. They include the Ghandour factory strike of late 1972 and the May 1973 army-*fedayeen* clashes. Both pitted leftist workers, sympathizers, and the Palestinian cause against the Lebanese state, army, and its supporters, like the Kataib Party. They collectively marked a rupture, backing the eventual parties to the war into more zero-sum, us vs. them stances, and mobilizing young ideologues to follow them to the front lines.

Imad Nuwayhid was one of these young men, who like thousands of others in the first years of the war, perished in battle. Death in war is both cruel and random; a certain person in a certain moment perishes while others who made similar decisions, who may have been in that same moment and same place, go on living. Yet, as I explain in the second half of *Beirut Radical*—a hard truth for some of his loved ones—Imad was ready for death. This end demonstrates the exact moment at which Imad ceded his quest for autonomy within a radically changing world to the cause he would die for: Palestine.

Movements, Students, and Unions in 1970s Lebanon

While Imad was away from home, again, from 1969 to 1971, between Lausanne, London, and Dublin, the "Palestinian factor" in Lebanon was on the rise.[5] Following the 1968 Israeli attack at Beirut International Airport (a violation of Lebanese sovereignty which resulted in over US$ 43 million in damages), the pressing question of the time was: what would the Lebanese state do to defend and support Palestinian liberation?[6] The November 1969 Cairo Agreement sought to address this question through "positive cooperation" between the Palestine Resistance and the Lebanese Army.[7] For all intents and purposes, it was quite favorable to *fedayeen* actions, an "explicit legitimization … of the Palestinian military presence in Lebanon."[8] Then there was Black September, 1970, where the Jordanian army looked to crush the Palestinian resistance there, forcing its hand to move to Lebanon. After this event, as Khalidi argues, Palestinian *fedayeen* "were deeply imbued with the idea that the only way to avoid what had happened [in Jordan] was to surround themselves with sympathetic formations of the Lebanese Left."[9] Indeed, they found a willing audience with leftists like Imad.

As the Palestinian resistance became more embedded in Lebanon in the 1970s—militarily, at the border in its incursions against Israel, and politically, predominantly in the capital among leftist forces—a counter-movement was birthed. Its representatives were Lebanese president Suleiman Franjieh (1970–6), his confidant in the army, General Iskander Ghanem, and a sympathetic party on the streets, the Kataib Party. Its leader, Pierre Gemayel, chastised the Lebanese Left's unlimited support for the *fedayeen*, which, he argued, ostensibly turned Lebanon into a battlefield for regional affairs. With every Palestinian attack into Israel (sixty-four in 1971–2) and every Israeli retribution into Lebanon (30,000 violations of Lebanese sovereignty between 1969 and 1974), the Kataib's anti-*fedayeen* stance solidified.[10] As the Kataib was a Christian, populist force, in defense of the Maronite Christian-led army and Christian president, the stance was understandably interpreted by the Left as sectarian. That is, the Kataib was dangerous, protecting a small, Christian-led Lebanon in the face of Arab and Palestinian solidarity.[11]

By the 1970s, the Lebanese face of that solidarity was Kamal Jumblatt, the leader of the Progressive Socialist Party.[12] As I described in Chapter 1, his revolutionary bona fides go back to the 1958 War, when he waged an armed campaign against the government and its, in his own words, "occidental alliance with the United States."[13] While meeting with Gamal Abdel Nasser in support of pan-Arab unification in 1958, a decade later he argued for a "stage of unification" between various Palestinian liberation groups working in Lebanon and the Lebanese Left.[14] At the same time, he sought to unify the ranks of the Lebanese Left. With the help of the Lebanese Communist Party in 1969, he created *al-Ahzab wa al-Quwwa al-Taqadumiyya fi Lubnan*, the Progressive

Parties and Forces in Lebanon.[15] Under Jumblatt's guidance, it placed domestic reform—most notably, the abolishment of political sectarianism in Lebanon—within a transnational program that linked Palestine liberation to other Third World causes, ranging from China to Vietnam. During the war years, Jumblatt's creation became known as *al-Haraka al-Wataniyya al-Lubnaniyya*, the Lebanese National Movement.[16]

Jumblatt's shift away from Pan-Arabism and toward Arab Marxism, was, as I explained in the previous two chapters, a product of 1967, where Nasser's Arab nationalism had lost. Imad and his comrades in the Union for the Lebanese Communists also made this turn. They were in full support of the Palestinian cause and "*fedayeen* actions."[17] They also linked Palestinian liberation to other causes, like Vietnam, as shown in the suggested reading list included at the end of Imad's translation of *The Jewish Question*. At the same time, they didn't think Jumblatt was the one who should guide them. Indeed, the charter for the Union of Lebanese Communists attacks the leader of the Progressive Socialist Party alongside the Lebanese Communist Party, criticizing Jumblatt for working too closely with "the ruling bourgeoise of the state."[18]

In sum, Imad was furthering, and being furthered by, a more leftist and transnational scene in seventies Beirut, or what Maasri refers to as "Arab Hanoi."[19] In particular, the city was becoming the political and cultural center of the Palestinian liberation movement. Young supporters like Imad were engaged in "literature, poetry, films, songs, and printed material" toward creating a "revolutionary discourse," circulated around Beirut and beyond, on, for, and by joint Palestinian-Lebanese solidarity, linked to a global decolonial movement.[20] Indeed, the Lebanese version of liberation was becoming more steeped in a rhetoric that pitted its populist vision for the future against a conspiracy, fronted by Zionism and Israel, backed by its global funders (most notably the United States), regional allies (so-called reactionary regimes, like Saudi Arabia), and its local supporters. By the early 1970s, "the plot" included the Lebanese state, the army, and the Kataib.[21]

But which party or organization could help realize joint Lebanese-Palestinian liberation and defeat its enemies? Imad's pre-Lausanne home, the Union of Lebanese Communists, ceased to exist as Imad returned to Beirut. For one, even if internationalist in outlook, it could not withstand the migration of many of its leaders and members, including Nabil and Imad. But there was a bigger blow at home: the creation of the Lebanese Communist Action Organization, the group that Imad joined next. While Imad was in London, the Lebanese Communist Action Organization had formed as a merger between a number of Marxist-Leninist movements, but *not* the Union of Lebanese Communists. As ex-union member tells me, "Instead of inviting us [as an organization to join their merger] they launched an attack [saying] you should join us but individually."[22]

When it was formally announced in July 1971, the Lebanese Communist Action Organization's two largest constituents came from *Lubnan Ishtiraki*, Socialist Lebanon—led by Lebanese sociologist Waddah Charara—and *Harakat al-Qawmiyyin al-Arab*, the Arab Nationalist Movement—founded by Palestinian George Habash in the 1950s as a transnational organization, but at this point, mostly Lebanese-based and led by Muhsin Ibrahim.[23] First and foremost, the organization leaned into the "entrance of Palestinian *fedayeen* into Lebanon as a lever for a popular [Lebanese] struggle." Like other movements of the New Left, it took the momentum of this cause, which it believed in, as the basis for a social and political revolution in Lebanon. Moreover, it formed in contrast to Old Left parties and institutions, "refus[ing] the path of the parliament of the Lebanese Communist Party," instead favoring "grassroots student, farmer, and worker struggles."[24]

One would not be misguided, to see this platform as very similar to that of the Union of Lebanese Communists: anti-elite, anti-party politics, populist, and pro-Palestinian. On one level, this signals how difficult it was for New Left groups to distinguish themselves from the field, given the growing centrality of the Palestinian issue in popular, leftist politics at this time. To do so was a matter of winning or losing new recruits, like Imad Nuwayhid. On another level, this is perhaps one reason the Lebanese Communist Action Organization only wanted the energy of past union members, but not its name. To take the latter, or officially merge, would only serve to challenge Muhsin Ibrahim, and, as I describe later, his sole control over the new organization. Regardless of these inter-Marxist squabbles, what came out of the unification, in Guirguis' estimation, was the "most significant New Left group in Lebanon."[25]

In an interview, Rida Ismael explains to me why he and Imad joined the Lebanese Communist Action Organization *c.* 1972. "Imad and I [were talking] what should we do," he tells me. "We do not only [care about] student sections but worker and neighborhood [local, grassroots] sections … so Imad and I agreed we will go to the Organization."[26] Over fifty years since, Rida is clear about what Imad and he wanted. There were no longer students at Raml al-Zarif high school. Imad was twenty-seven and Rida twenty-one. Student issues were only one of the litany of others they cared about. Like Nabil Khishin in Lyon, as I discussed in Chapter 3, they wanted to work with and mobilize workers. They also cared about where they lived, their neighborhood, the diversity of people that lived there, and also, in Rida's words "the Palestinian organizations."[27] Because they thought the Lebanese Communist Action Organization was—my words, not theirs—intersectional, they joined it.

Nevertheless, just because Rida and Imad entered the ranks of the Lebanese Communist Action Organization does not mean they were bound to them. Like Imad, other young leftists were studying and working. This means they could have multiple affiliations to groups on campus or in their workplace that served—or they wanted them to serve—their worldview. For Imad, although he left Europe disenchanted and less hopeful for his career, that did not mean he left the hotel industry. According to his family, Imad worked at Hotel Phoenicia Intercontinental as the head of reception, perhaps until his death.[28] Even if he learned in Europe that his career was not durable, he did not choose apathy. Instead, it appears his poor experiences as a foreign worker led him to seek better labor conditions for those in the industry. In one short reference, in Imad's obituary in *al-Nida'*, it reads that he "participated in the ranks of unions, especially in unions for hotels, restaurants, and amusement parks."[29]

But what were these unions like? Imad's profession would have been protected and unionized at least since the formation of the Union for Employees of Hotels, Catering Establishments, and the role of Entertainment in 1952.[30] Earlier in the decade, there was only one union federation for all of Lebanon. By the 1960s, there were multiple, representing over 100 some individual trade unions. And *c.* 1965, over 20 percent of the working population in Lebanon was unionized.[31] While there were many labor strikes during the 1960s, this growth of unions and federations was not free; it was tied up in the same Cold War that shaped Imad's coming of age. Some federations leaned toward Marxism, and may be supported by the Soviet Union, others were backed by the United States, which sought to "build a labor bulwark against communism."[32]

According to Bou Khater, labor politics in Lebanon "had always been subject to state intervention, which had systematical weakened its development and limited its influence since independence."[33] As the Lebanese state had been outwardly Pro-United States since independence, the main labor federation of the 1960s and 1970s, the General Confederation of Workers in Lebanon, was marked by a pro-United States agenda and funds, conservative on labor issues, and largely served the interests of private corporations and its executives.[34] The Union for Employees of Hotels, Catering Establishments, and the role of Entertainment, likely reformed and renamed in the 1970s, was under this confederation.[35] In short, this means if Imad was active in a union, its function would likely have run counter to his current politics.

This did not mean that the leftist movements and parties—ranging from the Communist Party to the Communist Action Organization—had no inroads in this confederation or, as I discuss in the case of the Ghandour factory strike, ties with particular workers. Moreover, labor politics writ large were also affected by the Palestinian cause. For example, a 1973 article in the newspaper *Nidal al-'Ummal*, Struggle of the Workers—released by the "voice of labor committees," apparently affiliated with the Lebanese Communist Party—called for "the Coalescence of the Lebanese and Palestinian masses to protect the nation and the [Palestinian] resistance."[36] The framing for such a call, in a paper dedicated to workers, was not only tied to labor, but a broader, popular solidarity. Hence, Imad's desire to be connected to workers and Palestine, did not have to come through a particular union tied to his profession. It could come through other affiliations that he and his comrades held.

More generally leftist, aligned with Imad's politics, were the student unions and the field of student politics in Beirut.[37] "The student movement after the 1967 war," per Anderson, "was characterized by demonstrations, strikes, and student occupations of campus buildings … as a tool for breaking the power of the establishment [and achieving] the return of Palestine."[38] These prevailing, "increasingly radicalized" dynamics were arguably most palpable at Lebanon's only public university, Lebanese University.[39] From 1972 to 1974, Imad was studying law and history there.

Historian and member of the Lebanese Communist Action Organization, Fawwaz Traboulsi, explains one protest movement that gives a sense of campus at the time:

> A fifty-day strike by both the students and teachers of the Lebanese University began in April 1968. The latter were demanding a wage increase and tenure, the former sought the building of a unified university campus, an increase in scholarships and the provision of university restaurants. None of these demands were met, but the students managed to impose the formation of the National Union of Lebanese University Students. As a sign of the radicalization of the student movement, the Left alliance [Progressive Socialist Party, the Lebanese Communist Party, and the Lebanese Communist Action Organization] gained control over [this student union], which in March/April 1972 launched a massive strike to press for its demands.[40]

Over the course of four years, what were once tenure and scholarship issues, were galvanized by leftist parties and turned into an unprecedented strike "supported by students from other [private] universities and secondary schools."[41] And this was all before Imad enrolled. By that time, strikes continued to widen at Lebanese University and President Frangieh considering closing the campus, arguing "university agitation might unleash a revolutionary situation."[42]

The president was right. 1972 became Lebanon's "Year of Rage," and "the student movement was at the fore ... [,] committing to labor and popular causes, supporting tobacco workers at the Régie (the monopoly tobacco company) defending tenants' rights and those of Palestinians to armed struggle."[43] Sociologist Halim Barakat captured the student movement for Palestine in a series of interviews conducted at Beirut universities throughout the 1970s. One of his main findings was that "political alienation and leftist radicalism are defined vis-à-vis the established order." While some students may "retreat from, or comply with" the system, the leftist radical seeks to "resolve their alienation by revolting against the system."[44] At Lebanese University in particular, Barakat found that those he identified as "rebellious activists" constituted a sizeable portion of interviewees, and that the mass majority of them supported the Palestinian cause. Of those pro-Palestinian, leftist radicals at Lebanese University, 38 percent supported armed struggle over other, more peaceful, and diplomatic solutions to liberate Palestine.[45]

Imad not only fit all of these categories. He likely encouraged other students toward these more radical stances.

The Lebanese Communist Party was active in campus politics, and especially at Lebanese University. Its 1974 pamphlet, titled *Jami'a Dimuqratiyya*, "Democratic University," with the subtitle "True participation for a wide student front, for the sake of democratic leadership for a national student union at Lebanese University" indicates as much.[46] Like Barakat, the party uses statistics to highlight the status and importance of the university. As of the 1972–3 school year, 60 percent of all university students in Lebanon went there, and the main demographic the party was trying to target, first year students, constituted 52 percent of the student body, a bigger percentage than at any other, private institution. Written more for party members than students themselves, the pamphlet criticized "non-national education," that is, foreign, private, and one-sect schools, grounded in "bourgeois ideology" and "elitist separation."[47] As the public institution, Lebanese University could play a pioneering role in what Mahdi 'Amal, Lebanese University professor and Lebanese Communist Party member, called "producing a national culture."[48] As I introduced in Chapter 1, these were principles Imad had supported since his choice to leave the French, private *Lycée Français de Beyrouth* and attend the public and national Raml al-Zarif High School.

So in the years preceding the Lebanese Civil War, the Lebanese Communist Party placed a huge emphasis on Lebanese University and its students. So did other parties of the Lebanese National Movement, most notably the Progressive Socialist Party. According to Maurice Nahra, Lebanese Communist Party official in the Mountain district, the two parties jointly held two festivals on Imad's campus during the 1972–3 and 1973–4 school years. Party brass, like Maurice, and affiliated students at Lebanese University, like Ghazi Aridi of the Progressive Socialist Party, gave speeches and looked to help organize—and recruit—students.[49] Being from the area near Ras al-Matn, Maurice already knew the Nuwayhids, but not Imad. He remembers walking with Imad, impressed by this man from "the vanguard of the youth."[50] It is possible Imad was already a party member at either of these festivals— Maurice tells me "he was communist at the time"—but if it was in the first year of his schooling, maybe he was still with the Lebanese Communist Action Organization.[51] Clearly whether in unions or student politics, the Lebanese

Communist Party was everywhere. That it, and not his organization, was showing up may have been a key indication to Imad that the Communist Party was the future of the Left and his future home.

The Lebanese Communist Party, like everything in Imad's orbit, was embracing the Palestinian cause. This was part of an attempt to come back to life. As described in the previous chapter, Imad's Union of Lebanese Communists framed its existence in opposition to the backwardness of the party. This was at the very same moment, 1968, that the Lebanese Communist Party was meeting for its second conference, updating its founding principles. Only one of the original tenets of the party pointed to the regional scene, promoting "fraternal solidarity between Lebanon, Syria, and the rest of the Arab countries and strengthening economic and cultural ties between them."[52] The lack of reference to political ties, or Palestine, was not disingenuous in and of itself. The charter was drafted in 1943, conceived of in a post-war and pre-1948 world. What was so egregious to young leftists of the 1960s was that the party's charter hadn't been updated since independence.[53]

In 1968, the Lebanese Communist Party finally named "the Palestinian issue" in their program.[54] However, at that juncture, the party was only ready to discuss the issue and confess that it had yet to "appreciate the concrete political and national impact of the Palestinian issue."[55] In its ten final action items of '68, only one mentioned Palestine. Number 8 was dedicated to "eliminate the effects of Israeli aggression" and realize "full restoration of the legitimate rights for the Palestinian Arab people [*lil-sha'b al-'Arabi al-Filistini.*]"[56] It appears the party had not yet caught up to the most radical elements of the post-1967 world. In its own words, it subsumed the issue under "a framework of more general struggle among the forces of Arab liberation." Yes, the 1968 program makes mention to "the current resistance movement" and "armed resistance," but the term "Palestinian resistance movement" or full support for it, was absent.[57] To not name Palestinian armed struggle, and consider it only as the extension of an Arab movement, must have read to some young leftists, like those in the ranks of Union of Lebanese Communists, as tone-deaf.

But things started to open up in the 1970s, perhaps one reason the party became extremely active in labor and student politics at that moment. Legal status was granted to the party in 1971, constituting the first time in its forty-seven-year history that it was allowed to operate in the open.[58] This was under

Interior Minister Kamal Jumblatt, whose decision also marked a closer union between the two parties and a new level of cohesion within the Lebanese National Movement. Then in 1972, the time of the next party congress, the Lebanese Communist Party adapted, again, its "missions of the next stage."[59]

Ismael and Ismael argue that although the party "added no fundamentally different ideas to the party's position on Palestine [in 1972] it did put additional stress on certain aspects."[60] While the Palestinian cause was still seen as "part of the Arab national liberation movement hostile to imperialism, Zionism and Arab reactionism," the charter positioned the party in full solidarity with the "Palestinian national liberation movement." In particular, the Lebanese Communist Party believed it had reached a level where now, it "participated in [the Palestinian cause] until blood mixed with blood."[61] Not only did it clarify the enemies it faced, linking Zionism, the United States, and backward regional powers, but that their subjugation of Palestinians was now the subjugation of Lebanese. The charter also, for the first time, named the "Palestinian National Liberation movement" and acknowledged it was "forcing the aggressors to retreat."[62] Stating this as a matter of fact, the Lebanese Communist Party now officially condoned the use of violence by the Palestinian National Movement against Israel.

The 1972 conference was well attended with international communist delegations from the United States, Brazil, France, Yugoslavia, Sudan, and India.[63] Furthermore, a host of Arab leftist parties either attended or sent greetings to voice their support for "Arab national liberation."[64] Regarding Palestine, in what appears to be a first, leadership were invited to speak at the conference. Most notable was Kamal Nasser on the Executive Committee of the Palestinian Liberation Organization (see Figure 4.1 below).

In his speech, Nasser celebrates the Communist Party, and the Lebanese National Movement it was a part of, for "exposing the Zionist imperial conspiracy against the Arab nation."[65] Nasser acknowledges that while the issues of the party and concerns of global communist visitors at the conference were important, the Palestinian revolution "was a complete liberation revolution" and necessitated complete attention and solidarity. Then he says:

> And everyone is aware of the nature of this stage, as it is the stage of national liberation where the true Left distinguishes itself in its ability to fight and struggle confirming its progressive identity for the sake of fighting and armed conflict which are the highest level of support.[66]

Figure 4.1 The 1972 conference of the Lebanese Communist Party. Among Soviet (right, front row), Mongolian, (back right), American (back left), and Arab delegates (middle front row), Lebanese Communist Party leader Karim Mroueh (far left), sits next to Kamal Nasser of the Palestinian Liberation Organization. Courtesy of the Lebanese Communist Party.

Nasser's words can be read as mere platitude, celebrating the Left. But they can also be considered a call to action. Nasser suggests that while it is great that the party had incorporated the resistance into their platform, it was now time to put their bodies where their rhetoric was. Nasser's 1972 conference appearance would become even more significant a year later when he was assassinated in Beirut by Israeli assailants. This event would lead to the first major clashes between Palestinian *fedayeen* and the Lebanese army, with the Lebanese Communist Party on the side of the former.

But a year earlier, in 1972, the young vanguard of the Left were looking for something similar to Nasser, a physical dedication to Palestinian armed struggle. To be clear, youth like Imad probably did not care how much the Lebanese Communist Party had transformed on the issue of Palestine since 1943, even if it had paved the way for Nasser's speech. In one of their founding documents, Imad's Union of Lebanese Communists chides that the Lebanese Communist Party 1968 program, "would not bring anything new" to the Palestinian struggle.[67] In this way Imad's reaction to the 1972 conference, if he had one, was similar to my interpretation of Nasser: it is good, you've come around, but have you put your life on the line for Palestine yet? This all changed in late 1972–3, giving the party fighting credentials to add to its official ones.

The Rupture of 1972–1973

On March 6, 1975, leftist leader Maarouf Saad died from gunshots he sustained a week earlier. The former mayor of Saida had led demonstrations alongside fishermen that ended in armed intervention. To the Left, these events demonstrated that the army would kill its leaders and citizens rather than defend them or the Palestinian cause.[68] The populist representative of the government, the Kataib, did not call for an investigation of the army's crimes in Saida (where eleven were killed), but notified readers in their newspaper that "today Lebanon demonstrates support for the army."[69] Its fighters would do more than support the army against the Left and Palestinians when, on April 13, 1975, it murdered twenty-seven Palestinian men, women, and children in Ain al-Rummaneh.[70]

While these were perhaps the most egregious and immediate sparks that set off the war, they were not the only or earliest ones. Two other events of the early Lebanese Civil War era that first transformed leftist activists, like Imad, into combatants, and specifically toward groups like the Lebanese Communist Party are the Ghandour factory strike of late 1972 and the May 1973 army-*fedayeen* clashes.

Imad never wrote about Ghandour, but many of his contemporaries have stressed its significance. Fawwaz Traboulsi sees the strike as the apex of "rank-and-file workers' struggles" leading up to the war.[71] Rida Ismael echoes Traboulsi: "The Ghandour strike was the biggest in Lebanon for us."[72] Walid Nuwayhid expands, saying as protests spread, at Ghandour and elsewhere, "there was some conviction that there was a possibility to change the Lebanese regime."[73] Scholars concur. While Bou Khater refers to Ghandour as "the crowning point" of the labor struggle, Saba summarizes what the broader moment meant to young people like Walid, Rida, Fawwaz, and Imad: "A segment of Lebanon's Leftist population assert[ed] that … Lebanon was on the verge of a social revolution."[74] Indeed, Ghandour held a very special place for the ranks of the Lebanese Communist Action Organization and Lebanese Communist Party.

Resentment was brewing at Ghandour Chocolate and Biscuits since the late 1960s. The company's 1200-plus workers across three factories—one inside the city in Shiyah, the others outside in Shweifat—represented the largest, non-unionized labor force in the country.[75] Work was hard, unregulated, dangerous, underpaid, and demoralizing.[76] Many workers were originally from south Lebanon, where labor conditions were not much better, but living conditions were. They were forced to what is referred to as Beirut's "misery belt," the suburbs around factories where housing was informal, tight, and provided many companies the cheap labor they coveted.[77] That was if these migrants were lucky enough to find a job in the first place.[78]

Primarily because the labor force was unrepresented, leftist parties sought to gain a foothold to represent Ghandour and mobilize disenfranchisement. This is something Mary Jirmanus Saba takes up in her documentary *Shu'ur Akbar min al-Hub, A Feeling Greater than Love*. It focuses on a series of protests from the 1930s to present in Lebanon, drawing throughlines and considering their legacy. Regarding the 1972 Ghandour factory strike, Saba interviews workers and leftist agitators. One person interviewed, Nadine, was a member of the Lebanese Communist Action Organization at the time. She tells Saba that she and a comrade named Rifaat helped organize workers. "Our goal was to recruit workers. So they would become comrades as quickly as possible."[79]

Rida Ismael's explanation on how he and Imad came to Ghandour is almost identical:

> In this period Imad, I and Rifaat al-Nisr he was a leader in the Communist Action Organization responsible for the labor sections … Imad and I had worker experience. We went to the factories … we started going to visit the houses of workers … [, including] Ghandour workers.[80]

In fact, Nadine's Rifaat is Rida and Imad's Rifaat.[81] The four were tasked with the same objective: meet with workers in an attempt to organize and link worker plights to that of their communist organization. Even though this may have been one reason Imad eventually soured on the Communist Action Organization—connecting with but not made up of workers—it appears that leftists were still willing to learn from the workers they recruited. One in Saba's documentary says "The workers were conscious. When I started to organize the workers, I am coming to explain their conditions to them [but instead] they explained to me. I learned more from them."[82]

On November 3, 1972, workers at Ghandour in Shiyah took the lead, staging a walkout. The following day, the headlines in *al-Nida'* read "Ghandour workers announce a strike after administration refused to increase wages by 5 percent."[83] The strike started with 200 workers, but a day later, it included those at the Shweifat location and apparently grew to 1,500.[84] In this moment and the coming weeks, "the worker movement transformed into a national political movement. It became a political, union and worker battle."[85]

Worker demands were published in leftist newspapers as such:

1. No workers dismissed after the end of the strike
2. Increase the living wage and give workers a [pay] cycle increase
3. Allow workers affiliation in the sweets and groceries union
4. Prohibit arbitrary calculation of overtime ages which [exceed] 9 ½ hours and create rebates in a special fund for social programs for the wellness of workers
5. Grant 17 holiday days
6. Pay wages for emergency injury days
7. Eliminate the terror which is directed toward workers and prohibit physical punishment
8. Give workers of Shweifat transportation wages.[86]

No retribution for striking, unionization, no exploitation or violence, and access to social welfare; while it is unclear if Imad was aware of these demands, based on his past writings, it appears he would be in solidarity with them. Throughout the course of his career, his pay was often unstable, overtime wages arbitrary, and he had to pay for transport to work. Indeed, in Hanover, it appears that the only time that his employers offered to increase his pay was when he told them he would be leaving.[87] Accordingly, I believe he would have supported and encouraged the words of Mustafa al-Aris, member of a labor federation associated with the Lebanese Communist Party, and columnist of *al-Nida'*. He asked of Ghandour, "Are any of these demands unreasonable?"[88]

Ghandour owners never heeded the apparent reasonable demands from its workers. As quoted in *al-Nida'*, a statement from the company reads, "We are not able to look into their [demands] except after they finish their strike and they return to work."[89] Workers were eventually dismissed, which led to more and larger demonstrations, and eventually clashes. On November 11, 1972, protests ended with the death of two workers, one of which was associated with the Lebanese Communist Action Organization, Yusuf al-Attar, the other,

Fatima Khuwajah, associated with the Lebanese Communist Party. Fatima was from Aitaroun in south Lebanon, and, according to the Lebanese Communist Party, was killed by, in scare quotes, "'stray' bullets" at the hands of unchecked internal security forces.[90] Two days later, labor federations called for a general strike as protests spread across the country and linked up with other, related labor concerns.[91]

Those who wrote into the Lebanese Communist Party's daily *al-Nida'* thought the company and state was coming for its own people. One woman who knew Fatima, Linda Maatar asks, "Do you think that the factory owners, no the cities of sweets, were more humane than the tobacco monopolists [that attacked workers in 1946]?" Her answer was a resounding no, but in the end she believes the "workers, [their] sweat, tears, and blood" would win out against the corrupt owners and the state.[92] In this moment of violence, leftists begin to narrate these events in increasingly zero-sum, populist terms: the bourgeois state, and its interests, against the workers and the people.

Linda and other leftists hoped for the "implementation of the good demands" of the Ghandour strike but that never came to pass.[93] Days later, the owners of Ghandour closed the factory, dismissed the workers, claimed to form a committee to negotiate, and then re-opened on November 16 once momentum from the strike had dissipated.[94] In the interim, the Lebanese Communist Action Organization and the Lebanese Communist Party were active. One member of the former claims that "without the [Lebanese Communist Action] organization there wouldn't have been a strike."[95] But to be clear, the Lebanese Communist Party just had more connections and worker representation in its ranks. It had been building out its party-labor union networks since it formed in the 1920s, including its deep connection with the first labor federation in Lebanon, something it had looked to expand since gaining official party status just a year before the strike.[96] While in a prior era, that long, old, and official history may have been considered a weakness, in this moment, the Lebanese Community Party was the most recognizable and rooted force linked to the largest labor strike in the country.

After its initial reporting on the death of Fatima, and the quashing of the strike, the Lebanese Communist Party stopped covering Ghandour—at least as a single event. Its newspaper framed it as part of a national social crisis and unified movement, covering other protests that picked up pace, including in other industries, and among taxi drivers, port, airport, agricultural workers, journalists, students, and teachers.[97] Like in other instances, the Lebanese Communist Party was coalescing multiple demands, from class to Palestinian solidarity, not just those of factory workers. Hence, Ghandour was an inflection point toward that unified, leftist movement, galvanizing young leftists like Imad.

Regardless of whether the party specifically drew attention to Ghandour after 1972, it stuck with the workers and moved new recruits to the Lebanese Communist Party. Nadine, the organizational operative mentioned above in Saba's documentary, argues that while the Lebanese Communist Action Organization's efforts were perhaps stronger than the Lebanese Communist Party in Ghandour, "Once things got tough and workers got fired from Ghandour factory and several others, the organization pulled out and left the workers to deal with the fallout some with work, some starving or whatever."[98] Nadine, like Imad, eventually moved to the Lebanese Communist Party. She does not mention why, but its historic and strong connections to workers were likely a reason. Rida's actions, or at least his retelling of those actions, run parallel to that of Nadine. He explains the terms by which he and Imad left:

> I began [to ask] why are there two communist organizations? Why the Lebanese Communist Party and the Communist Action Organization? Why aren't they united? One organization? There was a section of the leaders of the organization [saying] 'What is it that we are afraid of? There was a choice, we left' ... and the same thing, the same step for Imad and I.[99]

While Nadine mentions the Organization's neglect of Ghandour workers, Rida mentions redundancy and defections. Bardawil confirms the latter, stating that the Organization was "plagued by splits and expulsions" throughout the 1970s.[100]

Regarding the issue of redundancy, by 1972, there was a "growing consensus" between the Lebanese Communist Action Organization and Lebanese Communist Party.[101] The former had recently become a part of the Lebanese National Movement with the latter at the forefront. Hence, the Lebanese Communist Action Organization could no longer claim an anti-elite, anti-establishment, anti-party high ground. Accordingly, some, like Imad and Rida, began to consider if they are one and the same, why not join the party that is everywhere? The stronger party?

More immediate than Ghandour, and perhaps more consequential in leading young intellectuals to the mainstream Communist Party, and eventually toward war, was the May 1973 army-*fedayeen* clashes. Although Israel had regularly attacked Lebanese territory and interests since 1968, 1973 marked the first time they targeted specific, high-profile Palestinian officials working in Beirut.[102] On April 10, Israeli forces launched "Operation Spring of Youth," murdering three leaders of the Palestinian Liberation Organization in Beirut and evading without being caught.[103] One of those men was Kamal Nasser, executive for the Palestinian Liberation Organization and speaker at the 1972 Lebanese Communist Party conference.

The Lebanese National Movement immediately called for a general strike.[104] Nearly half a million people attended the funeral of the fallen Palestinian leaders. The Lebanese National Movement also joined calls for the resignation of Army Commander Iskandar Ghanem, blaming the army for their deaths and inaction in the face of Israel aggression. President Frangieh refused this call and the Prime Minister resigned.[105] The fall out wouldn't end there.

For the Lebanese Communist Party, spring 1973 was a pivotal moment. In certain ways, party rhetoric does not look that different than that of earlier crises. In an April 1973 statement titled, "The change needed to put an end to the politics of inaction and surrender," the party cites "collusion between the [Lebanese] powers and the Zionist abusers," claiming this was confirmed by the state's aloofness in the face of Israeli crimes. Also, like in the past, the Lebanese Communist Party links the immediate issue to concurrent crises, as the ruling powers "have turned away from the workers, tobacco farmers, students, and the crowds of the people."[106] In this way, Ghandour and the 1973 crisis were not separate issues, one labor, one military. They were wholly linked by a government that no longer cared for its people.

However, there is one way this statement marked a new era for the Lebanese Communist Party, and, I argue, signals a key reason leftist youth like Imad would join at this moment. It reads, "It has become the duty of the crowds to prepare to bear arms and personally resist the repeated Israeli aggression which will continue … [and] to preserve the dignity of the nation and encourage the

Palestinian resistance."[107] To my knowledge, this is the first call to arms from the Lebanese Communist Party preceding the beginning of the Lebanese Civil War in April 1975. Even if it was not asking members to fight directly against the government, if the government was facilitating Israeli aggression, the call to physically defend the Palestinian cause was implied.

Not only did President Frangieh not agree to the resignation of Ghanem. He let Ghanem turn his arsenal on Palestinian commandos. What unfolded was sixteen days of clashes between the army and *fedayeen*. It marked the first time the Lebanese Air Force was used to bomb Palestinian refugee camps in Lebanon (starting May 2nd).[108] This created outrage among the Lebanese Left. For its worth, the Lebanese Communist Party laid blame at the Lebanese government alone. A May 4 *al-Nida'* cartoon showed a Lebanese army tank firing towards Lebanon, in the opposing direction of Israel.[109] Given the prevailing state of affairs, the party called for "complete struggle to stop the massacres … against the *fedayeen*, residents of the Palestinian camps, and the Lebanese crowds."[110]

The *fedayeen* fought back. Perhaps most active of the groups in these clashes were the Popular Front for the Liberation of Palestine and Popular Democratic Front for the Liberation of Palestine—engaged in kidnappings of army officers—and Fatah—which ordered rocket attacks on the Lebanese Air Force.[111] What officially came out of these clashes was an update to the 1969 Cairo Agreement, including the creation of a "Joint High Commission of the Lebanese Army Command and the Palestinian armed struggle Command … to attend to all problems and misunderstandings between the two sides as they might emerge."[112]

Yet, pandora's box was opened. On the right, the Kataib which was surprisingly sympathetic to the Palestinian Liberation Organization after the assassinations—condemning government inaction in April—posted pictures of dead army soldiers, not commandos in the wake of the May clashes.[113] For the Palestinian Liberation Organization, they had thwarted a Jordanian Black September, but it was the closest thing to extinction experienced thus far in Lebanon. For groups like the Lebanese Communist Party, they joined the *fedayeen* on the front lines. Unlike their involvement on campuses or factories, this is not something the party confirmed—or denied—in their newspapers. Yet, Imad Nuwayhid's obituary reads that he joined the party in 1973 and "he participated in the battle of May 1973."[114] Indeed, for the Communist Party the war had already begun, and for young people like Imad, they were ready to fight.

Joining the Stronger, Non-Sectarian Party

In the abovementioned obituary for Imad, the Lebanese Communist Party notes his affiliation, in 1973, as a matter of fact—a foregone conclusion. But was it? Of course, Imad had the Marxist credentials, making him a great fit for the party, and with the party's standing in the Lebanese National Movement by '73, it was a good choice for him. But notwithstanding unaffiliating—which is hard to imagine for Imad at this point—there were two other options for him: stay with the Lebanese Communist Action Organization or join another leftist party, most notably one at the top of the pyramid, the Progressive Socialist Party.

I have already partially answered the former, reworded as why Imad left the Lebanese Communist Action Organization. Per Nadine, it sold out the workers, and per Rida, it was becoming obsolete. And while the country was in the midst of national and regional crisis, and in need of a unified Left, the organization was embroiled in infighting. In July 1973, Muhsin Ibrahim headed a push for "the Expulsion of the Boyish Leftist Band of Apostates." This included Waddah Charara, who, alongside Ibrahim, helped create the Lebanese Communist Action Organization only two years earlier.[115] This was at the same time that the Lebanese Communist Party and Progressive Socialist Party were either fighting (the former) or lobbying for (the latter) the Palestinian cause as a uniting force.

In contrast to the Lebanese Communist Action Organization was the Lebanese Communist Party's stature. Simply put, as Walid Nuwayhid tells me, on the eve of the war it was "the biggest and strongest in the Left."[116] In the age of counterculture and Marxist reading groups in the 1960s, this would have served as grounds for critique. Some, like Walid and Fawwaz Traboulsi, stuck with the Lebanese Communist Action Organization, favoring just that: a smaller, ideologically principled—even if draconian—type of organization.

Others, like the recently banished Waddah Charara, sought a third path, calling for "direct action among the masses and not through institutions" or any parties.[117] But by 1973, in the midst of state aggression on the people, the Lebanese Communist Party's infrastructure and connections to the masses would have been seen as an asset for many. Traboulsi perhaps put it best, arguing "Others [within the Organization and other leftist parties and movements] realized the weight and popularity of the Communist Party and its importance in the life of the working class."[118] The latter was important to Imad. Unlike Charara, an intellectual-meets-populist path was no longer appealing. He had been advocating something similar since his translation of Leon in 1969, to no avail. By 1973, it appears he wanted to stand by the masses with a party which had the capacity to fight for joint Lebanese-Palestinian liberation.

The first time I met Jawad Nuwayhid, Imad's closet brother, he chastised the working-class foundations of the Lebanese Communist Party. He argued that they recruited intellectuals, like Imad, to direct the poor, who, I speculate Jawad thought, were easily moldable. That is, the masses provided manpower, but did not really understand what they were fighting for.[119] Even if Imad would have agreed with this characterization, he would have seen their working class ranks as a plus. If the working classes were fighting for these causes, like Ghandour in 1972, he did not want to guide them, but join them.

Not only did Imad want to unite with workers in the fight, but the Palestinians, something the Lebanese Communist Party could facilitate. In the same conversation, Jawad told me that in 1973, Imad spent time in Jordan or Syria for military training with commandos of the Palestinian Liberation Organization.[120] The Lebanese Communist Party does not mention this in any remembrances to Imad. Nevertheless, if he did, it is likely that he trained with Fatah or the Popular Democratic Front for the Liberation of Palestine, who had the strongest connections to the Lebanese Communist Party. Moreover, as all *fedayeen* were tightly linked to the Lebanese National Movement by 1973, it is likely Imad never had to leave Lebanon for military training.[121]

Regardless of with whom, or where, Imad was training, his brother is emphatic that it was "for successive periods."[122] While in an earlier time, and with Fatah operatives in Syria, Gérard Chailand's account alongside *fedayeen* is useful in exploring what Imad would have done and seen during his training with resistance fighters. Chaliand writes:

> One hundred and twenty men are in training. They are dressed in camouflage and army boots; they run in close formation, led at rapid pace by an agile instructor. There are two hours of physical training every morning; basic exercises, combat training, jujitsu and karate. The standard is quite high[.][123]

At another training camp in Jordan, affiliated with the Popular Democratic Front for the Liberation of Palestine, Chailand details that trainees would match physical activities with intellectual ones: reading groups, political seminars, and public assemblies.[124] On top of these demands, Imad would meet Palestinians, like Ibrahim. Ibrahim was a sixteen-year-old *fidai*, a sacrificer of the *fedayeen*, interviewed by Chailand, who grew up in Amman but was originally from Jaffa. He tells Chailand, "I wasn't born in 1948, but my parents told me about Palestine and said we were exiles. When I was twelve I wondered why I didn't have a country. *Is there anyone in the world without a country of his own?*"[125]

While Imad had been arguing on behalf of the Palestinians for some time, to train with these youths had to have an impact on him. Unsurprisingly, Imad trained secretly, not telling anyone but Jawad what he was doing. Instead, he informed his parents he was pursuing another hotel job abroad. Even if his parents were sympathetic to the Palestinian cause, there were some things Imad could not tell them.[126] As he moved further and further from the career he had built in the previous decade, ceding his autonomy in real time, he leaned on the practical foundations that he knew they were still behind.

In sum, the Lebanese Communist Party was more popular, working-class, and had the capability to put Imad in direct contact, and action with, Palestinian *fedayeen*. At least in 1973, the Lebanese Communist Action Organization could not do that, so as Rida put it, Imad and him left.[127]

But why wouldn't Imad join another group that had even more institutional capacities within the Lebanese National Movement, the Progressive Socialist Party? While not as old as the Lebanese Communist Party, as of the 1960s it was as popular and had working class buy-in.[128] Its leader, Kamal Jumblatt had become the global face for the Left in Lebanon.[129] Like the Communist Party, his place within Lebanese bureaucracy may have once been a con, but was a benefit in this moment of polarization: the Left and the people versus the system, the Kataib, and the Army.

However, at least in 1973, the Lebanese Communist Party was directly engaged in the fight for Palestine. While the Progressive Socialist Party gave rhetorical support, it was not backed by action like the Communist Party after its 1972 conference. In fact, the Progressive Socialist Party did not get involved in the fighting until late 1975. Following the Ain al-Rummaneh massacre in April 1975, Jumblatt verbally attacked the Kataib, claiming that its actions represented an attempt to "liquidate the Palestinian resistance from Lebanese land."[130] But it was not until the Black Saturday Massacre—after Imad was killed, and hence why I do not discuss this event—that Jumblatt's party began to legitimize "revolutionary violence" to "break the evil" of the Kataib.[131]

Even if it is disputable—or at least not confirmable—that the Lebanese Communist Party engaged directly in the fighting of May 1973, by April 1975 its presence was less so. Salibi notes that the party immediately came to the armed defense of Palestinian commandos, particularly in the southern suburbs of Shiyah.[132] Hence, at most for two years, but definitely longer than the Progressive Socialist Party, Imad's Lebanese Communist Party was quicker to physically defend the cause he believed in.

Moreover, Imad was Druze, and even if he respected Jumblatt as a leftist thinker—socialist, but not communist—Jumblatt was a Druze leader. As I explained in Chapter 1, Imad had been critical of sect leaders and sect followers for some time.[133] If one thing appears constant about Imad through all his transformations it was his non-and anti-sectarian opinions. Imad saw himself as secular. The Lebanese Communist Party had always been just that, but, by 1975, the Progressive Socialist Party was not. While the sectarianization of the party had been in motion since 1958, by the start of the war, half of the rank-and-file membership was Druze, "the highest percentage attained of Druze membership since the party's inception."[134]

This would have been quite unappealing to Imad, Walid Nuwayhid tells me. He says "there is a small percentage [of Druze] that are independent in this atmosphere. And they don't need Jumblatt." The need Walid stresses is twofold: economically and politically. Economically, because Imad and Walid came from middle-class families, they did not depend on the financial support that Jumblatt provided Druze peasants and working-class families. Politically, because they lived outside Mount Lebanon—whether in Beirut or abroad, and went university, to work and beyond—they were exposed to different ideas. And Druze like that, in Walid's estimation, while "not against Jumblatt … they are out of it [the sect, the party, the leader] and they go to join the Communist Party, the Lebanese Communist Action Organization and other ideas, not traditional ideas."[135]

With its long-standing anti-sectarian credentials, Imad's long history of engaging directly with Marxism and communism, and the party's stature in the early 1970s, he joined the Lebanese Communist Party. He was a member of the party for two years, from spring 1973 through spring 1975. After the Ain al-Rummaneh massacre of April 13, 1975, the sectarian Kataib became the physical, local force that the party would fight and the enemy to Imad's anti-sectarian and pro-Palestinian credentials.

The Battle of Qantari

Where Imad was between April 13, 1975, the start of the war, and his death on October 28, 1975 is clear. He was residing in the neighborhood of Beirut he grew up in, Zaydaniyya. Yet, it is unclear exactly what Imad was doing during this period. After joining the Lebanese Communist Party in 1973, there is no written record of Imad. The only other thing that is referenced, in the party-produced biography written years after his death, is the book Imad was writing, titled *China After 30 Years*.[136] However, no one in Imad's life could confirm this work. The only thing I know, between 1973 and 1975, is that Imad was still working at the Phoenicia.[137]

After the Ain al-Rummaneh massacre, the first "round" of fighting followed in the neighborhoods of east and south Beirut.[138] Simultaneously, the official opposition within the Lebanese parliament looked to defang the Kataib Party. This included Kamal Jumblatt, who sounded the alarm in his party's newspaper, claiming Ain al-Rummaneh showed the true nature of "the Kataib isolationist conspiracy."[139] Because they were an enemy to the Palestinian cause, and by extension—à la the plot the Left had been framing since the late 1960s—the Lebanese people, Jumblatt also called for their disbandment and removal from parliament.[140]

Thereafter, the Kataib linked up with a number of right-wing Christian militias to make the putsch irrelevant. Starting in September 1975, its forces had pushed from its headquarters in east Beirut toward downtown, and by all accounts, led the ruin of the old downtown market area. Were they seeking to force the army's hand to intervene on its side? Attempting to show their strength and unwillingness to acquiesce to demands to dissolve and leave parliament? Regardless, as Salibi put it at the time, "if the Christian Lebanese … were trying to commit national suicide, they certainly seemed to be succeeding."[141]

After the switch flipped, destruction of downtown Beirut became more common and normalized. The Kataib then sought to control major vantage points across central Beirut, most notably its hotels. Qantari was the neighborhood closest to the grand hotels, like Hotel Phoenicia, as well as the closest neighborhood to Imad's home of Zaydaniyya. If the Kataib, which held the east, could secure the hotels, and Qantari, the perimeter south, it could corner the forces of the Lebanese National Movement into West Beirut. This made the battle of Qantari one of the most significant moments of the start of the war.

On October 26, the Kataib launched its Qantari campaign. Here are two reports from US Army intelligence on the fighting:

October 26, 1975
Forces: leftists/Muslims v. Phalangists
Sector: Kantari
Weapons: fire, heavy machine guns, rockets, rocket-propelled grenades
Structure: Holiday Inn, Phoenicia Hotel, Hotel St. Georges, Murr building
Comment: Kantari is a Muslim section but was regarded as a no-man's land militarily. Phalangists had been using flying roadblocks to kidnap people. The Muslim forces invaded in retaliation. No part of Beirut is safe.

October 27, Phalangists moved into the Holiday Inn, Phoenicia International, and the NLP [National Liberal Party, allied with Kataib] moved into Hotel St. Georges. In Ashrafiyeh, Phalangists attempted to get back the 40-story Murr building (uncompleted) lost to leftists. They fired recoilless rifles and machine guns at it. The leftists installed heavy machine guns, mortars, and snipers on the building's upper stories, which overlooked Kantari. Palestinian guerrillas were involved in the fighting. Al Fatah occupied Hamra. Heavy street fighting took place in most suburbs of the city. For the first time, the street fighting appeared organized; units of gunmen fought each other under commanders' maneuvering their forces to take territory. Much larger units were deployed than last spring.[142]

Army intelligence had not reported on developments since October 15, which in addition to the tone of this text, signals the uptick during the battle of Qantari. Of course, the framing is fraught (Muslims vs. the Phalangist, later using Muslim vs. Christian), but they were watching the Kataib home in on Qantari and observing a new level of armament and organization.

Others confirm these claims. Maurice Nahra said that in the moment, the Kataib were "not just [seeking] to be dominant here [in its area] but extend and fold up Beirut … Achraifeh, the port, the hotel [district]."[143] It was time for the Lebanese Communist Party and others of what would become known as *al-Quwwat al-Mushtaraka*, the Joint Forces of the Lebanese National Movement, to defend its people.[144] With both sides motivated, it was, in one observer's view the "worst [fighting] since the civil war began" with devastation to the grand hotels area.[145] In an ironic twist, what were once symbols of Lebanese development, and its discontents, were now being used as outposts, with rockets, snipers, and artillery fire, to—even if not the stated goal of either side—destroy Lebanon.[146]

It is unclear if October 28, 1975, was the first day Imad saw live fire. However, it is clear he decided to go to the front lines that day. Many of Imad's contemporaries tell me that this was the question of the day. Who would go to the front lines?[147] Leftists of different shades gathered in homes of Zaydaniyya and the Lebanese Communist Party office there. Rida Ismael tells me exactly how the conversation went between him, his brother Diyab, and Imad:

> [Zaydaniyya] was the political and party center and at the same time I oversaw military actions in the Qantari district. I recall a ray of brightness on the door. I don't know why [I felt] danger … Imad was talking with my brother Diyab at the window. 'We leave the center and go down to the front.' I told them drop going down there and [he said] 'no we go down.'[148]

As director of military affairs, Rida needed more volunteers. But he had a bad feeling about those closest to him doing just that. Telling me this story, vividly, forty-five years after, shows how this moment has stuck with him.

Figure 4.2 Imad Nuwayhid's last movements. It starts in the south, the Lebanese Communist Party office, and moves north, closer to the hotel district and Haigazian University where he was shot. The red pin on the far middle right is the Murr building, where Imad could expect backup from Joint Forces. Courtesy of Google Maps, 2024.

Diyab and Imad's route from the Lebanese Communist Party office to meet the Kataib would look something like one of the three paths in Figure 4.2.[149] Each seems plausible in its own way. Some variation of the middle path was most direct, but plateaus going north. This would leave them most exposed. The far-left path via Justinian Street slopes downhill and they would likely have the cover of Joint Forces in the West. However, since October 26, that street had been taken by the Kataib, making any movement dependent on minute-by-minute intel from Rida and the party office.[150] The right path would run closest to the Kataib line. At the same time, the topography becomes quite hilly moving further east down Spears Street. Terrain would be coupled with strong cover on that path, as the Murr building was also held by the Joint Forces.

US Army intelligence reports for the day make the above considerations moot. Any route would be dangerous:

October 28, Phalangists laid down a ring of fire around the Murr building to cut off supplies. Thousands-of Muslims besieged Christian-held hotels. They used jeep-mounted artillery. Muslims and Christians routinely fired at firemen putting out fires, if the fire was in an opposing section. Fighting spread north and south of the city; most major roads had been cut. The Holiday Inn was repeatedly hit by rocket and mortar fire.[151]

According to Jawad Nuwayhid, Imad, Diyab and Muhammad were shot near the intersection of Mexico and Jibran Khalil Jibran streets (indicated by the northern most pin in Figure 4.2 above).[152] This is right up the street from Haigazian University, which, per Kataib reports of the day, was recently taken and occupied by its forces.[153] According to Iyad Nuwayhid, another of Imad's brothers, Muhammad and Diyab were shot first in the open while Imad was under cover of a building. He then went out in the open to try and save his comrades. During this valiant effort, Imad was shot by Kataib snipers.[154]

Imad was taken to Barbir hospital, an eight-minute drive southeast of Qantari. Multiple people tell me that as Imad was in the ambulance, he shouted, *Ana Shuyuei ma bakhafa min mawt,* "I am communist and I am not afraid of death."[155] Brothers, cousins, and friends showed up at the hospital to donate blood to Imad. But it was too late. He died during operation, October 28, 1975.[156]

One day later, the Lebanese Communist Party responded and pushed the Kataib back, a story for the next chapter. For now, I want to note that this was the last day of fighting in Qantari for some time. According to those same US Army reports, there was a ceasefire days later.[157] On October 28, 1975, before the fighting ended, to Imad and others who went down to the line, perhaps it felt that there was no end in sight. In this context, he had to defend his neighborhood, his country, his cause. Whether he knew it or not, in this moment, he had ceded his autonomy. His job was no longer a career. He gave everything to the Lebanese Communist Party, risked his life, and for that, he was killed. But also for that, he became a *shahid,* a martyr.

5

Remembering, Forgetting, and Mobilizing a Martyr

Do They Look Alike?

Lancaster, Pennsylvania, early 2016

I felt guilty asking the above question. Was I profiling? Reducing two Arab men, pictures taken decades apart, to facial structure, hair lines, and expressions? The answer was yes. But alas, I still asked my spouse Nicole.

At this point, Nicole and I had been married for a year and were both working in Pennsylvania. A number of years earlier though she looked into pursuing a Master's degree in Public Health at the American University of Beirut. In the end, she chose the University of Arizona, where we finished our respective degrees in 2015. But our conservations on the program in Beirut were quite helpful for my own research, and like a lot of things in the story, serendipitous.

As I considered the possibility of converting my dissertation section on the martyrdom of Imad Nuwayhid to an article or book, I recalled that the Dean of the Faculty of Health Sciences at AUB, who oversaw the program in Public Health that Nicole had once considered, had the family name Nuwayhid. I then googled and found Iman Nuwayhid's faculty page. Iman is a Professor of Public Health who focuses on Environmental Health in the region and had served as dean from 2008 to 2020. I began to wonder, did I just find a living relative of Imad?

I then asked Nicole to take a look at Imad's picture from his 1975 obituary in al-Nida', side-by-side with Iman's faculty page. Honestly, I don't remember exactly what Nicole said. I'd like to think she said, "oh yeah," but more likely I got a "I can't say yes or no," a signature line from her. Either way, a research trip to Lebanon was on the horizon, so I set to get in touch with Iman Nuwayhid.

This was a tricky endeavor. If Iman was very close to Imad, perhaps his brother, I would be asking him to confront the past, the war, and his deceased sibling. To exercise caution, I first tried to find someone who knew the both of us who could vouch for me and arrange a meeting. That didn't work, so on April 5, 2016, I sent this introductory email:

Iman,

Hello and I hope all is well. My name is Dylan Baun, and I am an assistant professor of modern Middle East and Islamic World history at Franklin & Marshall College in the US. Although we have never met, we share some friends, including [omitted] and other faculty members at AUB. More specifically, my research is on youth clubs and political parties in Lebanon during the mid-20th century. I will be in Beirut this spring from May 11-June 9, conducting further archival research for a book project.

In a major section of my work, I focus on a man who has the same family name as you and lived during the 1940s-1970s. I know it is a long shot, but I am thinking you two may be related, and hence, if you feel comfortable that is, you could be of assistance to my work.

Out of courtesy, I thought it best not to include any biographical information on this man in this introductory email. But if you are comfortable, curious, and are ok with me sending you over some details about this man, and asking you a few questions over email about this potential connection, please let me know.

Thanks in advance and I hope to hear from you soon.

I didn't have to wait long. Two hours later, Iman wrote back, "It is difficult not to be intrigued and curious with such an introduction. Feel free to ask when you feel ready." After my response, Iman explained that Imad was his cousin, and that he would be happy to meet with me and connect me with some of Imad's family when I came to Lebanon. EUREKA! This was the breakthrough! Iman would be the first in a long line of Imad's family and friends—including Iman's brother, Walid Nuwayhid in 2016, then Imad's brothers Jawad and Iyad Nuwayhid in 2018, and then Imad's comrades Nabil Khishin and Rida Ismael in 2022—that I would meet and come to rely on to tell Imad's story.

Beirut, Lebanon, May 13, 2016

Iman Nuwayhid and I sit at a café, discussing basic information about Imad and his family. Imad was one of six kids. He came from a middle-class family. His father was a prestigious French instructor. And then this, per my notes:

> *Was some debate over [the] role of [the Lebanese Communist] party in funeral [of Imad]—immediate family considered this [a] death of [the] family, extended [family, Iman included] saw [him] as a symbol [for the Left and its cause in the war. Immediate family saw Imad as] Nuwayhid first, Communist second ...*

The funeral that Iman referenced took place in Ras al-Matn, one day after Muhammad Maki (22), Diyab Ismael (23), and Imad Nuwayhid (31) died in the Battle of Qantari. The description of the funeral that I provide below—based on sources from the days after Imad's death, as well interviews I have conducted— was derived from this single conversation with a man who (maybe?!) looked like Imad.

***

The Funeral

Immediately following Imad Nuwayhid's death, detailed in the previous chapter, his family sprang into action.[1] Adl Nuwayhid, Iman and Walid Nuwayhid's father, did his part by calling several Beirut-based newspapers— beyond the Communist Party's *al-Nida'*—to submit an obituary and notice of Imad's funeral.[2] The one in *al-Safir*, the Ambassador, reads as follows:

> The Nuwayhids and the people of Ras al-Matn mourned the martyr
> Imad Yusuf Nuwayhid
>
> He will be buried today [October 29] in the afternoon in his hometown. The family will accept condolences and guests after the burial and Thursday and Friday [October 30–1] in Ras al-Matn and Saturday and Sunday in his father's residence in Zaydaniyya [Beirut]—close to Cinema Aida, Salha Residence.[3]

The obituary in *al-Nahar*, The Day, has a few key differences.[4] For one, it does not give directions to Yusuf Nuwayhid's Beirut house. If Adl sent the same obituary text to both papers, Iman's assumption, this omission is likely because whoever edited it assumed that people reading it would likely not attend.[5] This is confirmed by the fact that *al-Nahar* did not run a correction, that *al-Safir* did on, November 1. It read, "The Nuwayhids, the people of Ras al-Matn, and the Lebanese Communist Party announce the martyr of the Matn, Imad Nuwayhid … The family will gather Saturday and Sunday [November 1–2, not October 30–1] in his father's residence in Ras al-Matn [not Beirut]."[6]

A more noticeable difference in obituaries is the language used. In no place does *al-Nahar* refer to Imad as *al-shahid*, the martyr. This was Adl's request, fulfilled by the leftist paper *al-Safir*, but not by the more moderate *al-Nahar*.[7] Iman "remember[s] vividly" his father's phone conversation with a rep from *al-Nahar*. "He insisted on the term martyr," and when *al-Nahar* informed him they would not do that, Adl raised his voice, telling whoever was on the other line that "That is your martyr."[8] For these obituaries to run on October 29, the day after Imad died, Adl had to make this call to the papers the day Imad. At the moment of his death, the politics of memorialization began, connecting papers, parties, and families. For its worth, the Lebanese Communist Party leaned into terms absent in either the *al-Nahar* or *al-Safir* obituary. Imad was a "comrade," "martyr," who died "fighting fierce battles against the fascist Kataib gangs."[9]

Imad's funeral on October 29 started in the courtyard of the home of Adl Nuwayhid.[10] Their house is right off the main street in Ras al-Matn, close to the Nuwayhid square. People could first visit the coffin and offer condolences in the courtyard, with overflow out into the main street (see Figure 5.1 below). There was a program of sorts at this gathering, including an opening statement by Ajaj Nuwayhid, an uncle of Imad.[11]

At some point, per Druze tradition, men carried Imad's coffin to the Nuwayhid burial plot nearby. Representatives of the Lebanese Communist Party were present at the procession. Maurice Nahra, regional director who had met Imad on Lebanese University's campus two years earlier, was there and told me "There was a big crowd, people from the Mountain, communists, [members] of the Progressive Socialist Party, people of the [Lebanese] National

Figure 5.1 Locations of Imad's funeral, including the Nuwayhid courtyard (left) and the Nuwayhid square (right). Pictures taken by author in 2016.

Movement [and a] group of young fighters [who] gave a military salute to Imad."[12] He does not, however, mention what happened next.

The story that follows has been told to me by at least three family members in interviews since 2016.[13] This is a composite of their recollections:

> *During the procession, a Lebanese Communist Party member tried to help Imad's family carry the coffin and draped it with a Communist Party flag. Jawad, angry by this display, pulled the flag off the coffin, and beat up this communist party member. He then said, 'Enough damage. You have done enough damage, get out of here, I do not recognize you, he is not part of you, he is us a Nuwayhid, enough is enough.' The Lebanese Communist Party acquiesced. They understood the situation and Jawad's grief. The flag was then no longer laid on Imad's coffin for the remainder of the funeral procession.*

Tense, tragic, and controversial. These descriptors and others have come to my mind over the years when I hear this story. The Lebanese Communist Party, however, does not use any of them nor mentions these events in subsequent write-ups. To start, the report on the funeral in *al-Nida'* dwells little on the procession or burial, just noting, similar to what Maurice Nahra told me, that there were "21 shots for the hero," Imad. It adds that women of the village scattered flowers for the fallen martyr.[14]

Instead, the party focuses on the ceremony that followed the procession. The people of Ras al-Matn, it reads, were "honoring the hero and pledging to continue the struggle and carry the torch of the communist and nationalist martyrs against the fascists and for the sake of a new Lebanon." And, per the report, Maurice Nahra himself "prais[ed] the struggle of Imad and his dedication in the battles for his people, for the great party, for giving his life [for the sake] of making victory … and the basis of a new Lebanon."[15]

~

This is the first divide in the immediate and long-term archival afterlife of Imad Nuwayhid. Was the funeral and procession a smooth, "normal" celebration of the martyr, the party, and the Left's war effort? Or was it a village, family-focused event, hijacked by a party that did not truly respect the trauma experienced by Imad's loved ones? The simple answer, and my core argument in the remainder of *Beirut Radical*, is that it was, and continues to be, both. The creation of a "martyr narrative"—that is, the party-sanctioned record on the fighter's death, its meaning, and future action in their name—is diffuse, contentious, and ever-changing.

This nuance is often lost in the scholarship on the Lebanese Civil War. This is largely because the field favors the study of collective memory, and often, exclusively party perspectives.[16] To be clear, I am not proposing that the only way to track the battles over memory during the war is through a single life and death, like that of Imad.[17] But I do find it is a more vivid and intimate way to do so, one that allows a level of detail that can complicate the very existence of martyr narratives.

What follows is an attempt to do just that. Through a mix of party sources and interviews I have conducted over the years, I focus on the Lebanese Communist Party's creation of Imad's martyr narrative, the role of comrades in its creation, and the family's place in all of this. This is for the sake of understanding the broader process and politics of memorialization in the midst of wartime (this chapter) and beyond (Chapter 6). One of the main trends I tease out across these two chapters is that as time moved away from

Imad's death, his martyr narrative, surprisingly, became more detailed, more nuanced, and more human. Stated differently, in the near aftermath of his martyrdom, the party created a largely depersonalized account of Imad to mobilize the living to fight.

At the same time, this finding in the party archive does not represent a dichotomy. That is to say, the party did not react just one way, and Imad's family the opposite. There are multiple points of connection and crossover between the martyr narrative and resistance to it. Taking the construction of Imad's martyr narrative, and changes to it, source by source, year by year, I believe, allows the reader to see the diversity of reactions created by his death, both immediately after and in the long term. Nonetheless, what is irrefutable is that with his death, the practical radical Imad—a communist hotel worker, a capitalist anti-Zionist intellectual, a proud and sometimes self-deprecating Arab leftist—was lost. Instead, he and others killed in the war became symbols, regardless of what that symbol was, who or what deployed it or how they mobilized it.

The Party

The comrades Imad Nuwayhid, Muhammad Maki, and Diyab Ismael
They were martyred for the life of their people and their nation
They counter the Kataib gangs in frontline sites in Qantari.[18]

This was the headline for the October 29, 1975, *al-Nida'* cover story that introduced me to Imad over a decade ago. Almost fifty years since his death, I was not the first to meet him. This story, and those that followed which constitute the martyr narrative, is how party sympathizers outside family, friend groups, and close political circles got to know Imad, his two fallen comrades, and the battle in which they died.

Regardless of whether it was the Lebanese Communist Party, the Progressive Socialist Party, later Hezbollah, or the Kataib on the other side of the war, martyr narratives often are commissioned, sanctioned, or at least approved by the specific party of the individual deceased. They include poems, songs, posters, statues, and events dedicated to them.[19] This way of recalling is not unique to wartime Lebanon. Missionary religions from Christianity to Buddhism have promoted their fallen for centuries.[20] And since at least the eleventh century in the Islamic world, biographical dictionaries and entries for venerated Muslim figures have been common forms of commemoration.[21]

Creating a martyr narrative is not solely a means of honoring the dead, however. It takes the death as a means to demonize the killer of the martyr as well as impel the living to fight in their name.[22] In the context of Lebanon before 1975, martyr narratives were common in the 1958 War.[23] One of the first martyr narratives from that conflict was created by the Progressive Socialist Party and is indicative of its form and intention. It is a newspaper article on the funeral for the second "martyr" of the party in the war, a young man named Sayd Malaab. As reported in *al-Anba'*, the News, Sayd was buried in April 1958 in his village of Basour before the war technically started in May.[24] The party was a central feature at his funeral, represented by its head Kamal Jumblatt, as well as Wadia Maalab, who is referenced as a "comrade" of Sayd. Whether Wadia is Sayd's brother or a distant cousin is not important. What is most crucial is what he vows that the living will do for Sayd: "crush the destructive elements and saboteurs."[25]

Party presence, a focus on future action, honorifics, and demonization are all on display here. Another thing that is common, especially in the first few years of the later Lebanese Civil War, is lack of personal details. It appears that the reader of this 1958 *al-Anba'* article, or the one who passes by a martyr poster in 1975, may not know much about the specific individual they were remembering. I consider this appropriation "an immediate marker of the party concerned," not the martyr themselves.[26]

So if the martyr narrative was where partisans learned about their fallen, what did they first learn about Imad and his death? In the first article following the battle of Qantari, *al-Nida'* declares that Imad, Muhammad, and Diyab "were defending the land and the people for the sake of a bright future, and a nation for all humans, defending the Palestinian resistance." This was in contrast to the "fascist Kataib, enemies of the people and enemies of the future." On one side of this battle, "gangs," on the other, "heroes."[27] Similarly, but months later, a Lebanese Communist party member wrote into *al-Nida'* with the pen/code name Ibn Shab, son of the people, distinguishing enemy from defender. The

Kataib were "scum," "protecting rapists," while "my people [that] will not knell, will not knell."[28]

This villainization of the Kataib was not new, for the party or the Lebanese National Movement. As I referenced in the last chapter, it had been in place since at least early 1975. What was new at this stage was the possessive claims that the party and its members made. In the case of Imad, Muhammad, and Diyab, they had died, per the first martyr report, for "our people" and "our dignity" against whatever macabre the Kataib represented.[29] The our here, or Ibn Shab's my, is the audience of *al-Nida'* readers and fighters, who the Lebanese Communist Party mobilized to fight for the people, nation, and party, against the Kataib.

On the other side of the battle, the Kataib engaged in something comparable. In a December 1975 edition of their newspaper, *al-'Amal*, The Action, a party member wrote in to remember his comrade Bassam, asking his fallen brother to "instill in us the intensity of your beliefs … to cleanse Lebanon from dirt [*qathara*]."[30] Like with the martyr narrative of the Lebanese Communist Party, the possessive us for the Kataib is contrasted to the putrid them. To print these words, or depict similar ideas in cartoons, I believe, was not merely reflective of a violent context.[31] Collectively, what can be thought of as "frames" around Imad's death—words and images of memorialization and dehumanization for the sake of mobilization—worked to make violence more plausible, actively transforming Lebanon.[32]

Returning to the initial *al-Nida'* article following the death of Imad, the focus quickly shifted from what the martyrs died for toward victory over their enemies. This is partial because of the nature of the martyr narrative—forward looking—but also the significance of the battle of Qantari itself. It marked the Kataib's first push into West Beirut and resulted in the death of at least twenty leftist forces, including Imad.[33] The battle loomed large in the press of the Left—an inflection point, one they won. After the initial Kataib campaign, "the neighborhood gangs [of the Kataib] incurred huge losses," as *al-Nida'* reports that the "forces of the Lebanese Communist Party and the National Movement were able to capture new frontline sites."[34]

The *al-Nida'* article does rest on the death of its fighters, at least at this moment when the war was still in limbo. Instead, the paper notes that as word traveled of the martyrdom of Imad and the others, "comrades, friends, fighters, and the people" came to the party office closest to the site of his death, in Zaydaniyya, where Imad's family house was located. This is a moment that several of my interviewees recall when discussing the death of Imad, something I take up in the next section. But here, in this October 29 article, *al-Nida'* makes sure to stress that those that showed up in Zaydaniyya were not just from nearby neighborhoods, but "all western areas."[35] It is not clear from the article if the counterattack from the Lebanese Communist Party was immediate, or after this huge impromptu rally. Nonetheless, the message is clear. We have already won back what territory was lost from the Kataib, so these martyrs did not die in vain.

At the time of Imad's death in October 1975, war was just entering its sixth month. Over the subsequent months, year, and decade, there would be many more martyrs and frontlines would change many more times. Accordingly, this posturing and staking of victory would become a mainstay in the wartime press of the Left. In late 1975, after the Black Saturday massacre—one of the most gruesome events of the early war, perpetuated by the Kataib and its allies—the Lebanese Communist Party ran a piece in *al-Nida'* titled "This is Our Reply." The story consists of ten pictures and captions showing just that. The first is of three communist fighters taking cover behind a building in downtown Beirut. They are moving toward the Starco Building, an office complex in the Central Business District that was occupied by the Kataib at this point of the war. It is followed by pictures of other nearby fronts that the Joint Forces of the Lebanese National Movement are now occupying. These pictures are bordered by a poem that contrasted the Kataib's sectarian actions, "emotional reactions," and "slaughter on the basis of identity," a reference to the Black Saturday massacre, to the anti-sectarian ones of the forces of the National Movement, which "carried weapons and fought honorably and triumphed."[36]

This tactic, what I think of as the "storming article," was not one of a kind. It built off of and was adapted by others among the Left and Right. Regarding the former, and also after Black Saturday, the Progressive Socialist Party's cover article for its December 1975 edition was titled "Our War and Their War." The cover was a split image. On the bottom half, corpses, victims of the Kataib's violence during Black Saturday. On the top were fighters, not that much younger than Imad. The story that followed explains the "savage acts" of the Kataib as well as the "dignified and manly war," of the Left, anchored in "principles of justice and love." Alongside this common difference making were a set of pictures, showing the advances of the National Movement. They were printed alongside the following caption: "from the barbaric Saturday massacres to the victorious battle of the hotels."[37]

The Kataib followed suit. In January 1976 it used images and words to justify its new military ventures in strategic areas of East Beirut.[38] A particular *al-'Amal* article shows its fighters traversing open streets during the "sweeping operation in the heart of Karantina," an enemy stronghold. One particularly interesting picture was that of a Kataib fighter, from the back, with an AK-47 in one hand and a flag in the other. The caption reads, "he raises a party flag over the occupied site."[39]

This foray into the frames of different parties to the war highlights that the martyr narrative did not exist in a vacuum. It was paired alongside articles like "This Is Our Reply," which showed the victory of their side. At this point, the Left and Right represented radically different visions for Lebanon. The latter, a strong Christian Lebanon separated from its regional context, the former, breathed through those like Imad, fully dedicated to reform and revolution within Lebanon and Palestine. Nevertheless, this war was not fought behind impenetrable walls. These groups took their cues from each other to memorialize their fallen, dehumanize the enemy, and declare victory.

Following the *al-Nida'* article on the Battle of Qantari, which, as its authors argued, the forces of the Lebanese Community Party had won, were the biographies of its martyred fighters, Imad, Muhammad, and Diyab. The brief text for Imad, which I included in its entirety in the introduction of this book, is what started my journey toward knowing him and telling his story. Brief, however, is the operative word. Like the other two, it is limited to where Imad was born, when he joined the party, and his physical participation in the war.[40] To be fair, it was information, a testament to their deeds, actions, and death. But this is juxtaposed to the detail and length on the enemy and what the party is doing to defeat it. Given this informational divide, it is hard not to consider this biographical information on Imad more than instrumental—an appropriation. In other words, his biography, and those of others martyred, was not too detailed, but just enough to get the living to fight in the name of the martyred.

That same day, also on the front page of *al-Nida'*, the party printed a poem dedicated to the fighters, titled "Three shining lanterns, Communists in the Qantari sky." Each of the three stanzas started with the names of the three martyrs, "Muhammad Yunis Maki, Diyab Ismael, and Imad Nuwayhid." Here are some excerpts from each of the three main stanzas:

> Three new torches progressing our party, the Lebanese Communist Party, on the trail of heroic martyrdom, purifying the streets in resistant Beirut of the vampires of darkness and the villains of the fascist Kataib
>
> They were martyred for the sake of drawing a smile on the children … for the sake of ensuring bread for the hardworking people … and for the freedom of all citizens
>
> And all you comrades, moving on the trail, [remember] Muhammad, Diyab, and Imad, for the complete elimination of this plague and salvation of our Lebanese people from the evils and their crimes[.][41]

The motifs of the first and third stanzas appear common enough. We are the strong party, they are villains, our cause is just, our enemy's motivation is villainous, and remember all of this as you fight on the street.

But the second stanza is not as common within the martyr narrative. It seeks to show that Imad's party considers themselves not only a fighting force but a provider. Even if unique in this forum, the Lebanese Communist Party was not alone in this venture. The Progressive Socialist Party and Kataib depicted caregiving during wartime.[42] Another party to the war on the Left, the Syrian Social Nationalist Party, published a lengthy report on its pre-war care efforts. Titled "Popular Social Services: The Clinics," the party explained why it started health clinics, what services they provided, and where they were located.[43] Like the poem for Imad, this publication was not without its propaganda purposes. Whether before the war or during, to show that the party cared and defended its people could serve as a recruitment and mobilization tool.

The first official party event to remember Imad, Diyab, and Muhammad took place on November 5, 1975. It was co-organized by the Lebanese Communist Action Organization, and hence, was also dedicated to its two fighters killed in the battle of Qantari, Nabil Hushar, and Said al-Dirani.[44] Collectively, the five were referred to as "the communist martyrs."[45] The rally took place at Cinema Aida in Zaydaniyya, right down the street from Imad's family house. From coverage of the rally in leftist papers, it appears that make-shift pictures and posters were erected around the walls of the cinema to commemorate the martyrs. But given that the pictures are at a distance to my eye, through a microfilm reader, it is very difficult to make out Imad's face. What is perceivable, however, is a banner next to the pictures that read "we avenged you oh our heroic martyrs," referencing the action of these two parties in the now victorious battle of Qantari.[46]

Hundreds of men, women, and children listened to words from a list of well-rounded and well-represented speakers: Fawwaz Traboulsi and Sahil Mashaqa, members of the Lebanese Communist Action Organization, Azat Harb, President of the Maqasid Islamic Society, Majid Abu Sharir, secretary of the Revolutionary Committee for Fatah, and Rafiq Samhoun of the Lebanese Communist Party. In an over two-hour event, the speakers delivered messages that should be familiar at this point of our investigation. Harb clarifies the rally was "not only for honoring the martyrs [but] to continue to struggle which is not yet finished."[47] Traboulsi calls the martyrs "five bullets in the face of colonization" and Samhoun, "five candlesticks along the road of the struggle."[48] Samhoun also took a shot at the enemies of the martyrs, the Kataib, who were guilty of playing a dangerous "game of violence." Sharir then reassures the audience that the martyrs "fell so the nation is not martyred."[49]

At least in print, at this stage of the conflict, there are very little personal details on these three fighters. While that changed by the late 1970s and early 1980s, something I explore in the next chapter, at this point in the construction of the martyr narrative, Imad and others were rarely spoken about as living people, but always as symbols. Nonetheless, to Imad's cousins, Iman and Walid, this rally was the most important event in the remembrance of their cousin.[50]

What does this say about party efforts to memorialize their fighters? In short, antagonism between family and party was not always fixed. Perhaps some family members took issue with the party, like Jawad at the funeral. But especially as time went on, these types of events with multiple speakers, and buy-in across the Left, were remembered favorably by some family members.

And in the family's moment of loss, the Lebanese Communist Party was there. After the initial funeral, the party was in attendance at a one-week remembrance to Imad held at the residence of the Nuwayhid family in Ras al-Matn on November 4, 1975. Unlike the rally it held in Beirut the next day, this event appears to be the most intimate event the party attended. The *al-Nida'* article that details the event provides no list of party delegates that were present or quotes from them. All it includes is words from Imad's mother on "their heroic martyr."[51]

Besides just being there, the party gave financial compensation to the family. According to Jawad, it was about 500 lira a month (or between US$ 120 and 220 depending on the year) for some time.[52] Like other realms in the memorialization meets mobilization of parties to the war, the Lebanese Communist Party's support to the family is not unique. As I have written elsewhere, "In the absence of sustained state welfare, multiple parties to the war, ranging from Hizbullah to the Lebanese Forces, filled the gap."[53] As Imad was from this group, and some of its top leaders knew him and his family—like Maurice Nahra, who, as I described in Chapter 4, Imad had met at a number of party gatherings at his university in the seventies—this support appears genuine. The parties cared about their members and their families, but as I demonstrate in the following chapter, showing up also ensured the parties would continue to have a seat at the table, even into today.

The Comrades

To introduce how Imad's contemporaries reacted to his death, let's return to the moment they introduce themselves in the archive: the gathering at the party office in Zaydaniyya following the battle of Qantari. This was first reported in *al-Nida'* the day after Imad's death, with words from one of his closest friends, who you first met alongside Imad in late 1960s Beirut: Rida Ismael. At this point, Rida was, by his own account, "a representative of the organization of the [Communist] party in Zaydaniyya." And even though he talks about him much less than Imad, Rida was the brother of the fallen Diyab Ismael.[54] In the *al-Nida'* report, Rida is quoted as follows:

> I was not surprised by the martyrdom of the comrades Imad, Muhammad and Diyab. They were martyred as brave heroes defending our people and our dignity. Their martyrdoms are torches lighting our path as communists

and all nationalists towards a bright future and a nation for its children. It is not for the communists to cry for the martyrs, for the path of the martyrs is our path.[55]

Even though Rida says he is not surprised, his last sentence acknowledges the potential trauma associated with the event. This consideration of grief is temporary, replaced quickly by the future call. Even if muted, this reaction from a comrade is not something I have seen expressed by other party officials. At the same time, Rida builds out the martyr narrative, very similarly to the party remembrances of the Lebanese Communist Party. At least in writing, Rida did not focus on who his brother Diyab, Muhammad or Imad were, but what their actions meant.

Rida's spoken words, today, some of which I shared in the previous chapter, complicate this initial reaction. Rida talks, at length, about Imad, the intellectual, the student, and the friend before this moment. In the moment, he stresses today that he didn't want Diyab and Imad to go to the front line. This speaks to the difference between the need for action, then, and the presence of nostalgia and pain today.

Nonetheless, I believe our conversations today are helpful to consider his reaction at the moment of Imad's death. In our interviews, Rida expresses shock: "I wasn't [having feelings] he will die, he will be martyred."[56] While he didn't admit this in the written word, it unearths the potential disbelief he had at that time. His comrades are gone, but given the task ahead, he pushes down that emotion. Moreover, even if not stated explicitly in our interviews, Rida hints to the courage he attested to in real time. Imad and his brother Diyab are "brave heroes" who went to the battlefield.[57] They were not called up, they were encouraged not to—by Rida—but did, given the magnitude of the moment.[58] As I describe in the next chapter, very few made that decision, and those who are still alive today explore the different paths they took, what ifs, and the sliding doors of life.

Many comrades met at the Zaydaniyya office of the Lebanese Communist Party in the wake of Imad's death, providing a different, immediate reaction. One of the most famous first responders was Khalid al-Habre. Habre wrote a song about this event, titled *Agniyya al-Qantari*, The Qantari Song. Today, Habre tells me he is merely a "friend of the party," but at the time, he was a member in the intellectual section of the Lebanese Communist Party and a professional musician.[59] His style is akin to the arguably more famous Marcel Khalife, who meshes Lebanese instrumentation and (Western) rock ballads under the umbrella of a leftist, radical politics.[60]

Habre describes that day at the party headquarters, where, immediately, comrades were singing songs. For party members to unite at the headquarters for ritual, song, and play was quite common, before and during wartime.[61] He tells me, "I had the idea to write a song for the youth and I said [out loud] 'Our song to our comrades our wounds were bandaged' [what became the chorus] … and in this song we were singing of the young men who were killed."[62] The lyrics of the song sprang from there.

While the song was originally recorded in 1975, all that is left today is a 2014 live recording.[63] I have included the original Arabic lyrics, per Habre, as well as my translation below.[64] Note that the song moves between the three martyrs singing (mostly in the verses) and the comrades singing (mostly in the chorus). The bolded lyrics indicate those words that were provided by Habre but are different/not in the 2014 recording.

Do not dig graves, because we are not dead	لا تحفروا قبورا فنحن لم نمت
We called [made known] where we were	دعونا حيث كنا
We embrace the message	نعانق الرسالة
We called where we were	دعونا حيث كنا
We weave the story	ننسج الحكايه
And we are not dead	فنحن لم نمت
Blind fate wanted us to disappear	شاء قدر أعمى أن نغيب
but we did not die	لكنا لم نمت
[Because] testimony [martyrdom] is not death	فالشهادة غير الموت
Martyrdom is life	**الشهادة حياة**
We write it with rifles	**نكتبها بالبنادق**
With bullets of rifles	**برصاص البنادق**
Martyrdom is a story	الشهادة حكاية
And the story is a legend	والحكاية أسطورة
And the legend is true	والاسطورة حقيقة
We are not dead	إننا لم نمت
Chorus (2x):	
Our song to our comrades	أغاني رفاقنا
Our wounds were bandaged	ضمدت جراحنا
Our songs to our comrades	أغاني رفاقنا
You gave us a rifle	اهدتنا بندقية

We planted chrysanthemums	زرعتنا اقحوانا
In the streets of Qantari	في شوارع القنطاري
Do not dig graves	لا تحفروا قبوراً
because we are not dead, we called	فنحن لم نمت دعونا
where we were	حيث كنا
We face history	نواجه التاريخ
We **wrestle with** history	نصارع[65] التاريخ
The fact that we were	بحقيقة اننا
We were martyred, we did not die	استشهدنا لم نمت
Chorus (2x):	
Our song to our comrades	اغاني رفاقنا
Our wounds were bandaged	ضمدت جراحنا
Our song to our comrades	اغاني رفاقنا
You gave us a rifle	اهدتنا بندقية
We planted chrysanthemums	زرعتنا اقحوانا
In the streets of Qantari	في شوارع القنطاري

There are some words in this song that bely direct transition. Most notable are the verb *da'a and* noun *shahada*. While simply meaning to call, and testimony, both have specific connotation in Arabic and within Islam. *Shahada* refers to the first pillar of Islam: to testify to the presence and oneness of God and the message of God brought by the prophet Muhammad. But it shares the same root as the verb *istashahada*, to be martyred, which is brought up later in the song. Hence, Khalid is playing with the connection between the two, for the sake of giving testimony to the martyrdom of these fighters.

Da'a specifically means to evangelize, to spread the word of God, to wish someone to be closer to God. This is quite important in two senses. Religiously, used in the past tense "we called," enshrines these three as martyrs of the faith—two Druze, one Shia—of Islam. Second, in a less religious sense, the use of the word points to future action. That they called necessitates that the listener of the song respond. No, the living will not forget what happened in the streets of Qantari, because these three are not technically dead. They were martyred and live on. Hence, the comrades must be mobilized in the future, to first remember their martyrs and to fight to defend them with words and rifles.

Also notable in this song is the use of the flower *uqhuwan*, chrysanthemums, white crown daisies, which are associated with death, dying, burying, and funerals, specifically in Islam. That these are planted on the streets is to mark the streets as a site of death and mourning. Here, Khaled's lyrics are similar to

Rida's words, focusing, even just for a moment, and in a muted fashion, on the loss itself. But both quickly turn toward action.

Perhaps most important for this section is the song's focus on comradeship, the first lyric that Khalid thought up: "Our song to our comrades, Our wounds were bandaged, Our songs to our comrades, You gave us a rifle." But comradeship to whom and for whom? No place in the song does the listener hear the three names—Imad, Muhammad, and Diyab—that are the namesake of "The Song of Qantari." Khalid admits to me he didn't really know the three martyrs, at least not in a "deep manner."[66] To highlight this is not to minimize what their deaths felt like to their comrades. To Khalid, Rida, and others, Imad's death meant something. But at least in the moment, that had to be subdued, minimized, and not dwelt on, given the fight ahead.

The comrade who perhaps wrote most personally about Imad was his cousin, Walid Nuwayhid. Walid had been a journalist since the late 1960s, and in 1974, he started working for *al-Muharir*, the Liberator. It was a leftist paper, not associated to any particular party or movement but the Lebanese National Movement more broadly.[67] He was in the education and culture section, reviewing books and films, until the war started. "They need us to help in the political section" of the paper, he tells me.[68] A week after Imad died, Walid penned the "week remembrance for the martyr Imad Nuwayhid." He writes, "frankly," directly to Imad, that you "said and acted and did not deviate from the goal." Walid articulates that goal. For ten years, Imad was "carrying the pen defending the right of the resistance to carry arms," and in battle "in 1975 you were at the forefront of carrying the gun in defense of the right of the Lebanese to carry the pen."[69] Here, Walid established Imad as a hybrid intellectual and fighter. While he once wrote about Palestine, the Jewish question, and the Palestinian right to liberate, Imad now put his life on the line for it.

In another line on Imad's credentials, Walid writes, "Since the first moments of your political commitments, you chose your profession and were not a political amateur." The choice of the word profession or calling, *mahana*, is telling. My investigation of Imad of the late 1960s to early 1970s demonstrated that the career he was pursuing was in the hotel business. On one level, this shows Walid replacing the practical radical with a leftist intellectual. On another and more nuanced plane it shows Imad as the practical radical he was. To Walid, it did not matter what his job was, even if he had one outside his "political commitments." To Imad's comrades, his calling was his dedication to the joint Palestinian-Lebanese leftist cause.

Even with these personal touches, Walid begins and finishes his remembrance much like the party Imad died fighting for. He starts with the following:

> I now write this not only because Imad was close to me, my friend and comrade, but because with the passing of hours and days there is a change with the rest of comrades of the martyrs towards a symbol for all of us that we have been looking for years.

It appears as if Walid wants to remind his reader, a potential defender or even fighter, that the fact that he knows Imad well is inconsequential. His death, in Qantari, is a symbol for what is ahead. Like Rida and Khalid did the day of Imad's death, Walid urges that his comrades must forge ahead, their action serving as a testament to Imad. To this end, Walid ends his piece of Imad's martyr narrative with the following: "You were the first but will not be the last on the path, which is still long and we are on the path."[70]

These were not Walid's last words in service of his comrade, the Left, and the Lebanese Communist Party. He spoke at the forty-day remembrance of Imad in his village of Ras al-Matn. Per an *al-Nida'* report, Walid was joined by a thousand attendees and the following representatives:

- Maurice Nahra, representative of the Lebanese Communist Party in the Mountain, who's following quote served as the headline for the story: "No solution [to the war] except fulfilling national demands."[71]
- Amr Gharz al-Din, representative of the Communist Party from Ras al-Matn, who discusses how Imad was joining the ranks of other famous communist party martyrs
- Salah Said, a representative of the Communist Party from Beirut, who notes "the Progressive and National Forces are fighting to win several victories which form the natural core for democratic expansion"
- Abu al-Abd, representative of the Palestinian resistance, who spoke of those "black [read evil] reactionaries" that future fighters would face

These were some heavy hitters. This event was not an impromptu festival that formed after Imad's death, like the one in Zaydaniyya. It was a party-orchestrated event. Yet, they asked Walid to speak, presumably because of his interesting position as a member of the family and comrade to the Left—a member of the Lebanese Communist Action Organization.

So how did he speak as the comrade? He discusses Imad's intellectual and physical struggles since his days of schooling in Beirut and Europe.[72] With no direct quotes provided, it appears that Walid's words were brief, at least shorter than any of the other speakers. Furthermore, like the other leaders, his words appear abstract, distant from the practical radical Imad. According to Walid, however, his speech was not short. He tells me he spoke for over fifteen minutes about Imad's character and personality, but only a sentence on this— that Imad was a "fighter in different planes"—was included.[73]

Adding the perspective of a friend and comrade to the official martyr narrative illuminates that the party was not forgetting the individual by accident, given the great task ahead. Rather, it edited words on Imad's personal characteristics and feelings on the magnitude of his death, ostensibly writing them out of the history of his death. I can only question, and imagine, what countless other fallen fighters of parties to the war met a similar fate? Reduced to a symbol?

But Walid, the comrade, does not take offense to this. He is not angry about it today. He was merely letting me know the difference between what he said and what was printed.[74] As his words through *al-Muharir* show at the time, comrades represented a unique, but largely confirming slice of the martyr narrative—to attest, to the past human, but only quickly, perhaps a second longer than the party, before moving on to the future struggle.

The Family

In sum, comrades contributed to the party-created martyr narrative on Imad, even when offering slight differences. At first glance, family reactions to Imad's death, from the time, would appear to run counter to both. Take, for example, the actions of Jawad at the funeral. He confronts a comrade of Imad's to assert the family name against the party name. He is not trying to appropriate Imad, but have space and time to grieve. Yet, the record here is equally mixed, complicating clear divides between party, comrades, and family, and providing a closer look at what it means to mobilize the dead.

I turn first to where the family first inserts itself in the afterlife, not the archive, of the martyr narrative: the funeral. I never really asked Jawad about his actions until recently. It could be my interviewing style (let the conversation flow, try not to lead too much) or my fear of not wanting to touch this contentious moment, directly. Accordingly, in the years since I found out about the funeral fight from Iman, it has often been refracted through others. In my conversations with Walid, he notes Jawad's rage. From his perspective, Jawad could not understand how someone as bright and talented as Imad was on the frontlines. He then saw the party member's placing of the flag on Imad's coffin as provocation, in his moment of loss.[75]

In Iman Nuwayhid's description of Jawad's actions, he stresses that Jawad was not a friend of the Communist Party. By Jawad's admission, he operated in similar circles to Imad in the 1960s. He attended the *Lycée Français de Beyrouth*, which, while perhaps too elitist for Imad, created many young leftists.[76] By 1975, in Iman's words, Jawad was trying to "disconnect … with his affiliation" to establish his career. Furthermore, most of the Nuwayhids were "actually anti-[communist];" Adl (Iman's father) was a Syrian Social Nationalist Party member, Adl's brother was a Progressive Socialist Party member, and Yusuf, Imad's father, was a non-affiliated Arab nationalist.[77] Jawad confirmed this point to me later, telling me, quite bluntly, "I don't like those people [the Communist Party,] personally I hate them."[78] Given the lack of strong support for the party among Imad's loved ones, and Jawad's feelings, some family at the funeral did not want Imad to be labeled a communist.

Beyond what some family did not want, it seems Jawad simply wanted his brother to be remembered as a Nuwayhid. Iman clarifies the different perspectives here, including the party's and Jawad's:

> And of course the Communist Party is declaring Imad as a martyr of the party and there are flags and they want to carry the coffin and then you have the Nuwayhids … who actually see Imad as a Nuwayhid and so his coffin should be carried by the Nuwayhids and not by the party … I think at that point Jawad and most probably members of the close family were sending the message that you cannot … take advantage or you cannot build on this … We lost him, he is our loss and we do not allow you to emphasize or promote or take advantage of that.[79]

Iman defends Jawad's actions, but also acknowledges, as a matter of fact, the party's strategy. In this way, Iman's words are some of the most telling I have heard since starting this project. On one level, the quote is my "smoking gun" for resistance to the martyr narrative, showing that logic, made most perceivable through this type of research. On another level, as I have written elsewhere, Iman's comments "add even more nuance to the politics of memorialization, demonstrating that there were, and continue to be, multiple positions in this encounter, including not absolutely for *or* against the party's claiming."[80]

But what about Jawad's perspective here? In recent conversations, I have asked him directly, and he describes his reaction to me as "very simple." "I was angry," he tells me.[81] Angry about his brother's actions, death, and a party that looked like they were trying to capitalize from this. Regardless of the necessary nuance captured by someone like Iman, emotion and grief are still parts of the equation that are missing—or reduced, omitted—from the official martyr narrative.

This is one corner of family perspectives, rendered through oral history. But the family is present in the archive at the time, having a say in the party-constructed martyr narrative. For one, Imad's mother, Umm Jihad, made an appearance. She is the only one quoted in the *al-Nida'* report of the November 4th, one-week remembrance in Ras al-Matn. She states, speaking to and from Imad, "Do not be selfish my mother. At my feet [I am] one of your five sons, for party, and the party for the people, and the nation."[82] In this one quote, she raises the potential anger, grief, and disbelief that her son is gone, that which Jawad embodies. But then she shifts. Like Rida in the initial *al-Nida'* report from Zaydaniyya, she pushes that feeling down, acknowledging that it is irrelevant in the scope of Imad's action for his party and Lebanon. To be fair, this could be a case of private grief vs. public stoicism. According to Iman, Umm Jihad was "practically disintegrated" by her son's death. "It wasn't easy on her."[83] There is, however, an alternative interpretation for family support of the martyr narrative: they had little choice but to participate in the party's claiming. As noted, the party physically showed up with their time, energy, and money. Unless they literally wanted to fight, the party was going to be there. So why not let them?

The last, and perhaps most intriguing, immediate family perspective is that of Imad's father, Yusuf. It is most interesting because of where it is found: in the pages of *al-Nida'*. A year after Imad's death, the non-communist allowed a letter that he wrote to his son to be published in the Lebanese Communist Party's daily. It is titled "The Longer the Time, the Closer the Distance," a theme carried throughout the letter. Like some comrades and family members, the letter holds an air of private grief, one that many fathers of "strugglers" could relate to in wartime. He starts, "My boy… a year has passed and I wait for you … a year has passed my boy and I wait for you to appear in the night … [.] And when it did not come I resorted to writing about you."[84] Walid tells me that Yusuf called him for weeks and months after Imad's death. He wanted to know more about his son, I presume, specifically his politics, his cause, that led to his death.[85] Although nothing could fill the void, Imad's father tries to cope with the loss of his son by talking with his son's comrades, those, as he writes in this letter, who "knew you." He also writes, "I ran to your papers to search for your remains."[86] These are the same letters and writings that were given to me decades later.

However, his father is not troubled by the public persona of Imad—how Imad has become a symbol to many in his death. He notes that through remembering Imad, his name is everywhere, on the streets, in Beirut, and in the mountain, in Ras al-Matn, as "Imad changes to thousands of Imad," one of many martyrs that inspires living comrades to "cut through the rocks." Indeed, Yusuf's letter is not only a means to remember. It sets out to build the momentum of his son as a spark to drive others to fight against the Kataib. One of his final messages in the letter is "the clock is ticking for the foes," signaling that violence is justified, especially to avenge his son.[87]

While perhaps as close as one could get to Imad at the time, Yusuf's message is not wholly personal. Like the mass majority of party, comrade, and family perspectives, at least in the party archive, it focuses on the cause ahead in a depersonalized way. This call for future action, arguably the most salient aspect of martyr narratives, is likely why the party published it.

Yet, this was not a conspiracy. The party did not fabricate Yusuf's feelings. It appears that Yusuf accepted the appropriation of his son to the Lebanese Communist Party. To be clear, I caution against seeing one person's reactions to Imad's death as more or less authentic than another. Regardless of Yusuf's beliefs, or grief, it appears through this letter that he accepted Imad's actions. Others did not, at least not fully, including, as I explore in the final chapter, Imad's siblings. They seek to mobilize him in another way: by cleaning the slate.

6

The Politics of Memorialization in Death's Aftermath

Googling Imad in Beirut

Beirut, Lebanon, Fall 2013

There is one organization in Lebanon doing the work, the "memory at work" as they call it. The UMAM Documentation and Research Center opened in its current form circa 2010. Its purpose is to "boost discussion of specific facts and episodes related to Lebanon's war and its legacy while overcoming the self-imposed boundaries of good and evil."[1] When I was a graduate student living and researching in Beirut, I decided to visit UMAM to see how they could aid my current research on the politics of memory at the hands of parties to the war.

Like many archives within Lebanon, you don't just show up during business hours, at least not with the expectation that you will get anything done. I had already had a taste of this at the National Archives, leaving empty-handed—besides a coffee or tea—several times before I was able to look at anything related to my project. Leaving with no sources from UMAM was not my only concern. UMAM is located in Haret Hreik, the top part of the Dahiya, the southern suburb of Beirut, an area that I'd never visited but surely heard of. Hizbullah, the hybrid party-social movement-military organization, holds support in this area today. While mapping my visit, thoughts of Hizbullah's mass kidnappings of foreigners in the eighties surely crossed my mind.

As I rode in the taxi on my way to UMAM, any unfounded nerves I had completely eased. I saw a new side of the city, a vibrant one. Those who have spent time in Beirut since the 1990s know that many places feel, well, fake. After the war, real-estate mogul and Prime Minister Rafiq Hariri launched a development plan in downtown that, in my opinion, sucked the life out of it. Depending on the time of day you are walking in this area, you could be alone in what feels like a concrete jungle.

But this was not the case in the Dahiya. Sometime in the morning of a random weekday, I look out my cab window to see people were out, running errands, talking, just living. The experience at UMAM that day was less memorable. Yes, I found some documents for my research, and the UMAM space, a converted old villa, was bright and beautiful. But more memorable was the drive. Three years since my first trip to Lebanon, I felt I had finally found Beirut.

Beirut, Lebanon, Summer 2022

Nine years had passed and a lot had changed since my last trip to UMAM. For starters, I knew Beirut much better, including the exact mini-bus route that would get me to Haret Hreik and UMAM. After a bit of research there one day, I head over to the newer UMAM Hanger, an exhibition space next door. There I see "Memory of a Paper City: An Installation by Alfred Tarazi." The exhibit is an ode to the history of print in Beirut, "following the thread of over a hundred publications from the nineteen thirties till the end of the eighties."[2] I recognize a lot of media in the exhibit and am thoroughly impressed with its presentation and scope. Although I am not a visual artist like Tarazi, I collect things that underscore UMAM's mission to remember. Perhaps, I ponder, UMAM would want to pair with me on my book project on the life, death, and memory of Imad Nuwayhid.

So I send an email. It is short and informal, I attach an article I had written on Imad, and ask if they would like to collaborate. I don't hear back, but the next time I come to UMAM a week later, one of the archivists and researchers recalls my email and asks me back to their office. Maybe this is the start of something! It was, just not what I thought. Immediately, I can tell that the archivist is just there in a supportive, not collaborative, role. They check their database to see if they have any documents on Imad. They don't, which I already know. So they go on the internet and Google, in Arabic, عماد نويهض, Imad Nuwayhid.

To be honest, I am underwhelmed by all of this. I had been coming to Lebanon for the past twelve years, working on this project for about nine, published an article on this research, sent it to them, and now their assistance is to do what I have clearly already done? Search his name on the internet in his own language?

However, what I had never done was google عماد نويهض *in Beirut—a different IP that yields new and slightly different results. The first was a fan site, dedicated to the "Martyrs of the Lebanese Communist Party" (see Figure 6.1 below). Its entries appear to be reproductions from books like the 1980 Martyrs of the Lebanese Communist Party, which includes the entry on Imad that launched this project. A current party member later told me this site was compiled by some interested party members, not on initiative from the party center.*

No, UMAM wouldn't be collaborating with me—at least not at the time of writing—but they opened me up to a new world. Members and supporters of the Lebanese Communist Party today take their own time to create a space, online, to remember their fallen comrades, like Imad. No one tells them to do it. Perhaps they see it as their duty. Since that search in Beirut two years ago, it has become harder to find Imad's page online. More or less, you need to be looking for him to find it. Yet, even if only for a few of his comrades, and one researcher, his memory lives on in the digital realm.

Figure 6.1 First result when googling Imad at UMAM: A fan site dedicated to the "Martyrs of the Lebanese Communist Party." Courtesy of the Lebanese Communist Party.

***

A lot had changed since Imad Nuwayhid's death in October 1975. No longer defending its headquarters in West Beirut, the Joint Forces of the Lebanese National Movement had, as of early 1976, "established control of over two-thirds of Lebanon and appeared on the verge of defeating their opponents outright and establishing a new regime."[3] A US-backed Syrian intervention dashed those hopes, and by 1977 they were no longer just an intervening force in the war. Syrian troops occupied the entire northern and eastern part of the country.[4] By 1978, Israel had invaded most of southern Lebanon, its first attempt to dislodge the Palestinian Liberation Organization from its de facto headquarters.[5] And while the possibility of reform looked possible in late 1975 to early 1976—between the Palestinian Liberation Movement and the army, between the Lebanese National Movement and the government—two invasions complicated any hope for real change. In the interim, the casualty and injury count had merely risen from roughly 18,000 killed and 15,000 injured by the end of 1976, to 21,000 killed and 18,000 injured by 1978.[6] These counts nearly doubled in 1982, the year of the second Israeli invasion and the bloodiest year of the war.[7]

This new context permeates party-produced martyr narratives on Imad, other leftist fighters, and beyond. Like I charted in Chapter 5, parties to the war continued to use death to mobilize the living to fight. At the same time, with the length of the war and devastation it had wrought by the late 1970s and into early 1980s, parties began to reflect on the war and what it became. These changes mark the first major shift in the martyr narrative. Details on the lives of martyrs—like those included in my first lead on Imad, the 1980 volume dedicated to martyrs of the Lebanese Communist Party—empathy for the families, and nostalgia began to creep into party memorizations. The latter was especially true as the righteousness of the causes that martyrs died for was being tested by the fact that they, years later, still remain unfulfilled.

Today, thirty-plus years since the war ended, the landscape for remembering and evoking the past is radically different. Post-war growth, the growth of Hizbullah, Syrian withdrawal, Syrian War, parliamentary shifts, anti-parliamentary protests, incursions with Israel, and then, revolution in 2019, pandemic in early 2020, blast in late 2020, and an economic crisis and a regional war over/on Palestine that is still unresolved as of writing.[8] This new world must be accounted for when discussing how the politics of memorialization around Imad unfold today, differently than the seventies or eighties. But, alas, the memory game continues. This chapter then takes as its background these shifting grounds to assess the ever-evolving afterlife of Imad Yusuf Nuwayhid.

~

When I started studying Lebanon's war and its legacy two decades ago, the prevailing "collective amnesia" argument was already unraveling. The first article I remember reading that debunked it was Oren Barak's 2007 "Don't Mention The War." He argues that the trauma from the war, coupled with the 1991 amnesty law that absolved militia leaders of war crimes, did little to stop the public from wanting to talk about the war.[9] Others have built off of this thesis, demonstrating that civil society actors, political parties, artists, and even state officials, have resisted any form of state-sponsored ambivalence or amnesia, even as they create their own versions, a sort of amnesia, of the war, its perpetrators, and victims.[10] My research confirms these findings and takes them to the micro-level. It may have taken a few years, but I cannot get the Nuwayhids or Imad's friends and comrades to stop talking about the war as they create their own version of events.

Others working at the micro-level have reaped similar rewards. In his wonderful 2017 book, *War Is Coming: Between Past and Future Violence in Lebanon*, Sami Hermez interviews Lebanese of today, a number of which are ex-fighters, to argue for just that title. His subjects live in between conflicts, in his own words, "in the meanwhile."[11] Within this context, he has witnessed what he calls "active forgetting," a concept very useful for our exploration of how people today evoke Imad. "The forgetting … [they] were engaged in was associated more closely with forgetting past ideals one held, and with the type of person one was during the war."[12] Stated differently, they choose to forget, not passively, or under state direction, but as a form of agency, disassociating themselves with the aspect of their identity that is wrapped up in the war, one they would rather forget.

In my conversations with those around Imad, I have witnessed active forgetting but with some twists. Many distance themselves from the war, as an event, but they actively remember their brother and comrade, as a human or a symbol. The first variety I have witnessed is what I have elsewhere termed "cleaning the slate."[13] There are those that recast Imad in a way that is more sympathetic to their beliefs today. This way of recalling wipes clean what those see as Imad's indiscretions, specifically the most radical and traumatic components. The slate cleaners may be forgetting Imad's actual roles in the war, but they hold him and their memories of him near.

Furthermore, what they tell me combats a certain way of remembering, the party-created martyr narrative. This form of claiming is most clear with Imad's siblings, specifically Jawad and Iyad, whose words today stand to serve as a corrective. Yes, Jawad was resistant to the party narrative in the moment of Imad's funeral, discussed in Chapter 5, but I argue the resistance has continued into the present as he and others seek to honor Imad as more than a leftist intellectual and communist martyr.

The other variation of active forgetting, is, in a word, nostalgia. There are some of Imad's comrades and family who do not disassociate from the war—at least I have not observed this—but rather use Imad as a reference point for better times when the Lebanese Left was more robust. This is where I return to the wiseness of Javier Cercas, and his investigation of his deceased great uncle and his actions in the Spanish Civil War. In one eye-opening exchange, he found his mother was quite celebratory of who he had once seen as an embarrassment, "secretly horrified and ashamed" of his Francoist, fascist family. He writes:

> What I understood then [after hearing his mother's approval] was that Manuel Mena's death had been seared into my mother's imagination in childhood as what the ancient Greeks called *kalos thanatos*: a beautiful death … demonstrat[ing] his nobility and purity by risking his life for all or nothing in the front line for values greater than himself[.][14]

While perhaps not a memory from childhood, Imad similarly becomes a symbol of bravery for those close to him who today agree with the causes he died for. Moreover, Imad becomes a representation of what so many gave up once—their lives—and what they, as the living, noncombatants today, chose not to give up.

Actively forgetting one thing, wiping the slate clean of another or nostalgic of other things. These are the multiple, complicated, and contradictory ways that Imad lives on today. In the remainder of this chapter, I explore those reactions and pair them with earlier memorializations of Imad and others, paying close attention to how memory shifts in different contexts, and under different people, into the present day.

Nostalgia for the Last Living Left

The 1980 volume dedicated to *The Martyrs of the Lebanese Communist Party*, the one where I first learned about Imad's time in Europe and his translation of *The Jewish Question*, was unprecedented. At over 300 pages, the volume was not merely dedicated to fighters. Noncombatant men, women, and children were memorialized.[15] To be blunt, increased casualties meant more martyrs, and a new level of density of martyr narratives. In the first year of the war, the Lebanese Communist Party counted and remembered sixty-three martyrs, Imad being one of them. This tripled by 1976, the second-most violent year of the entire war.[16]

One may assume that this escalation would render the martyr narrative less personal over time. That is, the more death, more destruction, and no end in sight would desensitize party officials, making martyr narratives even more propagandistic and cold. At least for the Lebanese Left, the exact opposite happened. As the war unfolded in the 1970s and 1980s, its martyr narratives became more detailed, nuanced, and empathetic. In short, I believe this is a product of nostalgia creeping in, for a simpler time and single cause, as things became more violent and more hopeless.

Also changing were the mediums in which the martyred were introduced to the public. As shown in Chapter 5, leftists who were contemporaneous to Imad met him through obituaries and newspaper write-ups on events dedicated to him. But those in the 1980s would encounter fallen comrades through compiled volumes, like the one mentioned above, and posters, which were now more pervasive at the hands of well-oiled propaganda departments of parties.[17]

Perhaps most distinct and impressive of this new era were films made by leftist sympathizers that took up the theme of martyrdom. One of the most famous was created by the Lebanese Communist Action Organization in 1978 and is titled *Ajmal al-Ummahat*, "The Most Beautiful of Mothers." The title is a reference to the song by Marcel Khalife, which was featured, for the first time, in the film. Khalife converted a poem from Hassan Abdallah, member of the Lebanese Communist Party, into song.[18] Its most iconic lyric is its namesake: "The most beautiful of mothers is that who waited for her son and he returned a martyr."[19]

The song sets the tone for the opening scene. Members of the Lebanese Communist Action Organization carry a coffin of one of their martyrs, as a woman, presumably his mother, cries in despair and rage. She is flanked mostly by children, all male, that look on at this grieving woman.[20] In a 2013 documentary about the making of the film, Habib Sadiq, General Secretary of the Cultural Council of South Lebanon, describes the significance of the song in this context: "it had an active role in expressing people's feelings and thoughts and opinions and at the same time serves as an eye opener and provides more motivation."[21] Those feelings and thoughts were of sadness, anger, and loss. By Sadiq's own admission, martyr narratives were now balancing these complex emotions with the call for mobilization observed in earlier productions.

The film was directed by Maroun Baghdadi, one of the most celebrated of Lebanon's new leftist cinema.[22] His thirty-some-minute film flips between two formats. One is a documentary, interviewing the loved ones of fallen comrades of the Lebanese Communist Action Organization, including mothers, fathers, brothers, sisters, and comrades. The other feels more, and was, "performed" cinema.[23] The focus is a staged military operation from south Lebanon into Israel, which in actuality was conducted the night before by members of the Lebanese Communist Action Organization.

These reenactments were not wholly new by 1978.[24] For example, a 1976 edition of the Popular Front for the Liberation of Palestine's magazine, *al-Hadaf*, The Target, takes up a mission from south Lebanon into Israel, before it even happened. The cover of the edition is a staged picture of four young fighters: Ahmad (twenty years old—born in Homs), Najim (twenty-eight years old—born in Kuwait), Bassam (twenty-one years old—born in Aleppo), and Hussein (nineteen years old—born in south Lebanon). They hold their rifles in different positions like props, as the caption reads, the "'Hunayn' [Arabic name of the now Israeli village] Suicide Mission."[25] Indeed, staged productions like this are meant to show what the youth are actually doing, in real time, to stop the enemy. But they were paired with a personal touch. For one, all four young men who gave up their lives were profiled and given space to leave words for their living comrades.

Like this level of detail, loss and trauma were traits absent in earlier martyr narratives, circa Imad's in 1975. But they were on display in the dedication to martyrs in *Ajmal al-Ummahat*. The first mother interviewed in the film describes her son, holding back tears. "My dear Ali," she says, "the light of my eyes. He was a role model for the youth. 20 years old, blond, tall." Another mother admits that she and her family "had no idea" that their son, now a martyr, was training and fighting.[26]

The film captures many responses from loved ones of the martyrs, but centers mothers in a way that is somewhat new. Yes, as noted in Chapter 5, Imad's mother was quoted in a 1975 write-up. But in comparison, Imad's father was commissioned by the party to remember him a year after his death. By 1978 and beyond, something had changed. For example, the entry for Muhammad Maki in the 1980 volume dedicated to communist martyrs is written by his mother. This martyr narrative of the man who died alongside Imad in Qantari is one of the more illuminating ones I have read in its mixing of loss, nostalgia, and propaganda.

Throughout the entry, it becomes clear that Muhammad's father did not approve of his son's role in the Lebanese Communist Party. But his mother did, and they developed a special bond through their joint support for leftist causes. At the same time, her relationship with her husband soured. Muhammad came home one day to inform his mother "this is my last bath," and he never returned thereafter. According to the mother's story, at the funeral of Muhammad, her now ex-husband approached her, shouting "You left me for him … and now he is gone and you [what will you do]?" The mother replies, "I am *Aghoub* [Muhammad's code name] He did not die he has been martyred for your sake. He was fighting for you and your likes."[27]

Muhammad's mother takes on his *nom de guerre* and his cause. She ends the martyr narrative, declaring "And I will carry the weapon instead of him."[28] On one level, this story confirms Muhammad's dedication, the importance of loving mothers, and feminizes those who do not support, like Muhammad's father. At the same time, to write on what was lost—her son, her husband, her marriage—was unique, in and of itself, even if that pain was trumped by the necessity of future action. And through that dedication, Muhammad's mother becomes a living embodiment of Khalife's song, "The most beautiful of mothers is that who waited for her son and he returned a martyr."

Returning to *Ajmal al-Ummahat*, another interviewed mother contrasts the trauma and pride she feels in the starkest of terms. As she sits with her six children, she laments:

> I had cooked mloukhieh [a dish made of cooked Jute leaves] and he ate [his final meal] … I never cooked mloukhieh ever again … Every time I see any of the comrades I imagine his face right in front me. I remember him in everything. Wherever I go, whatever I do, whenever the time..[pause] I remember him in everything. His memories were numerous. I no longer recall anything in this life.[29]

Grief is clear here and Baghdadi seeks to capture it. When she says, "I never cooked mloukhieh ever again," his camera slowly zooms in on her face. She fans herself any time she is close to tears, as her children do the same.

But this woman also voices longing, nostalgic for a time when her son was alive. In fact, it is all she can recall. The present means little to her unless her son's comrades are with her. From one reading, this sounds like a line in Imad's father's 1976 *al-Nida'* letter. As I relayed in the previous chapter, Yusuf sees his son everywhere, especially in his comrades as "Imad changes to thousands of Imads" that fight the good fight.[30] Like Yusuf, then, this mother is acquiescing that the youth need to continue the cause of her son. There is another reading here, however, especially given the turn she takes toward his memory, alone, toward the end. Perhaps she is lamenting for a past time when their comradeship felt strong enough to attain anything. That has passed, replaced by a sort of bitterness. Now, like her son, all is lost in life.

These humanizing trends in the Lebanese Communist Action Organization's 1978 *Ajmal al-Ummahat* continued into the 1980s, across other parties, and into the Lebanese Communist Party and its compilation *Martyrs for the Lebanese Communist Party*. Imad's entry was not written by his mother, but, as Maurice Nahra, party representative in Mount Lebanon, informs me "by his comrades in the mountain … and those who knew him well and had connections with his family and his father." While his comrades may have been the main authors, Maurice tells me they sought to fill in the dots they did not know by working with those who knew him "before he entered politics and the party."[31]

Before the entries of Muhammad Maki, Imad Nuwayhid, and the some 200 other martyrs, Secretary General of the Lebanese Communist Party, George Hawi, introduces the volume. It includes motifs that the readers of that book, and this book, know well at this point. Hawi calls for "revolutionary violence" by the living comrades in the face of "imperialism, Zionism and fascism," in the name of the fallen martyrs.[32] Yet in his final lines, he mentions the Hassan Abdallah poem, Khalife song, and partner organization film, confirming some of the newest features in remembering the fallen. Hawi admits, this period, the beginning of the decade, represents a "turning point" one where things were bleaker. The pivot was 1978, the "current Israeli occupation" of south Lebanon, the death associated with it, and the "politics of inaction in front of the Zionist enemy."[33]

The turning point, perhaps most importantly, was also communicated through Hawi's honesty and empathy. He starts his introduction with an acknowledgment. This book would stir "contradictory feelings" of "pure sadness mixed with pride," "love and hate united" in the moment of death and memorialization. To be clear, these words did not change the reality of "sacrificing towards the road of victory" in the name of the dead.[34] But breathing life into trauma, I would think, was important for readers, their families, and their comrades. It is not to argue that in 1975—a context when martyr narratives like those of Imad were bereft of detail—the party did not care about loss. Nonetheless, as I have shown, a meditation on the dead, as living humans, and the emotions it could stir, was not palpable after Imad's death at the start of the war. But as the war continued, a space for a longer pause was growing. It was a space to discuss not only what was lost individually, but also what the parties had lost: Lebanon and the war.

After Hawi's introduction, a poem titled "A fighter's death for the sake of peace," and a number of other martyr narratives, Imad's entry came on page 64.[35] The first thing the reader sees is Imad's picture, his name, and his birth and death years. The picture that was chosen for this volume was the same as the initial obituary in *al-Nida'* (see Figure 0.1). It was likely taken toward the end of Imad's life, perhaps during his time at Lebanese University in the early 1970s.[36] I do not know whether the picture was provided by Imad's father or the party selected it. Regardless, the choice is noticeable when compared with a host of other pictures of Imad that I have seen. When I have shown some of Imad's comrades the picture that was used in *al-Nida'* and the 1980 volume, they almost didn't recognize him. One person tells me that Imad did not always look like this, so formal.[37] They aren't wrong (see Figure 1.2 for example), but this may be how Imad's comrades see him today, fun-loving, suave, and not so stiff. That is, however, precisely how the party, and perhaps Imad's father, wanted to represent him: structured, formal, and dedicated.

Below is Imad's entry, in its entirety, paragraph by paragraph. The bolded words note areas of discrepancy. The first paragraph reads:

> There are few who in a short life assembled as much as comrade Imad Nuwayhid, all this richness in culture and struggle. Imad was born in 1944 in Ras al-Matn, **he studied until the end of secondary school in "the lycée"** and this is where he begun to open in his thinking … and in 1966 he obtained his degree in Philosophy and **joined the College of Law and the College of Literature, History Branch, at Lebanese University, then he traveled to Lausanne** for study in hotel administration for two years, **moving after that to Hanover,** where he **studied German and then to Dublin where he perfected English**. He returned to work at Hotel Phoenicia and received a certificate in law and not long before his martyrdom a certificate in history?![38]

This was the first biographical information I saw on Imad, and it has been indispensable to this book. But we know already, from the sources and people it opened me up to, that it is factually incorrect in multiple places. First, it reads as if Imad only attended "the *lycée*," almost positively a reference to the *Lycée Français de Beyrouth*. But he completed high school at Raml a-Zarif. And yes, he finished high school in 1966, but did not attend Lebanese University until after his return from Hanover, which is placed after his stay in Lausanne. The timeline is jumbled here: he worked at Hotel Phoenicia Intercontinental first, then Hanover, then Lausanne, then London—not mentioned—and then Dublin. Finally, his main purpose in Hanover and Dublin, working at hotels, is not mentioned.

This all may seem minor. Maybe it is. Maybe I am too close. Most of the information is here, and its writers likely did not fuss over the exact order of life events. If, like Maurice believes, Imad's entry was compiled in conjunction with the family, it is possible they could have gotten the timeline wrong, or it was mixed up in communication.[39] But the fact that neither his family nor the entry mentioned that he was in Germany or Ireland for more than language study, training in hotels specifically, leads me to two possible conclusions.

One is that the writers interviewed a family member—an uncle or cousin maybe—in Ras al-Matn who knew generalities, but not specificities. Maurice said it was his comrades in the mountain who wrote this entry, but Imad spent much more time in Beirut. These people would just know less about Imad. Equally plausible is that the party wanted to allude to job training, as a young man, but not working as a career seeking adult in Europe. If this is the case, the party was writing out of Imad's history the practical radical he was. Regardless of what the omission means, the entry shows that by 1980, family, comrades, and readers wanted to know the details of their martyrs' lives. They were nostalgic of who they were. Yet, these details were balanced with a message. To establish who Imad was, learned and globetrotting, proved what he was willing to give it up for his party.

The second paragraph moves toward the causes Imad held dear. Bolded, again, are some inconsistencies:

> Imad grew up with parents who surrounded him with care and attention and encouraged him to think freely and to be committed to popular and national issues … Imad got involved in the national struggle then in the party struggle committed to determination, courage, and depth of awareness. From the side of the rifle, Imad carried his pen and translated the book **"The Jewish Case according to a Materialist Understanding"** (twice printed) **as he was preparing a book for publication "China after 30 Years"** until the day of his death.[40]

The stress on Imad's parents should not come as a surprise. Yes, parents were becoming a fixture of martyr narratives, but from Imad's letters in Europe through interviews I have conducted today, family support for Imad is one of the most tangible features I have observed. Still, to mention this was also a means to an end, showcasing that he was nurtured to pursue the "right" ideas.

For inconsistencies, while I wish I could see this book on China, no one I know has ever heard of it. The entry also slightly mistitles Imad's translation, using the Arabic word for "case" (*qadiyya*) over the correct "question" (*mas'ala*). The error—even if minor—either highlights a lack of knowledge on the specifics of Imad's translation or an appropriation of his work for the current moment. The former seems unlikely, given that the writers of the entry knew, and referenced, that the book had been published in Arabic twice. Interestingly enough, that second, 1973 edition does not include Imad Nuwayhid's name as translator nor his translator's introduction.[41] The party was then actively writing Imad back into one his most important milestones and contributions to the Arab Left.

The current moment of the early 1980s, before the 1982 Israeli invasion, was a point at which cohesion between the Lebanese Left and Palestinian cause was at its apex. In this context, the word *qaḍiyya* was more politized than question, paired with *Filastiniyya*, to mean "the Palestinian issue." So yes, details on Imad, and other martyrs, were important as a matter of presence by this period. However, I cannot help to think that when parties attempt to dig deep, within the context of balancing future action with past greatness, sometimes they would miss, minimize, or shift the latter. This is because the mark was always defeating the enemy, as the entry's final paragraph demonstrates: "On October 28 Imad was with his comrade Diyab Ismael and Aghoub [Muhammad Maki] in the front of the ranks of liberation in Qantari from the fascist gangs, where their martyrdom launched a new stage in the sacrifice and gave new reasons for steadfastness and victory."[42]

This information on Imad was reproduced in a 1985 volume. It was published by the Lebanese Communist Party, dedicated to fighters from Mount Lebanon, like Imad, and titled *Difa'an 'an al-Jabal Difa'an 'an al-Watan*, *Defending the Mountain, Defending the Nation*. The context had, once again, shifted and is important for interpreting the nostalgia of the Left presented in this volume. Following 1982, and a widening loss of hope in Palestinian liberation, fighting had shifted from the south of the country, with Israel, to the interior among different Lebanese factions. This war for the hinterland— mostly fought between the Progressive Socialist Party and the Lebanese Forces, but also including a smattering of leftist forces—resulted in a win for the Lebanese National Movement in 1984, but not before 1,300 people perished.[43]

Like the 1980 volume, this 1985 one starts with an introduction, and shows many continuities but also the shifting context in which martyr narratives were created. Nadim Abdel Sammad, deputy Secretary General of the

Lebanese Communist Party, wrote this volume's introduction, and starts with the balance of loss and future action that one had come to expect in these productions. The martyrs were "bright flares on the road to our own struggle." At the same time, there was a "deep bitterness and feeling of loss" even if that feeling was less important than "feelings of pride for them." Samad confirms that, "We preserve their names, engraved their pictures in our memory," both of which are nods to memorization. He also acknowledges pain, as we "learn from them how to be tender."[44]

Sammad was from Mountain Lebanon, and given the present volume, he stresses that those martyrs included in the volume defended the "mountain of my father" against the fascists that "came to the mountain."[45] Imad did not fight in the mountain, but the capital as a part of the defense of a particular neighborhood. He was not alone here as the book includes many fighters who died in battles all over the country, well before the war was centralized in the mountain. This, it appears, does not matter. To be from the mountain, in this moment in the War of the Mountain, regardless of what battle you died in, meant Imad died for the mountain.

What is not mentioned in Sammad's introduction is perhaps most telling: Palestinian liberation. To be clear, the Lebanese Communist Party was still supporting the Palestinian Liberation Organization by 1985 when this volume was produced. But in the wake of the Israeli invasion of 1982, and abdication of key PLO leadership in Lebanon, sanctioned under American empire—through military action, not tourism or education like in an earlier age—the cause for Palestine was much more fractured. In 1984, for example, the Amal Movement, Syrian armed forces, and its Syrian-backed Palestinian factions of the Palestinian Liberation Organization waged a war on other Palestinian factions in the refugee camps of Beirut.[46] Even if the Lebanese Communist Party was not directly involved in this fight, the Palestinian cause, as a united one, had much less currency by the time Sammad wrote his introduction. This was the end of an era. The fallen, like Imad, who died for Palestinian liberation, were now represented as martyrs for Lebanese sovereignty alone. By 1985, a time when the territorial unity of Lebanon was in serious doubt, Samad instead emphasizes "true national unity" and a need, in the name of those Lebanese Communist martyrs, to "increase belief in national working unity."[47]

As time moved further from 1975 and Imad's death, so did the Communist Party. Besides the contemporary website I referenced at the beginning of this chapter, this 1985 memorialization was the last party one for Imad. The battle continued, more "martyrs" dedicated themselves to the cause (whatever that cause was in a given moment and time), and memorialization of new martyrs remained a key component of the war. By 1990, the war had ended, but as Hermez argues, people continued, and continue to, live in the meanwhile of war, actively forgetting their past roles. Clearly, no one I talk to forgets Imad, even if they recast certain things, and downplay or ignore others. But specifically, how do his closest comrades of the Left remember him today?

Rida Ismael tells me, "When Imad was martyred by the sword I lost my other half."[48] Walid Nuwayhid echoes this sentiment, stressing "we really lost him, really."[49] Gilbert Achcar refers to Imad's death as "premature."[50] Rida's connection, as Imad's best friend, may be the strongest of the three. But Rida, Walid, and Gilbert all communicate grief, trauma, and a loss. Moreover, his death becomes a stand-in for what was lost more broadly for the Left in the long decade of defeat.

This is most palpable for Rida, given who he is today. As explained in Chapter 3, Rida works for a publisher that necessitates he move away from his former politics. As academics and journalists, Gilbert and Walid do not have those same pressures. Rida is a practical radical, but unlike Imad, he had to substitute the former for the latter in the wake of the war. Accordingly, he is quite nostalgic for that time when he could be a part of those causes. "He was the model of a leftist struggler," Rida laments, "the model of the secular and democratic personality not sectarian not doctrinal not religious."[51] But with the war, and Rida's need to distance from the Left, that model disappeared, and died, abruptly, with Imad.

Nabil Khishin, Imad's co-translator, is also nostalgic for a lost past embodied in Imad. One of the first emails I received from him was on what the death of Imad meant to him. "He was a true revolutionary," Nabil writes, "full of optimism and enthusiasm, and his demise at an early age was a serious loss for all his comrades."[52] One way Nabil's memory of Imad and the war is different from Rida's is due to his status as an active communist party member today. He leans more toward party opportunity and retribution than full loss like Rida. He tells me, his "main concern is to revive the enthusiasm of the comrades because many of them are not very happy about the current state. It reminds me of my youth experiences when I joined the party with Ghassan Fawaz."[53]

What Nabil is referencing is that period in the late 1960s when the Lebanese Communist Party was stale, but the causes had merit. Hence, people like him, Ghassan, Gilbert, and those they recruited, including Imad and Rida, reorganized around other groups, like the Union of Lebanese Communists. The Communist Party today, per Nabil, is in a similar state: feeling archaic, swaying little influence in politics, and slow to change. However, unlike before, when Nabil went outside Lebanon, he sticks with the party. He is disillusioned, but hopeful it can be reformed within. One of the more memorable things Nabil has ever said to me was this: "I know we [the Left] will win. I think it's too late for me. I hope it's not for you."[54] With his actions and words, I see a man longing for a time when these causes seemed closer to being realized than currently. Alas, he holds out hope that they can happen, even if not within his lifetime.

It is in part too late for Nabil because what was lost, and who would be in his ranks if he were around today: Imad. When I ask Nabil what he thinks Imad would be like today, he gives me a simple answer. Imad would be like him.[55] To recast the fallen through one's current life and eyes is a common occurrence. For Nabil, nostalgia is the driver—nostalgic for the causes that felt young, vibrant, and achievable in the 1970s. For Imad's brothers, it is what I discuss as cleaning the slate in the next section. Beyond these politics of memorialization, I still find it a fair question, one I keep asking and considering: what would Imad's politics and position be in the current context?

Here, I am guided by Jihane Sfeir's article on the pathways of two leftist activists from the 1970s. One was a member of the Popular Front for the Liberation of Palestine, the other a member of the Communist Party, but both left their respective groups. She argues that "the aftermath of 1982 transformed their fight, their ideologies and their partisan commitments."[56] If Imad had lived through the Israeli invasion of 1982, and the destruction it wrought to leftist, pro-Palestinian causes, would he have done the same?

Walid gives me a more measured answer than Nabil. When I ask him about his comrade and cousin, and what he would be like today, "as a guess," he replies:

> I think if Imad was still alive he would be a prominent figure, as a thinker,
> translator, maybe one of the leaders in the communist party … I think he
> will be important[,] but you know many people they were strong, but they
> change their minds, maybe he would change his mind after 10 or 15 years.
> I don't know.[57]

The former is closer to what Nabil would think, but Walid later adds that Imad could be "one of the writers" or "a teacher in the university."[58] These are positions more closely to his now, as an unaffiliated leftist journalist. Walid also echoes Sfeir's activists, who either left politics entirely or joined Hizbullah. Both paths are possible for Imad, especially the latter. Today, several scholars track a shift in Lebanon, from Marxist-Leninism, à la the Arab Left in the 1960s, to political Islam, à la the Iranian Revolution and Ayatollah Khomeini in the 1980s.[59]

There is another alternative. Imad would have become a hardened fighter, one that was no longer driven by cause, but need. The transformation from leftist, or right-wing, young intellectual to *sheikh al-shabab*, youth militia leader, is a common theme in literature and film on the war.[60] Perhaps the most famous one to depict this shift is *West Beyrouth*. In Ziad Doueiri's film, there is a young man, who, before the war, is depicted as being with the working-class residents of the neighborhood. He sits with them, drinks coffee with them, listens to their issues, and tells them his positions.[61] In sum, he is a hero of sorts in the neighborhood of West Beirut where the film takes places. Given Imad's interest in being with the workers, and spirited discussions and intellectual exercises with whoever would listen, this pre-war representation seems within the realm of possibility for Imad.

Once the war begins in *West Beyrouth*, the young man transforms into a hero of battle, given the code name *Abu Hanash*, Papa Snake. He then turns on his neighborhood, because the people will not give him what he wants. In one of the most chilling scenes of the film, Papa Snake assaults an older man, a baker, and destroys his flour supply, because the man insists on distributing it fairly. A once-celebrated figure is exposed as an exploiter of the masses as the war continued and the just principles he once embodied were a distant memory.[62] *Abu Hanash*, then, comes to symbolize the "predatory dimension of militia rule" that terrorized noncombatants in civil war Lebanon.[63]

Staying strong, leaving, exploitation, and more are all possible outcomes for Imad. But in the end, even if they help build out the pathways for fighters, post-war, they are purely speculation. Any perspective on Imad from Rida, Nabil, or Walid says more about how people today cope with death, the splintering of the Left, and what befell their country. Take Imad's sister, Lina, for a final example here. The first time I met her in 2018, she showed me a picture of Imad. He looks quite handsome, at ease, joyful, and smiling. She tells me this photo was taken the morning that Imad died.[64] Whether or not that is actually the case, I find, is irrelevant. Lina chooses to remember her brother the way she wants to remember him, and that is at peace, content with life. And sometimes memory can defy reality.

Cleaning the Slate

So like Lina, others, especially family members, aim to restore Imad as an individual, with a smile, hopes and dreams, and perhaps most pointedly, life beyond the Communist Party. I am sympathetic to these responses on multiple levels. First, simply put, Imad is their sibling (or comrade for that matter), they can choose how to remember him however they want, and what I am to say otherwise? Second, Imad did have a life before the Lebanese Communist Party, one that I tracked and tried to give meaning to through the concept of "practical radicals." That is, although I truly believe Imad ceded his autonomy to that party and the cause it championed at that time, there was a period before this when Imad's hopes and dreams were not purely ideological. Hence, to remember him beyond that ideology is nuanced and necessary.

Still, sometimes these types of comments do not always reflect how Imad lived, even in his life before the Communist Party. This, in a similar way to the martyr narrative, is an act of meaning making, what I call cleaning the slate. While this is most observable in Imad's family—those who knew Imad the longest and in a personal, not always political sense—some of his comrades choose to purge Imad's history of some of its more unsavory elements. Per Hermez, this may be to absolve their decisions in wartime, but they are not, in any way, forgetting Imad. They are creating a new narrative, one that competes with the martyr narrative, and constitutes an analogous form of claiming toward the individual away from the collective. It is a corrective, a counter-narrative on who Imad was and what he died for.[65]

Over years of conversations, cleaning the slate has come to the surface through four discussion points:

- Imad's political affiliation
- His status as a fighter
- His actions, or orders, the day of his death
- His legacy and what he would be like today

The first was probably the first I observed in this phenomenon. Whether through insinuation or communication, some family members—and only family—claim Imad was never a member of the Lebanese Communist Party. The implication is a worse-case scenario for the party: their appropriation of Imad was not merely unjustified, but fabricated. When I first met Jawad in 2018, he was emphatic that Imad never joined the Lebanese Communist Party. It is the first thing I wrote in my notes from that day, and I can only assume his comment was prompted after I said something like, "Imad was a member of the Lebanese Communist Party" as a matter of fact. But Jawad stopped me, and said no, he was a part of the Lebanese Communist Action Organization. In this conversation, Jawad actually stressed Imad's student days more so. He was part of the Student Forces Front at Raml al-Zarif, a leftist, but not singularly communist, group.[66] This is something Jawad continues to think as of the writing this book, telling me in 2023, "Imad was not part of the Communist Party, he was part of the Communist Action Organization."[67]

Walid disagrees with Jawad, something I saw him do in person.[68] Once being a member of that group, Walid remembers Imad's shift to the stronger fighting force of the Lebanese Communist Party that I discuss in Chapter 4. Actually, Walid tells me that Imad never joined the Lebanese Communist Action Organization, contradicting some of his own comrades.[69] Others in Imad's family dismiss party affiliations altogether. For example, amidst these discussions in 2018, one family member said to me, quite sarcastically, "welcome to our communist family!"[70] The Nuwayhids were not, nor are today, a communist family. But regardless of Imad's particular party, he was affiliated with communists. So I interpret this joke of sorts as a nervous reaction to a conversation they would rather not be having about one of the Nuwayhids' less than ideal associations.

To be clear, as I hope this book has proven, Imad joined the Communist Party in the early 1970s. Iman Nuwayhid, Imad's cousin, who I have known to always strive for balance, says "We all knew that he was a communist[,]" "related to the Lebanese Communist Party."[71] In contrast are those perspectives of the family that wipe Imad's slate of his last affiliation, the one that marked his shift from practical, but radical, to armed struggler. The words of Jawad and others like him must be viewed through a contemporary lens, where today communism and the Lebanese Communist Party are not very popular—particularly in parliamentary politics—with a "sense of dislocation from a previous age."[72] Consequently, some who have lost faith in these ideas, if they ever had them in the first place, reposition Imad's affiliations, while others laugh them away.

This is a similar dynamic to the one Saba highlights in her documentary, *Shu'ur Akbar min al-Hub,* largely on the Ghandour factory strike that I described in Chapter 4. One of the casualties of that strike was Fatima Khuwajah, a Communist Party member. While the newspapers and comrades are clear on the fact that Fatima was a communist, this is what a cousin had to say:

> She was like any child. She still played hopscotch, jump rope, and so on. Shots were fired from the main road … She thought [the strike] was a wedding. Her mother told her to hang the clothes and forbade her from going. She snuck off, between two buildings and reached the main road. There was a sniper, or a stray bullet. She was hit in the heart and in the head … The Communist Party claimed her. Her parents refused their support.[73]

When Mary presses him, likely similar to myself, confused with this perspective, he says "No, no," she was not part of the Communist Party, "she was in third grade. She wasn't politically involved. She didn't know what politics was."[74]

In a similar vein, Saba writes that "none of the women workers [of Ghandour] whom I have managed to track down can (or will) recognize their former militant selves—or any of their coworkers—in the photos."[75] The latter appears to me a clear example of active forgetting. No, these women are not divorcing themselves from actions in a war, but forgetting their more radical days, especially in an entrenched masculine political world today. But with the former, I do wonder, does Saba's interviewee have a score to settle with the Communist Party? At the very least, it appears her family does. I know Jawad and some of his family do. Like Fatima's family, some attempted to resist the party in the moment and continue to today. Cleaning the slate today, then, is somewhere between a means to cope and a means to hold responsible those who put their loved ones in harm's way.

Those who are firm about Imad's party affiliation, comrades here, downplay that he was actually a fighter. The party-created martyr narrative and the family counter-narrative actually overlap in claiming that Imad was shot trying to save Muhammad and Diyab, regardless of who was fighting or not.[76] However, there is a third narrative here, that a younger communist, Omar Deeb, tells me. Supposedly a fourth man who is still living, Marwan Matarji, dragged Imad, Muhammad, and Diyab's bodies off the street. Omar tells me Matarji is no longer a Communist Party member, perhaps one reason this story has been forgotten.[77] While I am unsure what this exactly means for Imad's death, it shows how the politics of memory are always unfolding, serviced to new interventions and information.[78]

But parties to this conversation clarify that regardless, Imad was not actually a fighter. For one, Walid tells me, "Imad was not a fighter he is just a political comrade in the party."[79] He goes on: "Imad he is not a fighter because in the battle you have two parts the fighter on the ground and the political."[80] Making a distinction between the political and fighting class is common among party members and officials. When I met Maurice Nahra in 2022, he stresses to me Imad was not "professional," not part of the "military fighters."[81] Rida confirms, "No he got excited, he would go down sometimes, he would carry a gun, but no he didn't have military training..he wasn't a fighter."[82] To "go down," means go down to the battle, as Imad did on October 28, 1975. But to Rida, Maurice, and Walid, Imad was unprepared for battle.

On one level, these sentiments contradict what Walid voiced in late 1975. Imad was a "fighter in different planes."[83] Yes, he was an intellectual but also, Walid wrote, Imad was "carrying the gun" to defend the Palestinian cause.[84] On another level, these reactions from comrades run counter to both what other family and the party states. Even if Jawad denies Imad's affiliation, he was the one who told me—in that same 2018 conversation—Imad trained with Palestinian *fedayeen*.[85] And the party writes that Imad "participated in the 1973 battles and every battle since April 13 [1975]."[86] To remember Imad as a leftist intellectual, alone, is to forget that Imad and others of the Lebanese Communist Party were not just theorizing armed struggle, but actively participating in liberating the Palestinians. In the end, Rida, Maurice, and Walid may engage in this as a form of active forgetting, to divorce their roles, intellect, and political actions from those of actual fighters. But in correcting Imad's actions, they also seek to clean his slate, distinguishing him from rank-and-file fighters who, at least in their minds it appears, were less a part of the intellectual class.

This question of his status as a fighter is tied to his actions. While Jawad acknowledges that the details are scant here, he believes that Imad was pressured to go to the battlefield. In his mind, because the three men were killed together, they must "have been sent by a leader to inspect [Qantari] then the [Kataib] shot them. Definitely there is an organization behind [this decision]."[87] Walid puts it this way: "He [Jawad] was astonished, why did they send his brother Imad to a battle to fight and he is not a fighter in the end, he is a thinker … they can use them in other ways."[88] To send a top-notch intellectual like Imad was both irresponsible and unforgivable.

Imad's comrades think differently. While Maurice is clear that Imad was "not military trained," he believes he "volunteered." He says "Imad was from the vanguard of the youth, they went down to the confrontations [to fight against] the Kataib to dominate Beirut."[89] Rida is similar here. "All the youth at that time would get excited to carry guns [and] the battle of Qantari was close to the headquarters."[90] Imad was a part of this trend. Lastly, an acquaintance of Imad, and friend of Walid, remembers that day in Qantari vividly. In 2022, he told me that he asked Imad why he was going to the front lines? Even more emphatically, he inquired why he was fighting for someone else, for the Lebanese Communist Party? Imad assured him that this was his battle and his issue.[91]

My best guess is that Walid's friend is right here. Taking up arms was Imad's final move toward ceding his autonomy. He was not just wrapped up in the moment. He had been dedicated to Palestinian liberation and its place within

Lebanon for years. The two main reactions though—he was sent vs. he went—however, muddy this reality because they focus on the moment in a vacuum. Jawad is communicating a certain type of loss, one unfulfilled. Jawad does not agree with what Imad died for, so he recasts Imad as not having this decision to make in the first place. He was exploited by the party, period.

On the other side, there are those individuals who want to stress Imad's bravery, but also, I believe, want to address what they see as their lack thereof. I have heard several people say, what if I had gone down to the frontlines that day? Rida deals with this today, as he told his brother Diyab and his brother-in-arms Imad not to go.[92] In another instance, a conversation in 2016 with Walid and some of his comrades, one asks what would have happened if "Walid went with Imad."[93] They all laugh, uneasily. This is how they cope. Whether Imad was a fighter or not is inconsequential to them. He was willing to die in that moment, and they weren't, having to hold that burden today. Here, they do not clean Imad's slate, but rather use the bloodied version as a stand in for what they didn't or couldn't give up.

The final aspect of cleaning the slate is the flipside of Nabil's comments on what Imad would be like if he lived. Some family members do not think he would be a communist had he survived through the war. I quote here at length from an earlier article I wrote on this subject and particularly my conversations with Jawad and Iyad:

> several family members today stress that Imad would be different had he lived through the war. Reflecting on Imad's actions in the 1970s, Jawad says, 'I never thought he would do this.' Imad's radical ideas were one thing, but to Jawad, that he acted upon them went too far. If his brother was still alive today, Jawad believes Imad's beliefs would reflect his own, which are that the war, the Lebanese Left, and the Palestinian resistance movement were a waste. Iyad thinks his brother would have become a writer, but not a political one.[94]

These outcomes, as I explored above, are certainly within the realm of possibility. Yet, like with Nabil, their comments also can be seen as an attempt to recreate Imad in their image.

Iyad works in global sales, Jawad is a retired architect. They are both well off, living between Ras al-Matn and Beirut. Iyad's Beirut flat is in one of the most expensive parts of town.[95] Providing these details is in no way meant to criticize their life choices. Indeed, I have benefited from them when in Lebanon. I have been cared for and taken in by these two men. However, and I hope they understand, I see it as my job to balance their commentary on who Imad would be and provide context for it. To them, unlike others nostalgic for the lasting living Left, the Lebanese Left's platforms, whether on how to solve the Palestinian question or the crisis of capitalism, did not and cannot work. Accordingly, they believe Imad, like them would, have shed any of his more youthful, radical ideas.

However, no one I have interviewed considers whether Imad would still work at his last employer, Hotel Phoenicia Intercontinental, which is still owned and operated by the Salha family. Unlike Nabil, who doesn't recall Imad mentioning his employment there, his brothers know this was his job. In this act of cleaning the slate, Imad is no longer as radical, but also, he is no longer a practical one either.

The Party Strikes Back

The above conversations serve as a reminder that the war is not forgotten. Its legacy is still unfolding, disputed, and ever changing. This, again, has been made clear to me at the micro-level through the case of Imad. Families, comrades, and the party still battle over his memory today. Nevertheless, the Lebanese Communist Party is a former shell of itself. At its peak, it had over 40,000 members.[96] Today, with little sway, there is a new generation of leaders, including Omar, who are trying to resurrect its core principles: Marxist-Leninism and support for oppressed peoples, close and far. Yet, the party has also ceded ground in the politics of memory, not officially memorializing Imad since 1985. In its place, other, more active parties attempt to claim him.

In early 2018, the Progressive Socialist Party got in the mix. The first time I met Iyad in Ras al-Matn, he told me how just a few days earlier, the party presented him and the Nuwayhid family with a gift (see Figure 6.2 below).[97] It was a small bust of their fallen leader, Kamal Jumblatt, and a certificate celebrating the "martyr Imad Nuwayhid." In the background of the certificate is a picture of Kamal Jumblatt, wearing a *kufiya*, the scarf adorned by Palestinian

Figure 6.2 The plaque and certificate, gifted to the Nuwayhids in 2018. The certificate reads: "A token greeting and thanks on the centenary of Kamal Jumblatt to [written in pen] the martyr Imad Yusuf Nuwayhid. And to all the freedom fighters for their sacrifices and struggles." Courtesy of the Nuwayhid family.

fedayeen. In the forefront of the certificate is the signature of Kamal's son, current leader of the Progressive Socialist Party, Walid Jumblatt. The certificate slides into a leather sleeve that has the party symbol: a hammer and a rifle.

It has been over forty years since Imad's last breath. From the year after his death, until the end of the war in 1990, there were at least 50,000 more casualties, people that I can only assume have been memorialized in some shape and form.[98] I find it remarkable that any party can identify any individual fighter and find their family. Granted, the Progressive Socialist Party may have an easier time than others, especially in Ras al-Matn. Today, it holds almost full support there. When you come into town you see a much larger obelisk statue to the "martyrs of Ras al-Matn" with words from Kamal Jumblatt: "And one of the things I honor is crossing over the bridge of death to life which aims to revive the others."[99] Even if Imad is one of those martyrs from Ras al-Matn, Jumblatt, as well as his party, has become the symbol for all of them.

This is an instance that shows how these groups, in wartime and beyond, hold the resources and mobilize capital (cultural and monetary) to claim individuals, incorporating them into their narratives, and collective identities. Whether it was the Lebanese Communist Party at Ghandour in 1972, any party to the war, or the Progressive Socialist Party today, to incorporate the fallen is to stay relevant and in the minds of the living. This legacy perhaps continues on most today with groups like Hizbullah.[100] Passersby in areas of their support will find posters dedicated to their martyrs. Yes, the wars are different—whether Hizbullah's involvement in Syria or its recent wars with Israel—and so is the rhetoric. For example, one Hezbollah poster that I saw while walking around Beirut in 2013 was dedicated to those that "fought for the sake of God and the Shia."[101] Despite these shifts in memory framing, the throughline, from 1975 to 2013 and beyond, is the medium: a martyr narrative with the dual goal to remember and recruit.

Returning to Imad, while there might be some disagreement on Imad's role within the Communist Party, everyone agrees Imad was never a member of the Progressive Socialist Party. As I explained, in the late 1960s, Imad was part of organizations that were critical of Jumblatt and his role in successive Lebanese governments. In the 1970s, Imad would not have considered joining the group given its sectarian—largely Druze—affiliation. By 1975, as Jumblatt was the undisputed leader of the Left, he was likely sympathetic to him and the party's role in the war. But still, it wasn't his group.

Iyad tells me that he first received a call from the party's representative in Ras al-Matn letting him know of the gift and then three party members stopped by his house.[102] The party dropped it off in the lead-up to the 2018 parliament elections in an attempt to secure votes. The family therefore chuckles at this gift. Nonetheless, they accept it, Iyad takes a picture with it alongside party representatives and presumably votes for the Progressive Socialist Party.

This event reminds me of an earlier episode: when, in 1975, the Lebanese Communist Party showed up for Imad's family, making it easier to accept them, even if tenuously. Now, the Progressive Socialist Party is here to recognize Imad, and given their support in Ras al-Matn, as well as Iyad's standing in the community, he says "What else could I do?"[103] He's right here, as today, an almost an exclusively Druze party, in a Druze town, is honoring a Druze individual and family. To contest the present could risk ostracization.

The party's bet here represents how politics in Lebanon has changed today: from ideological to purely sectarian claiming. Furthermore, the Progressive Socialist Party's appropriation represents another, new interpretation of who Imad was: a member of general leftist, progressive causes, not specifically communist ones. Akin to cleaning the slate, this may be a representation of Imad that the family finds more acceptable. Thus, in addition to his life, his death, and immediate afterlife, today there are multiple afterlives of Imad. It has been my intention in this book to shine a light on all of them, balance them with the archive, and link them to a broader analysis of the experiences and memories of the Lebanese Civil War.

Coming to Terms

Through a decade of research on Imad, I have changed. I used to think it was about me, the researcher, the writer, the historian. I wanted to find the most interesting documents, meet the right people, and ask the best questions. This project has made me question a lot, coming to terms with who I am professionally and what it is I do. Should I be the one researching Imad, meeting the family, asking uncomfortable questions, and writing their stories? As I conclude this book, I am in the same place as I started: intrigued, conflicted, but bounded by fate. Yet, in the course of meeting Imad, I have become more aware of all of this. Aware of my positionality, my biases, and the ethical concerns tied to bringing back the dead. It is my hope that coming to terms has led me to write a well-researched, balanced, empathetic book with the least emotional trauma attached to it.

My assumptions on Lebanon have also been upended through this project. I used to think that the local dimensions of conflict were the most important, the regional more rhetorical.[104] I used to have a pretty black-and-white view of the war: the party was the exploiter, the family the victim. I used to study causes over people. Imad, through the lens of global microhistory, has shattered all of this. He was a young man, a practical radical, living in two overlapping worlds: city and village, Druze and pan-Arab, sixties Europe and Lebanon, career and liberation, intellectual and activist, human and symbol. As it relates to the history of modern Lebanon, it is my hope that through his story, his life, his death, his legacy, the reader's sense of what the country was, and is, has changed. Whether it be Lebanon's status under global capitalism and American empire, the shifting conditions of the war, who its combatants were, and how the fight over their memory continues, my perspective surely has.

But again, it's not just about me. Imad's friends, family, and comrades have changed too. Recall that initially, some of Imad's immediate family were hesitant to meet me. Now, they host me for lunches, for the night, they have met my spouse, and answer any question I ask. And the questions, oh, they have been incessant. Jawad once told me, and I am paraphrasing here, "Dylan you kept on poking, you kept digging." On first hearing this, I felt bad, thinking of the potential harm my constant questions have caused. Maybe my questions unearthed feelings that his family would rather not have to live through again, and subject Imad to as well. To be blunt, I can't change this. I already did it, and still do it, as I ask follow-up questions to finish the final words of this book. I would have had to take a step back years ago, but Imad kept coming back.

As fate has been a major theme of *Beirut Radical*, I thought I should end with perhaps the most serendipitous aspect of this project. In late 2022, I met some of Imad's cousins who live in Huntsville where I teach. Yes, that is right; in a town of 170,000 in northern Alabama, there are Nuwayhids. One morning about a year earlier, I was jogging around an area of town with a lot of office buildings and saw a sign with "Ramsey Nuwayhid dentist" on it. While I still have not met Ramsey, a year after that, Jawad told me he had a cousin, Nadim, in Huntsville, Alabama.

Nadim's brother, the father of Ramsey, went to the University of Tennessee, received a degree in civil engineering and asked his brother to follow. This was in the 1980s during the war. Like many others, Nadim left Lebanon for new opportunities. He started his own businesses, bought some pharmacies and now owns one that I drive by on my way to work every day. His son is the head pharmacist there.[105] From Beirut-to Ras al-Matn-to-Switzerland-to Miami-to Pittsburgh-to-Huntsville. Each of these encounters pushed me forward. And my hope is that through my questions, reframing through each humbling experience, my work has helped all the contacts that I have come to terms with who Imad was.

I believe this is the case with at least one of my contacts, perhaps the closest to me and this project: Jawad Nuwayhid. Last time I was in Ras al-Matn with him and Nabil, visiting Rifaat Nuwayhid and Sami Ghazali as I started Chapter 1, Nabil was telling Jawad and me about the story of Imad's death. As noted in Chapter 4, he heard that as he was being taken away in the ambulance, Imad said, "I am a communist, I am not afraid." I am not sure how I thought Jawad would react here, but I was surprised to say the least. He agreed with Nabil that this happened. It may have been for the sake of avoiding argument, knowing Nabil loves a good one. But I'd like to think Jawad is, in some small way, coming around to who his brother was, not only how he wants to remember him, the more he talks to people about it. Again, a part of me feels awful as I am forcing Jawad to confront this. But, if I am to believe in fate, as I have come to, maybe Imad would want his brother to meet halfway—for his siblings and others to come to terms with the choices of his life and death.

Speaking on behalf of the dead is definitely not how I thought I would end this book. I hope that I have made it clear that I cannot speak on Imad's behalf, but synthesize the archive, interviews, and the world that these places and people have opened up. Through that synthesis, where am I left? Who is Imad? Did he play a part in destroying the country, like some Lebanese today would think? Is he an inspiration, a sign of a Global Sixties politics that has since died, but could be resurrected? Or is he a cautionary tale, what can happen when one cedes their autonomy to a radical cause with an unknown future?

And what should we call him? An intellectual? A fighter? A hotel employee? A victim or a martyr? Iman Nuwahyid and I had a conversation like this recently. We discussed, as I explained in Chapter 5, how his father called the newspapers in 1975 asking for Imad to be called a martyr. Iman told me that there was a similar conversation unfolding today about this. The August 3rd blast of 2020 in Beirut killed over 200 people. Iman and I discuss, were they martyrs? Or does that miss the point, given that their deaths were the result of state negligence? Are they victims?

Living in the meanwhile in Lebanon today—as another war over Palestine and in Lebanon continues—forces those to connect past crises to present ones. Like Iman, living in the now, and like Javier Cercas, and his uncle, the fascist "hero," I, 200-some pages later, go back and forth here. I am left with multiple, overlapping Imads: martyr, victim, radical, and optimist. I hope I have shown that none of these single Imads works. None, alone, do justice to his memory. Only when they are strung together do we get a more composite picture of who he was, is, and what his life and death mean.

But even though I respect those who clean the slate, today, I do not question Imad's dedication or those young Arab leftists of his generation. He is a window. He is unique. He is representative. He is impressive. And whether he should be or not, he will now be remembered by more than he was before I decided to write this book.

Nabil seeks, in some small way, to do the memory work. He hopes to re-release Imad's translation of *The Jewish Question*, error free I may add. I'd like to think this decision has something to do with us connecting over the last few years and him reconnecting with the Nuwayhids. But when Nabil explains why he wants to do this, he says, "Just to keep the memory of Imad alive."[106] Nabil does not think that this will have some outstretched significance, admitting the re-release will likely have little intellectual impact today.

Maybe that is it then. It doesn't matter if Imad is representative, if Imad is exceptional, or whether or not Imad will be remembered by many. Fate has driven all of us, together, to keep him, his work, and his memories alive.

Notes

Introduction

1 *al-Nida'*, October 29, 1975.

2 To be clear, Imad is no more important than Diyab or Muhammad. Through a number of chance encounters which I describe throughout the book, I came to focus on Imad. So while Diyab and Muhammad are not the focus of this book, I do reference them and discuss their significance, largely in Chapters 4–6.

3 *al-Nida'*, October 29, 1975.

4 The obituary is referencing the 1973 clashes between the Lebanese Army and fighting forces of the Palestinian Liberation Organization, and the Ain al-Rummaneh massacre of April 13, 1975, marking the beginning of the war.

5 While pictures and obituaries of martyrs were not uncommon in late 1975, to see pictures and names on the front page of a newspaper, like that of Imad, Muhammad, and Diyab, was unique. This is likely one reason I paused, stopped, and later, continued to think about Imad.

6 A similar argument is made in Zeina Maasri, *Off the Wall: Political Posters of the Lebanese Civil War* (London: I.B. Tauris, 2009), a central influence of my own work.

7 Theodor Hanf, *Coexistence in Wartime Lebanon: Decline of a State and Rise of a Nation* (London: The Centre for Lebanese Studies, 1993), 341.

8 Lebanese Communist Party, *Shuhada' al-Hizb al-Shuyu'i al-Lubnani 1975–1980: min Ajalak ya Watani* (Beirut: Manshurat al-Hizb al-Shuyu'i al-Lubnani, 1980).

9 Ibid., 64.

10 See Kamal Salibi, *Crossroads to Civil War: Lebanon 1958–1976* (Ann Arbor, MI: Caravan Books, 1976), Samir Khalaf, *Civil and Uncivil Violence in Lebanon: A History of the Internationalization of Communal Conflict* (New York: Columbia University Press, 2002), and Fawwaz Traboulsi, *A History of Modern Lebanon* (London: Pluto Press, 2007).

11 See Oren Barak, "'Don't Mention the War?' The Politics of Remembrance and Forgetfulness in Postwar Lebanon," *Middle East Journal* 61, no. 1 (2007), 49–70.

12 I thank Joseph Ben Prestel for this recommendation.

13 Javier Cercas, *Lord of All the Dead* (London: MacLehose Books, 2019). John Paul Ghobrial and Laila Parsons ask similar questions in their micro-historical explorations and have also been helpful in my study of Imad. John Paul Ghobrial, "The Secret Life of Elias of Babylon and the Uses of Global Microhistory," *Past & Present* 222 (2014), 51–93 and Laila Parsons, *The Commander: Fawzi al-Qawuqji and the Fight for Arab Independence 1914–1948* (New York: Hill and Wang, 2016).

14 I thank Jadwiga Pieper Mooney for this reminder.

15 Saidiya Hartman, "Venus in Two Acts," *Small Axe* 26 (June 2008), 4 and 2. I thank Elizabeth Holt for this recommendation.

16 Ibid., 1.

17 Ibid., 9 and 12.

18 Ibid., 11.

19 Ibid., 13.

20 The micro-level work of Jennifer Marglin is helpful here too, connecting a nineteenth-century transregional story (spanning from Tunisia to Italy and France) to questions of the utility of place-based citizenship today. See Marglin, *The Shamama Case: Contesting Citizenship across the Modern Mediterranean* (Princeton, NJ: Princeton University Press, 2022).

21 Iman Nuwayhid, interview with author, Beirut, Lebanon, June 1, 2016.

22 Jawad Nuwayhid, WhatsApp correspondence, November 6, 2023.

23 To be clear from the onset, sectarianism, as a frame or approach, does not figure into this book much, especially in the earlier chapters. This is because I find sectarianism as negatively defined (i.e., sect supremacy, narrow thinking) was not something Imad communicated or embodied.

24 See Kamal Salibi, *A House of Many Mansions: The History of Lebanon Reconsidered* (Berkeley, CA: University of California Press, 1988).

25 See Jens Hanssen, *Fin de Siècle Beirut: the Making of an Ottoman Provincial Capital* (Oxford, UK: Oxford University Press, 2005).

26 See Agnès Favier, Logiques de l'engagement et modes de contestation au Liban: genèse et éclatement d'une génération de militants intellectuels, 1958–1975 (Ph.D. dissertation, Université Paul Cézanne Aix-Marseille III, 2004).

27 See Elizabeth Thompson, *Colonial Citizens: Republican Rights, Paternal Privilege and Gender in French Syria and Lebanon* (New York: Columbia University Press, 2000).

28 See Ussama Makdisi, *Artillery of Heaven: American Missionaries and the Failed Conversion of the Middle East* (Ithaca, NY: Cornell University Press, 2008) and

Beth Baron, *The Orphan Scandal: Christian Missionaries and the Rise of the Muslim Brotherhood* (Stanford, CA: Stanford University Press, 2014).

29   Unlike with Imad's time in Hanover, Lausanne, or London, I have been unable to find any documentation of his time in Dublin beyond family confirmation that he was there, *c.* 1972. With little there, and little to explore, I have made the decision to not cover that (seemingly brief) period of his life.

30   See Paul A. Kramer, "How Not to Write the History of U.S. Empire," *Diplomatic History* 42, no. 5 (2018), 911–31.

31   See Dennis Merrill, *Negotiating Paradise: U.S. Tourism and Empire in Twentieth Century Latin America* (Chapel Hill, NC: University of North Carolina Press, 2009), Victoria de Grazia, *Irresistible Empire: America's Advance through Twentieth Century Europe* (Cambridge, MA: The Belknap Press of Harvard University Press, 2005), and Jenifer Van Vleck, *Empire of the Air: Aviation and the American Ascendancy* (Cambridge, MA: Harvard University Press, 2013).

32   See Yezid Sayigh, *Armed Struggle and the Search for State: The Palestinian National Movement, 1949–1993* (Oxford, UK: Oxford University Press, 1997).

33   To be clear, radical and leftist currents, movements, and groups pre-date the sixties Arab Left, almost by a century. See Ilham Khuri-Makdisi, *The Eastern Mediterranean and the Making of Global Radicalism, 1860–1914* (Berkely, CA: University of California Press, 2013).

34   Fadi A. Bardawil, *Revolution and Disenchantment: Arab Marxism and the Binds of Emancipation* (Durham, NC: Duke University Press, 2020), 13.

35   See Yusri Hazran, "Lebanon's Revolutionary Era: Kamal Junblat, The Druze Community and the Lebanon State," *Muslim World* 100 (January 2010), 157–76 and Maasri, *Off the Wall.*

36   See Ibid and Zeina Maasri, *Cosmopolitan Radicalism: The Visual Politics of Beirut's Global Sixties* (Cambridge, UK: Cambridge University Press, 2020).

37   Nathaniel George, "Jabal 'Amil between the Palestinian and Iranian Revolutions," in *The Fate of Third Worldism in the Middle East: Iran, Palestine and Beyond*, eds. Rasmus C. Elling and Sune Haugbolle, (London: Oneworld Publications, 2024), 148.

38   Arthur Marwick, *The Sixties: Cultural Revolution in Britain, France, Italy, and the United States c. 1958–1974* (Oxford, UK: Oxford University Press, 1998), 7.

39   Ibid., 17–8.

40   Burleigh Hendrickson, "Finding Tunisia in the Global 1960s," *Monde(s)* 11, (2017), 62. See Andrew Ivaska, *Cultured States: Youth, Gender, and Modern Style in 1960s Dar es Salaam* (Durham, NC: Duke University Press, 2011), Heather

Stur, *Saigon at War: South Vietnam and the Global Sixties* (Cambridge, UK: Cambridge University Press, 2020) and Eric Zolov, *The Last Good Neighbor: Mexico in the Global Sixties* (Durham, NC: Duke University Press, 2020).

41 See Paul Thomas Chamberlin, *The Global Offensive: The United States, The Palestine Liberation Organization, and the Making of the Post-Cold War Order* (New York: Oxford University Press, 2012), Jeffrey James Byrne, *Mecca of Revolution: Algeria, Decolonization & the Third World Order* (New York: Oxford University Press, 2016), and Anne Garland Mahler, *From the Tricontinental to the Global South: Race, Radicalism, and Transnational Solidarity* (Durham, NC: Duke University Press, 2018).

42 Burleigh Hendrickson's recent book is instructive here. It takes up student activism, but not student studies or careers. While I do not argue this is a problem—the book is on student activism after all—it is a gap I seek to address. See *Decolonizing 1968: Transnational Student Activism in Tunis, Paris, and Dakar* (Ithaca, NY: Cornell University Press, 2022).

43 Maasri, *Cosmopolitan Radicalism* and Robyn Creswell, *City of Beginnings: Poetic Modernism in Beirut* (Princeton, NJ: Princeton University Press, 2019).

44 See Julie Stephens, *Anti-Disciplinary Protest: Sixties Radicalism and Postmodernism* (Cambridge, UK: Cambridge University Press, 1998).

45 See Khalaf, *Civil and Uncivil Violence in Lebanon.*

46 Two great studies on the war and its memory that fall into the above criticism (capturing collective memory, but little beyond that) are Lucia Volk, *Memorials and Martyrs in Modern Lebanon* (Bloomington, IN: Indiana University Press, 2010) and Sune Haugbolle, *War and Memory in Lebanon* (Cambridge, UK: Cambridge University Press, 2010).

47 Mohammed El-Kurd, *Perfect Victims and the Politics of Appeal* (Chicago, IL: Haymarket Books, 2025), 35–6.

48 I borrow this term from David Cook and use it in my 2021 article "Claiming an Individual: Party, Family and the Politics of Memorialization in the Lebanese Civil War," *Middle East Critique* 30, no. 4 (2021), 353–71.

49 Besides those cited above and below, my micro-level approach is indebted to the work of James Gelvin, Edmund Burke III, and Dana Sajdi. See Gelvin's chapter on Wasif Jawhariyyeh in *The Modern Middle East: A History*, 5th ed. (New York: Oxford University Press, 2020), Burke III and David Yaghoubian, eds., *Struggle and Survival in the Modern Middle East*, 2nd ed. (Berkeley, CA: University of California Press, 2006), and Sajdi, *The Barber of Damascus: Nouveau Literacy in the Eighteenth-Century Ottoman Levant* (Stanford, CA: Stanford University Press, 2013).

50   Carlo Ginzburg, *The Cheese and the Worms: The Cosmos of a Sixteenth-Century Miller* (Baltimore, MD: Johns Hopkins University Press, 1982), xx.

51   John Paul Ghobrial, "The Secret Life of Elias of Babylon and the Uses of Global Microhistory," 6 and 59.

52   Jill Lepore, "Historians Who Love Too Much: Reflections on Microhistory and Biography," *The Journal of American History* 88, no. 1 (2001), 133.

53   Ghobrial falls into this trap. See "The Secret Life of Elias of Babylon and the Uses of Global Microhistory," 56.

54   I thank Fadi Bardawil for this realization.

55   I thank Laila Parsons for this reminder.

56   Cercas, *Lord of All the Dead*, 50.

57   Maya Mikdashi, *Sectarianism: Sovereignty, Secularism, and the State in Lebanon* (Stanford, CA: Stanford University Press, 2022), 53.

Chapter 1

1   The Daniel and Emily Oliver Orphanages. *"Seeing Is Believing"* (Philadelphia, PA: George F. Lasher Printing Company, 1930). Daniel and Emily Oliver Papers, 1907–1960. Courtesy of Haverford College Quaker and Special Collections.

2   Carolyn Gates, *Merchant Republic of Lebanon: Rise of an Open Economy* (London: I.B. Tauris, 1998).

3   See Malcolm H. Kerr, *The Arab Cold War: Gamal Abd al-Nasir and His Rivals, 1958–1970*, 3rd edn (New York: Oxford University Press, 1971).

4   Much of this argument, the source work, and some prose are adapted from Dylan Baun, "A Contentious Empire: Pan Am, Intercontinental, and Hotel Phoenicia in Beirut," *Journal of Tourism History* 16, no. 2 (2024), 191–206.

5   See Richard H. Immerman, *Empire for Liberty: A History of American Imperialism from Benjamin Franklin to Paul Wolfowitz* (Princeton, NJ: Princeton University Press, 2010) and Daniel Immerwahr, *How to Hide an Empire: A History of the Greater United States* (New York: Farrar, Straus and Giroux, 2019).

6   See Christine Skwiot, *The Purpose of Paradise: U.S. Tourism and Empire in Cuba and Hawai'i* (Philadelphia, PA: University of Pennsylvania Press, 2011) and Emily Conroy-Krutz, *Christian Imperialism: Converting the World in the Early American Republic* (Cornell, NY: Cornell University Press, 2015).

7   Great studies on these topics that fall short of using the logic of American empire include Ussama Makdisi, *Artillery of Heaven: American Missionaries*

and the Failed Conversation of the Middle East (Cornell, NY: Cornell University Press, 2008) and Begüm Adalet, *Hotels and Highways: The Construction of Modernization Theory in Cold War Turkey* (Stanford, CA: Stanford University Press, 2018).

8   See Dennis Merrill, *Negotiating Paradise.*

9   Nuwayhid, *Dossier de L'Élève*, Personal File, 1971. Courtesy of EHL archives, physical and digital collections.

10 Letter from Daniel Oliver to US Quakers, November 6, 1944. All letters from Daniel Oliver, as well as all documents on the Daniel and Emily Oliver Orphanages—unless noted otherwise—are from Daniel and Emily Oliver Papers, 1907–1960. Haverford College Quaker and Special Collections.

11 Letter from Daniel Oliver to Algernon and Anna R. Evans, September 5, 1945.

12 See Stephen Hemsley Longrigg, *Syria and Lebanon under French Mandate* (London: Oxford University Press, 1958).

13 See Eyal Zisser, *Lebanon: The Challenge of Independence* (New York: I.B. Tauris & Co Ltd, 2000).

14 Jawad Nuwayhid, WhatsApp correspondence with author, July 9, 2022.

15 Jawad Nuwayhid, email correspondence, December 18, 2020, Walid Nuwayhid, WhatsApp correspondence, November 7, 2023, Iman Nuwayhid, interview, Beirut, June 1, 2016, Nabil Khisin, WhatsApp interview, February 3, 2021, Iyad Nuwayhid, WhatsApp correspondence, August 29, 2024, and Rida Ismael, interview, Beirut, June 22, 2022.

16 Jawad Nuwayhid, WhatsApp correspondence, November 7, 2023.

17 See www.youssefnoueihed.com.

18 Author conversations with the Nuwayhids, Ras al-Matn, Lebanon, June 3, 2018.

19 Iman Nuwayhid, interview, Beirut, June 1, 2016.

20 Nuwayhid, *Dossier de L'Élève.*

21 Zaydaniyya is close to neighborhoods that are historically Armenian and Kurdish. See Karim al-Hakim, *Zokak el-Blat: Memories from a Beirut Neighborhood* (Beirut: UMAM Videotech, 2009).

22 Tramway Map, Beirut, 1961. Wikimedia Commons.

23 Walid Nuwayhid, WhatsApp correspondence, August 23, 2023.

24 Iman Nuwayhid, interview, Beirut, June 1, 2016.

25 Kais Firro, *A History of the Druzes* (New York: E.J. Brill, 1992), 3.

26 See Anis Obeid, *Druze and Their Faith in Tawhid* (Syracuse, NY: Syracuse University Press, 2006).

27 Firro, *A History of the Druzes*, 13 and 353.

28 There is a picture of these men meeting in the 1960s in one of the Nuwayhid homes in Ras al-Matn.

29 Author conversations with Jawad Nuwayhid and Nabil Khishin, Ras al-Matn, June 19, 2022.

30 See Firro, *A History of the Druzes*.

31 Letter home, February 19, 1967. All letters home cited below are from the same collection and were written in Europe. Located in Imad Nuwayhid, Personal Sources: Letters and certificates, 1965–1971. Courtesy of the Nuwayhid Family.

32 See Dylan Baun, *Winning Lebanon: Youth Politics, Populism, and the Production of Sectarian Violence, 1920–1958* (Cambridge, UK: Cambridge University Press, 2021).

33 Conversations with Iman Nuwayhid, Beirut, May 13, 2016.

34 Conversations with Jawad Nuwayhid and Nabil Khishin, Ras al-Matn, June 19, 2022.

35 Albert Hourani, "Ideologies of the Mountain and the City," in *Essays on the Crisis in Lebanon*, ed. Roger Owen (London: Ithaca Press, 1976), 33–41.

36 See Sara Fregonese, *War and the City: Urban Geopolitics in Lebanon* (London: I.B. Tauris, 2020).

37 This is at least what his family has told me. When I ask about Imad as a child, they end up talking about their shared childhoods in Ras al-Matn.

38 The Daniel and Emily Oliver Orphanages, "We've Been—We've Seen!" Philadelphia, PA, 1930[?].

39 Memo from Daniel Oliver to Friends Chapter of Philadelphia, 1934 (?), General Items.

40 Iman Nuwayhid, interview, Beirut, June 1, 2016.

41 Ibid.

42 Walid Nuwayhid, WhatsApp correspondence, August 28, 2023.

43 See Akram Fouad Khater, *Inventing Home: Emigration, Gender, and the Middle Class in Lebanon, 1870–1920* (Berkeley, CA: University of California Press, 2001).

44 See Zeina Maasri, "Troubled Geography: Imagining Lebanon in 1960s Tourist Promotion," in *Designing Worlds: National Design Histories in the Age of Globalizations*, eds. Kjetil Fallan and Grace Lees-Maffaei (Oxford, UK: Berghahn Books, 2016).

45 William Bacon Evans to sister, August 8, 1925. All letters from Evans, are from Daniel and Emily Oliver Papers, 1907–1960. Haverford College Quaker and Special Collections.

46 See Makdisi, *Artillery of Heaven* and Sir James Craig, *Shemlan: A History of the Middle East Centre for Arab Studies* (London: Macmillan Press LTD, 1998).

47 Lettice Jowitt, *Quaker Biographies: Daniel Oliver and Emily, His Wife* (London: Friends Home Service Committee, 1955) and *The Daniel and Emily Oliver Orphanages Ras-El-Metn, Syria* (Philadelphia, PA: George F Lasher Printing, 1930). Latter courtesy of Haverford College Quaker and Special Collections.

48 Memo from Daniel Oliver to Friends Chapter of Philadelphia, 1931 (?), General Items.

49 Letter from Daniel Oliver to Thomas and Ethel Potts, July 6, 1908. The school, eventually, took on girls for a period.

50 The highest recording of orphans that I can find was during the Second World War, at 65, 43 percent of the student body. Letter from Daniel Oliver to Mr. and Mrs. Marriot C Morris, July 1938.

51 Letter from A. Douglas Oliver to Friends Chapter of Philadelphia, December 13, 1954.

52 Author conversation with Sami Ghazali, Ras al-Matn, June 18, 2022.

53 Sami Ghazali, WhatsApp correspondence, July 17, 2023.

54 Conversations with Sami Ghazali, Ras al-Matn, June 18, 2022.

55 Letter from William Bacon Evans to Sister, August 1, 1926.

56 The Daniel and Emily Oliver Orphanages, "Information Relating to the work of Daniel and Emily Oliver" (George F. Lasher Printing: Philadelphia, PA, 193[?]). Daniel and Emily Oliver Orphanage, Ephemera, 1921–1956. Courtesy of Friends Historical Library of Swarthmore College.

57 For more on Salha, see Muhammad Khalil al-Basha, *Muʿajim Aʿlim al-Druz fi Lubnan*, vol. 1 (Beirut: Dar al-Taqadumiyya, 2010), 76–7.

58 Letter from William Bacon Evans to three sisters, November 19, 1926.

59 The Potts family invested in Farid Nibhan for seven years and stayed in touch with him for over twenty. Letter from Daniel Oliver to Mr. and Mrs. Potts, March 18, 1907 and Letter from Daniel Oliver to Ethel Potts, January 3, 1931.

60 Letter from Daniel Oliver to Thomas and Ethel Potts, August 17, 1910, and Oliver to Thomas and Ethel Potts, September 17, 1912.

61 Walid Nuwayhid, WhatsApp correspondence, November 7, 2023.

62 Letter from Daniel Oliver to Algernon and Anna R. Evans, September 5, 1945.

63 *The Daniel and Emily Oliver Orphanages Ras-El-Metn, Syria*, 193[?].

64 See Sylvester A. Johnson and Stephen W. Angell, "Quakers and Empire," in *The Creation of Modern Quaker Diversity, 1830–1937*, eds. Stephen W. Angell, Pink Dandelion, and David Harington Watt (University Park, PA: The Pennsylvania State University Press, 2023), 18–36.

65 See Zisser, *Lebanon: The Challenge of Independence*.

66 See Baun, *Winning Lebanon*.

67 Walid Nuwayhid, WhatsApp correspondence, September 14, 2023.

68 See Baun, *Winning Lebanon*.

69 Khalaf, *Civil and Uncivil Violence in Lebanon*, 146. Also see Jeffrey Karam, ed., *The Middle East in 1958: Reimagining a Revolutionary Year* (London: I.B. Tauris, 2020).

70 Randi Deguilhem, "Turning Syrians into Frenchmen: The Cultural Politics of a French Non-Government Organization in Mandate Syria (1920–1967)—the French Secular Mission Schools," *Islam and Christian-Muslim Relations* 13, no. 4 (2002), 449.

71 See Nadya Sbaiti, "'If the Devil Taught French': Strategies of Language and Learning in French Mandate Beirut," in *Trajectories of Education in the Arab World: Legacies and Challenges*, ed. Osama Abi-Mershed (New York: Routledge, 2010).

72 Jawad Nuwayhid, WhatsApp correspondence, November 9, 2023.

73 Nabil Khishin, WhatsApp correspondence, January 17, 2024.

74 See Hanssen, *Fin de Siècle Beirut*.

75 See Alejandro J. Gomez-del-Moral, "Refashioning Spain: Fashion, Consumer Culture, Gender, and International Integration under the Late Franco Dictatorship," in *The Global 1960s: Convention, Contest, and Counterculture*, eds. Tamara Chaplin and Jadwiga E. Pieper Mooney (New York: Routledge, 2018).

76 Walid Nuwayhid, WhatsApp correspondence, January 14, 2021.

77 Mike Featherstone, *Undoing Culture: Globalization, Postmodernism and Identity* (New York: Sage, 1995).

78 Jawad Nuwayhid, email correspondence, December 18, 2020 and Walid Nuwayhid, WhatsApp correspondence, January 14, 2021.

79 Omar Deeb, WhatsApp correspondence, January 12, 2024.

80 Favier, *Logiques de l'engagement et modes de contestation au Liban*, 113.

81 Thompson, *Colonial Citizens*, 106.

82 Conversations with Nuwayhids and friends, Ras al-Matn, June 3, 2018.

83 Bardawil, *Revolution and Disenchantment*, 29.

84 Nabil Khishin, WhatsApp correspondence, January 17, 2024.

85 Ministry of National Education of Lebanon, *Baccalauréat Libanais De L'Enseignement Secondaire* for Imad Nuwayhid, August 10, 1966. All educational and work certificates are from Personal Sources: Letters & certificates, 1966–1971. Courtesy of the Nuwayhid Family.

86 Ministry of National Education, Youth and Sports, *Philosophy and Civilizations, Secondary Education, Second Year, Humanities Section* (Sin El-Fil, Lebanon: National Center for Educational Research and Development, 1999).

87 Walid Nuwayhid, WhatsApp correspondence with author, August 28, 2023 and Omar Deeb, WhatsApp correspondence, January 12, 2024.

88 Janet Sfeir, "The Disenchantment of the Left: Two Memories of the Palestinian Struggle," *TRAFO—Blog for Transregional Research* (2018), https://trafo. hypotheses.org/9905.

89 Author conversations with Nuwayhids and friends, Ras al-Matn, June 3, 2018.

90 Favier, *Logiques de l'engagement et modes de contestation au Liban*, 157, 282, and 284.

91 Ibid., 365.

92 Ibid., 490.

93 Conversations with Nuwayhids and friends, Ras al-Matn, June 3, 2018.

94 A later letter home indicates as much. Letter home, Hanover December 12, 1966.

95 Tania Hadjithomas Mehanna, *Le Phoenicia un hôtel dans l'Histoire* (Beirut: Tamyras, 2012), 46.

96 Phoenicia work certificates and badges for Imad.

97 See Baun, "A Contentious Empire."

98 Van Fleck, *Empire of the Air*, 7.

99 Ibid., 83–7.

100 *The New York Times*, "Roger Lewis, Amtrak's First Chief and an Executive in Many Fields" (November 15, 1987), https://www.nytimes.com/1987/11/15/ obituaries/roger-lewis-amtrak-s-first-chief-and-an-executive-in-many-fields. html.

101 Roger Lewis, "Received from H. Preston Morris the following documents," June 6, 1957, Intercontinental Hotel Corporation, Box 3. All Pan Am- and Intercontinental-related primary sources, unless noted otherwise, are from Pan American World Airways, Inc. records. Courtesy of Special Collections, University of Miami Libraries, Coral Gables, Florida.

102 James Potter, *A Room with a World View: 50 Years of Inter-Continental Hotels and Its People 1946–1996* (London: Weindenfeld & Nicolson Ltd, 1996), 8.

103 "Intercontinental Hotels," 1960[?], Intercontinental Hotel Corporation, Box 11.

104 Outlined in internal memo, "For Your Information …" 1948, Intercontinental Hotel Corporation, Box 11.

105 See Christopher Endy, *Cold War Holidays: American Tourism in France* (Chapel Hill, NC: University of North Carolina Press), 2004.

106 See Annabel Jane Wharton, *Building the Cold War: Hilton International Hotels and Modern Architecture* (Chicago: University of Chicago Press, 2004).

107 "For Your Information …"

108 Ibid.

109 US Congress, House of Representatives, Committee on Foreign Affairs, H.J. Res. 350: "To promote the foreign policy of the United States by Fostering International Travel and the Exchange of Persons," 83rd Cong., 2nd sess., February 8–March 31 (Washington, DC: Government Printing Office, 1954), 260.

110 See, Adalat, *Hotels and Highways* and Napawan Tantivejakul, "The State Railway of Siam and the origin of tourism public relations in Thailand (1917–1941)," *Corporate Communications: An International Journal* 29, no. 1 (2024), 9–23.

111 Skwiot, *The Purpose of Paradise*, 3.

112 "To promote the foreign policy of the United States by Fostering International Travel and the Exchange of Persons," 260.

113 "Impact of the Jet Age upon the Hotel Industry," Delivered by Mr. Peter Grimm at Cornell University, May 6, 1957, Intercontinental Hotel Corporation, Box 1.

114 Ibid.

115 MoVitty to Bixby, Beirut and Damascus as Intermediate Points, August 2, 1945, Geographic locations, Middle East, General and others, Box 4.

116 Campbell to Cummings, June 14, 1946, Geographic Locations, Box 6 and Formal opening of Beirut New Airport at Khalde, July 2, 1950, Pinkerton to State department, Geographic Locations, Box 6.

117 "William Campbell, Pipe-Line Executive," *New York Times* (December 29, 1963), https://www.nytimes.com/1963/12/29/archives/william-campbell-pipeline-executive.html and "William Alexander Campbell," https://www.aramcoexpats.com/obituaries/william-alexander-campbell/.

118 Irene L. Gendzier, *Notes from the Minefield: United States Intervention in Lebanon and the Middle East, 1945–1958* (New York: Columbia University Press, 1997), 109 and 211.

119 See Hicahm Safieddine, *Banking on the State: The Financial Foundations of Lebanon* (Stanford, CA: Stanford University Press, 2019).

120 Resume-Hotel Deals, H.M.B, 195[?], Intercontinental Hotel Corporation, Box 11.

121 Ronen Shamir, "British Interwar Airspace in the Middle East: The Forgotten Airport of Lydda," *Journal of Historical Geography* 76 (2022), 32. I thank Cyrus Schayegh for his work and guidance to make this connection.

122 See Judith Rowbotham, "'Sand and Foam': The Changing Identity of Lebanese Tourism," *Journal of Tourism History* 2, no. 1 (2010), 39–53.

123 Samir Kassir, *Beirut*, trans. M.B. DeBevoise (Berkeley, CA: University of California Press, 2010), 114–5.

124 Janina Santer, "'Open Your Eyes onto these Unexploited Treasures': *The Société d'Encouragement au Tourisme* and the Making of a Lebanese Nation in the 1930s," *Journal of Tourism History* 16, no. 2 (2024), 174 and Jasmin Daam, *Tourism and the Emergence of Nation-States in the Arab Mediterranean, 1920s–1930s* (Leiden, Netherlands: Leiden University Press, 2023), 270.

125 Marwan Buheiry, *Beirut's Role in the Political Economy of the French Mandate, 1919–1939* (Oxford, UK: Centre for Lebanese Studies, 1990), 10. I also thank Phillip Lee for the research here, compiled from English-language newspapers and hotel fan sites.

126 Baun, "A Contentious Empire," 198.

127 Hotel Phoenicia brochure, 196[?], Intercontinental Hotel Corporation, Box 10.

128 I thank George Arbid, President of the Arab Center for Architecture, for a host of documents that help tell this story before Salha began negotiations with Intercontinental.

129 "Interiors to Come," *Interiors* 116, no. 6 (January 1955).

130 Architectural Plans, June 7, 1954. Courtesy of the Department of Technical Installation, Ministry of Tourism.

131 Edward Durrell Stone, *The Evolution of an Architect* (New York: Horizon Press, 1962).

132 Mehanna, *Le Phoenicia un hôtel dans l'Histoire*, 53.

133 New York School of Interior Design, *Designing the Luxury Hotel*, https:// nealprince.omeka.net/.

134 George Arbid, "Phoenicia Hotel, 1954–1961," https://blfheadquarters. com/2019/08/14/modern-architecture-in-lebanon-phoenicia-hotel/.

135 Daniel Oliver, Memo, Report of the Year's Work, 1949.

136 Dammam Hotel Project, August 15, 1952, Intercontinental Hotel Corporation, Box 5.

137 Hiatt to Whittaker, July 20, 1952, Intercontinental Hotel Corporation, Box 5.

138 Miami Herald, "M Dayton Obituary" (September 12, 2002), https://www.legacy. com/us/obituaries/herald/name/m-dayton-obituary?id=13839085 and Potter, *A Room with a World View*, 38–9.

139 Dayton to Calhoun, July 3, 1956, Intercontinental Hotel Corporation, Box 5.

140 Dayton to Calhoun, March 16, 1956, Intercontinental Hotel Corporation, Box 5.

141 All direct quotes from "Technical Assistance Agreement," August 14, 1956, Intercontinental Hotel Corporation, Box 12.

142 Ibid.

143 "Operating and Management Agreement," September 26, 1956, Intercontinental Hotel Corporation, Box 12.

144 Ibid.

145 Dayton to Calhoun, January 28, 1956, Intercontinental Hotels Corporation, Box 5.

146 See Asher Kaufman, *Reviving Phoenicia: In Search for Identity in Lebanon* (London: I.B. Tauris & Co Ltd, 2004).

147 Dayton to Salha, September 26, 1956, Intercontinental Hotel Corporation, Box 12.

148 "Breakdown of Bookings Originating in Each Geographical Area, July–December 1966," February 15, 1967, Intercontinental Hotel Corporation, Box 2.

149 Potter, *A Room with a World View*, 69.

150 Fact sheet for Phoenicia Intercontinental, 1966[?], Intercontinental Hotel Corporation, Box 1.

151 Intercontinental Hotels brochure, 1966[?], Intercontinental Hotel Corporation, Box 6.

152 See Maasri, "Troubled Geography."

153 *al-Siyaha*, September 1965.

154 Ibid.

155 Ibid.

156 Hotel Phoenicia brochure, 196[?].

157 "Breakdown of Bookings Originating in Each Geographical Area."

158 Phoenicia work certificates and badges for Imad.

159 See Mehanna, *Le Phoenicia un hôtel dans l'Histoire*.

160 Pan American Airways, *New Horizons World Guide: Pan American's Travel Facts About 138 Countries* (New York: Simon and Schuster, Inc., 1970), 605.

161 Raymond Morineau, *Lebanon Today* (Paris: Editions Jeune Afrique, 1974), 200–1.

162 Baun, "A Contentious Empire," 201.

163 Hotel Phoenicia brochure, 196[?] and Mehanna, *Le Phoenicia un hôtel dans l'Histoire*, 227–31.

164 He does mention several times in his letters, as matter of fact, that he can return to his job at Phoenicia, at any time it appears.

165 Ministry of National Education of Lebanon, *Baccalauréat Libanais De L'Enseignement Secondaire* for Imad Nuwayhid.

166 *al-Siyaha*, July 1965.

167 Eliyahu Kanovsky, "The Economy of Lebanon: Postwar Prospects," *Middle East Review* 16, no. 2 (1983), 29.

168 Kassir, *Beirut*, 347.

169 "World without Strangers: 10,000 Rooms around the World," 1966 [?], Intercontinental Hotel Corporation, Box 2.

170 Traboulsi, *A History of Modern Lebanon*, 120.

171 Cited in Waleed Hazbun, *Beaches, Ruins, Resorts: The Politics of Tourism in the Arab World* (Minneapolis, MN: University of Minnesota Press, 2008), xii.

172 Sara Fregonese, "Between a Refuge and a Battleground: Beirut's Discrepant Cosmopolitanisms," *Geographical Review* 102, no. 3 (2012), 318.

173 Khalaf, *Civil and Uncivil Violence in Lebanon*, 161.

Chapter 2

1   See Marwick, *The Sixties*.

2   Hendrickson, "Finding Tunisia in the Global 1960s," 64.

3   See Timothy Scott Brown, *West Germany and the Global Sixties: The Antiauthoritarian Revolt, 1962–1978* (Cambridge, UK: Cambridge University Press, 2013).

4   Imad's experiences abroad align with two sets of scholarship: one on adult foreign workers, the other youth studying abroad in sixties Europe. However, given that he was neither, it also expands those fields. See Rita Chin, *The Guest Worker Question in Postwar Germany* (Cambridge, UK: Cambridge University Press, 2007) and Quinn Slobodian, *Foreign Front: Third World Politics in Sixties West Germany* (Durham, NC: Duke University Press, 2012).

5   See Richard Ivan Jobs, *Backpack Ambassadors: How Youth Travel Integrated Europe* (Chicago, IL: University of Chicago Press, 2017).

6   See Eric Zolov, "Introduction: Latin America in the Global Sixties," *The Americas* 70, no. 3 (2014), 349–62.

7   David Gerber, *Author of Their Lives: The Personal Correspondence of British Immigrants to North America in the Nineteenth Century* (New York: New York University Press, 2006), 2.

8   Claire Makepeace, "Correspondence as a Historical Source: Clare Makepeace on Researching the Experience of Prisoners of War," *On History*, https://blog.history.ac.uk/2018/08/correspondence-as-a-historical-source-claire-makepeace-on-researching-the-experience-of-prisoners-of-war/.

9   See Penny Summerfield, *Histories of the Self: Personal Narratives and Historical Practice* (London: Routledge, 2019).

10   See Bruce Redford, *The Converse of the Pen: Acts of Intimacy in the Eighteenth Century Familiar Letter* (Chicago, IL: University of Chicago Press, 1986).

11   Letter home, September 16, 1966.

12   See https://population.un.org/wpp/.

13   Jawad Nuwayhid, WhatsApp correspondence with author, August 14, 2024.

14   *Encyclopedia Britannica*, "Hannover," https://www.britannica.com/place/ Hannover-Germany and "The Hotel Hannover Intercontinental—Showplace of Hannover, November 1965, Intercontinental Hotel Corporation, Box 11.

15   Brown, *West Germany and the Global Sixties*, 91.

16   See Jobs, *Backpack Ambassadors*.

17   Axel Schildt and Detlef Siegfried, eds., *Between Marx and Coca-Cola: Youth Cultures in Changing European Societies, 1960–1980* (New York: Berghahn Books, 2006), 10–11.

18   See Martin Klimke, *The Other Alliance: Student Protest in West Germany and the United States in the Global Sixties* (Princeton, NJ: Princeton University Press, 2010).

19   Mathilde Von Bulow, *West Germany, Cold War Europe and the Algerian War* (Cambridge, UK: Cambridge University Press, 2016) and Slobodian, *Foreign Front*.

20   Letter home September 16, 1966.

21   Ibid.

22   Ibid.

23   Letter home, September 6, 1966.

24   Letter home, September 16, 1966.

25   Ibid.

26   This is what some scholars refer to as state feminism. See Margot Badran, *Feminism in Islam: Secular and Religious Convergences* (Oxford, UK: Oneworld, 2009).

27   KayAnn Johnson, *Women, the Family and Peasant Revolution in China* (Chicago, IL: University of Chicago Press, 1983), 89.

28   Letter home, December 12, 1966.

29   Ibid.

30   See Thompson, *Colonial Citizens*.

31   See Safieddine, *Banking on the State*.

32   Letter home, December 23, 1966.

33 Ibid.

34 Letter home, March 28, 1967. Rather, he attributes it to institutions, like the Catholic and Protestant churches, that often prohibit intermarriage.

35 See Yoav Di-Capua, *No Exit: Arab Existentialism, Jean-Paul Sartre & Decolonization* (Chicago, IL: University of Chicago Press, 2018).

36 Letter home, December 23, 1966.

37 See Khater, *Inventing Home.*

38 Letter home, December 23, 1966.

39 Letter home, April 27, 1971.

40 In a March 28, 1967 letter he mentions recently buying one.

41 Letter home, September 16, 1966.

42 See Julia Sneering, *A Social History of Early Rock'n'Roll in Germany: Hamburg from Burlesque to The Beatles, 1956–69* (New York: Bloomsbury Academic Press, 2018).

43 See Eric Zolov, *Refried Elvis: The Rise of Mexican Counterculture* (Berkeley: University of California Press, 1999) and Lauren D. Whitley, *Hippie Chic* (Boston, MA: MFA Publications, 2013).

44 Letters home, September 16, 1966.

45 Letter home, March 28, 1967. See Sneering, *A Social History of Early Rock'n'Roll in Germany.*

46 Letter home, March 28, 1967.

47 Letter home, December 23, 1966.

48 See Dagmar Herzog, "Between Coitus and Commodification: Young West German Women and the Impact of the Pill," in *Between Marx and Coca-Cola,* eds. Schildt and Siegfried (New York: Berghahn Books, 2006), 262–86.

49 Letter home, December 12, 1966.

50 Jawad Nuwayhid, WhatsApp correspondence, August 15, 2024.

51 Letter home, March 28, 1967.

52 Letter home, October 28, 1966.

53 Letters home, September 16, 1966, October 24, 1966, October 28, 1966, December 12, 1966, and May 22, 1967.

54 Letter home, January 9, 1967.

55 Letter home, December 12, 1966.

56 Letter home, December 23, 1966.

57 Ibid.

58 Schildt and Siegfried, *Between Marx and Coca-Cola,* 12.

59 Letter home, October 28, 1966.

60 See Marwick, *The Sixties*.

61 Eric Hobsbawm, *The Age of Extremes: A History of the World, 1914–1991*
(New York: Vintage Books, 1994), 259.

62 Certificate of employment at the Hanover Intercontinental Hotel, October 15,
1967. Located in Imad Nuwayhid, Personal Sources: Letters and certificates,
1965–1971. Courtesy of the Nuwayhid family. All certificates and letters of
recommendation for Imad cited below are from the same collection.

63 "Hotel Hannover Intercontinental" 1966, Intercontinental Hotel Corporation,
Box 1.

64 "The Hotel Hannover Intercontinental—Showplace of Hannover," November
1965, Intercontinental Hotel Corporation, Box 12.

65 Certificate of employment at the Hanover Intercontinental Hotel, October 15,
1967.

66 Letter home, October 24, 1966.

67 Ibid.

68 Bernard Kayser, *Cyclically-Determined Homeward Flows of Migrant Workers and
the Effects of Emigration* (Washington, DC: Organization for Economic Co-
Operation and Development, 1972), 7.

69 Rita C.K. Chin, "Imagining a German Multiculturalism: Aras Ören and the
Contested Meanings of the 'Guest Worker,'" *Radical History Review* 83 (2002), 46.

70 Chin, *The Guest Worker Question in Postwar Germany*, 2. Imad comments on
working with Italians, Slavs, and Turks. Letter home, October 28, 1966 and
October 1, 1967.

71 See Chin, *The Guest Worker Question in Postwar Germany* and Jennifer A. Miller,
*Turkish Guest Workers in Germany: Hidden Lives and Contested Borers, 1960s to
1980s* (Toronto: University of Toronto Press, 2018).

72 Chin, *The Guest Worker Question in Postwar Germany*, 41. Imad mentions
having to pay rent, but it is unclear if that was subsidized by his employer. Letter
home, May 22, 1967.

73 Letter home, September 16, 1966 and May 22, 1967.

74 Chin, *The Guest Worker Question in Postwar Germany*, 41.

75 Letter home, September 16, 1966. This is confirmed by the Hannover City
Archives, which supplied me the only address they had for Imad, likely his first
residence, set up by the hotel: Jacobistraße 28, 4 km north of the hotel and city
center.

76 Chin, "Imagining a German Multiculturalism," 52.

77 Slobodian, *Foreign Front*, 42.

78 One of Imad's comrades confirms this inactivity. Nabil Khisin tells me he didn't think Imad was too politically active in West Germany, attributing Imad's politicalization to a post-1967, Beirut context. Author conversations with Jawad Nuwayhid and Nabil Khishin, Ras al-Matn, June 19, 2022.

79 Letter home, May 22, 1967.

80 Letter home, March 28, 1967.

81 Prestel discusses something similar in the Palestinian case, where because of the lack of bilateral relations between West Germany and Jordan, Palestinian workers arrived as "tourists without work permits." Joseph Prestel, "A Diaspora Moment: Writing Global History through Palestinian-West German Ties," *American Historical Review* 127, no. 3 (2022), 1196.

82 Chin, *The Guest Worker Question in Postwar Germany*, 10.

83 Prestel, "A Diaspora Moment," 1195.

84 Letter home, December 12, 1966.

85 Letter home, January 9, 1967.

86 In a March letter, he discusses his Egyptian friend, who also still did not have a permit, and said "it is as if he is in my place completely." Letter home, March 28, 1967.

87 Letter home, November 4, 1966 and September 19, 1967.

88 Letter home, November 4, 1966.

89 Letter home, December 12, 1966.

90 Letter home, February 19, 1967.

91 Letter home, October 1, 1967.

92 Jawad Nuwayhid, interview with author, Ras al-Matn, June 3, 2018.

93 Letter home, December 12, 1966.

94 Letter home, October 28, 1966.

95 The average response time for his family was about ten days.

96 Letter home, May 22, 1967.

97 Letter home, October 28, 1966.

98 Letter home, January 9, 1967.

99 Letter home, November 4, 1966.

100 Letter home, September 16 and October 28, 1966.

101 Letter home, October 1, 1967.

102 Letter home, December 12, 1966.

103 Letter home, March 28, 1967.

104 Letter home, September 16, 1966.

105 Jawad Nuwayhid, WhatsApp correspondence, April 12, 2021.

106 See Steven Hyland, *More Argentine Than You: Arabic Speaking Immigrants in Argentina* (Albuquerque, NM: University of New Mexico Press, 2017) and Stacey D. Fahrenthold, *Between the Ottomans and the Entente: The First World War in the Syrian and Lebanese Diaspora, 1908–1925* (Oxford, UK: Oxford University Press, 2019).

107 Letter home, December 12, 1966.

108 Letter home, October 1, 1967.

109 Letter home, November 4, 1967.

110 Letter home, October 28, 1966.

111 Ibid.

112 Letter home, December 12, 1966.

113 *Annexe au Prospectus: directives et renseignements,* August 1971, in Course Programs and Educational Plans, 1949–1972. Courtesy of EHL Archives.

114 Letter home, June 26, 1967.

115 See Slobodian, *Foreign Front.*

116 Letter home, January 9, 1967.

117 Ibid.

118 Cited in Prestel, "A Diaspora Moment," 1199.

119 See Wm. Roger Louis and Avi Shlaim, eds., *The 1967 Arab-Israeli War: Origins and Consequences* (Cambridge, UK: Cambridge University Press, 2012).

120 Letter home, May 22, 1967.

121 Ibid.

122 Ibid.

123 Ibid.

124 Ibid.

125 In Imad's June 26, 1967 letter, he references a letter he sent, one in which he received no response. Either he is referencing his May 22 letter or another letter in the interim that no longer exists. Regardless, it appears he had not heard from his family since before the war.

126 Circulation appears to begin after Imad left Hanover. For example, *al-Hadaf,* the newspaper of the Popular Front for the Liberation of Palestine, based in Beirut, ran letters from Europe, but only since its first edition in July 27, 1969. I thank Joseph Prestel for his help here.

127 Letter home, February 19, 1967.

128 Letter home, June 26, 1967. See Louis and Shlaim, *The 1967 Arab-Israeli War.*

129 See Sadik al-Azm, *Self-Criticism after the Defeat,* trans. George Stegois (London: Saqi Books, 2011).

130 Walid Nuayhid, WhatsApp correspondence, July 3, 2024.

131 Nabil Khishin, WhatsApp correspondence, July 3, 2024.

132 See al-Azm, *Self-Criticism after the Defeat*.

133 See Baun, *Winning Lebanon*, for my discussion on the use of "crisis" alongside other terms in the 1958 War.

134 Letter home, June 26, 1967.

135 Fawwaz Traboulsi, *Surat al-Fata al-Ahmar: Ayyam fi al-Salam wa al-Harb* (London: Riad El-Rayyes Books, 1997).

136 Walid Nuwayhid, WhatsApp correspondence, July 3, 2024.

137 Letter home, June 26, 1967.

138 See William B. Quandt, *Peace Process: American Diplomacy and the Arab-Israeli Conflict since 1967* (Berkeley, CA: University of California Press, 2005).

139 See Zach Levey, "The United States' Skyhawk Sale to Israel, 1966: Strategic Exigencies of an Arms Deal," *Diplomatic History* 28, no. 2 (2004), 255–76.

140 Letter home, February 19, 1967.

141 See Douglas Little, "The Making of a Special Relationship: The United States and Israel, 1957–1968," *International Journal of Middle East Studies* 25, no. 4 (1993), 563–85 and Elizabeth Stephens, *US Policy towards Israel: The Role of Political Culture in Defining the "Special Relationship"* (Brighton, UK: Sussex Academic Press, 2006).

142 Letter home, June 26, 1967.

143 Nabil Khishin, WhatsApp correspondence, July 3, 2024.

144 Yoav Di-Capua, "The Slow: Revolution: May 1968 in the Arab World," *American Historical Review* 123, no. 3 (2018), 733–8.

145 See Baun, *Winning Lebanon*, specifically my work on the Arab Nationalist Youth in the 1950s, formed by George Habash, eventual leader of the Popular Front for the Liberation of Palestine.

146 Vania Markarian, *Uruguay, 1968: Student Activism from Global Counterculture to Molotov Cocktails* (Berkeley, California: University of California Press, 2016), 1–2.

147 Letter home, September 19, 1967.

148 Ibid.

149 Ibid.

150 Ibid.

151 The latter is per the Hannover City Archives.

152 Letter of recommendation for Imad Nuwayhid, October 15, 1967.

153 Kayser, *Cyclically-Determined Homeward Flows of Migrant Workers and the Effects of Emigration*, 13.

154 See European Central Bank, "The 'Great Inflation': Lessons from Monetary Policy," *Monthly Bulletin* (May 2010), https://www.ecb.europa.eu/pub/pdf/other/mopo_strat_art1.pdf?b19aa418314b36e5c21fe296a788b20b. Interestingly, Najib Salha was the acting chair of Intra Bank at the time, which crashed in 1966 and was at the center of an economic downturn. See Safieddine, *Banking on the State*.

155 Letter home, October 1, 1967.

156 Letter home, October 15, 1967.

157 Ibid.

158 Ibid.

159 Charles Sabel, *Work and Politics: The Division of Labour in Industry* (Cambridge, UK: Cambridge University Press, 1984), 13 and 18.

160 Letter home, September 6, 1966.

Chapter 3

1   Maasri, *Cosmopolitan Radicalism*, 85.

2   Tal Elmaliach, "The 'Revival' of Abram Leon: The 'Jewish Question' and the American New Left," *Left History* 21, no. 2 (Winter 2017/18), 88 and 73.

3   *Course d'administration hôtelière, certificat*, March 15, 1971, Imad Nuwayhid's personal file. All material related to *École Hôtelière de Lausanne*, unless noted otherwise, is courtesy of EHL archives.

4   See Philippe Gindraux, *L'Art et La Manière: L' École hôtelière de Lausanne* (Lausanne: Editions Payot Lausanne, 1993) and "QS World University Rankings by Subject 2023: Hospitality & Leisure Management," https://www.topuniversities.com/university-subject-rankings/hospitality-leisure-management.

5   Some of the argument, source work, and some prose are adapted from the following articles: Baun, "An Arab, Jewish, and Inter-Generational Tradition: The History of a Scholarly Critique against Israel," *Jadaliyya* (2021), https://www.jadaliyya.com/Details/43141/An-Arab,-Jewish,-and-Inter-Generational-Tradition-The-History-of-a-Scholarly-Critique-Against-Israel and Baun, "Claiming an Individual."

6   See Bardawil, *Revolution and Disenchantment* and Michaelle Browers, "Beginnings, Continuities and Revivals: An Inventory of the New Arab Left and an Ongoing Arab Left Tradition," *Middle East Critique* 30, no. 1 (2021), 25–40.

7   See George, "Jabal 'Amil between the Palestinian and Iranian Revolutions."

8   See Klimke, *The Other Alliance*, Makram Rabah, *A Campus at War: Student Politics at the American University of Beirut, 1967–1975* (Beirut: Dar Nelson, 2009), and Betty Anderson, *The American University of Beirut: Arab Nationalism and Liberal Education* (Austin, TX: University of Texas Press, 2011). In many ways, Anderson's book is the exception, but in the chapters on student activism in 1960s, the studies of AUB students recede to the background.

9   Letter home, October 1, 1967.

10   Letter home, February 19, 1967.

11   *Hawl Itihad al-Shuyu'iyyin al-Lubnaniyyin*, April 1, 1968. All Union of Lebanese Communist sources, unless noted otherwise, are from Lebanese Radical New Left of the late 1960s–70s Collection. Courtesy of International Institute of Social History, Amsterdam, Netherlands (online).

12   Hotel Phoenicia Intercontinental certificates, February 13, 1969.

13   See Hassan al-hassan, *al-Siyaha fi Lubnan: Madiyyan wa Hadiran wa Mustaqbilan* (Beirut: Matba'a Salim, 1973).

14   Mehanna, *Le Phoenicia un hôtel dans l'Histoire*, 140.

15   Lebanese General Commission of Tourism, Summering, and Wintering, Consent Request Agreement and building plans (April 25, 1965). Courtesy of the Department of Technical Installation, Ministry of Tourism.

16   Mehanna, *Le Phoenicia un hôtel dans l'Histoire*, 86.

17   "New 600 room economy class Hotel Planned in Beirut" (January 22, 1966), Intercontinental Hotel Corporation, Box 2. This plan was never realized.

18   Sayigh, *Armed Struggle and the Search for State*, 89.

19   See Ibid.

20   Sfeir, "The Disenchantment of the Left."

21   Walid Nuwayhid, WhatsApp correspondence with author, July 3, 2024.

22   Nabil Khishin, WhatsApp interview, August 14, 2023.

23   Rida Ismael, interview, Beirut, June 22, 2022.

24   *Fi Sabil Hizb Shuyu'i Lubnani Muhad*, December 1968, 1.

25   See Baun, *Winning Lebanon*.

26   See Tareq Y. Ismael and Jacqueline S. Ismael, *The Communist Movement in Syria and Lebanon* (Gainesville, FL: University Press of Florida, 1998).

27   Nabil Khishin, WhatsApp interview, August 14, 2023.

28   Gilbert Achcar, WhatsApp conversations, August 11, 2023, and WhatsApp interview, April 9, 2024.

29   Nabil Khishin, WhatsApp interview, August 14, 2023.

30   See Matthew D. Rothwell, *Transpacific Revolutionaries: The Chinese Revolution in Latin America* (New York: Routledge, 2013).

31   See Bardawil, *Revolution and Disenchantment.*

32   Walid Nuwayhid, WhatsApp interview, June 22, 2022.

33   Lebanese Communist Party, *Shuhada' al-Hizb al-Shuyu'i al-Lubnani 1975–1980.*

34   Ismael and Ismael, *The Communist Movement in Syria and Lebanon,* 64.

35   Gilbert Achcar, WhatsApp interview, April 9, 2024.

36   *Hawl Itihad al-Shuyu'iyyin al-Lubnaniyyin,* 1–2.

37   Di-Capua, "The Slow Revolution," 734 and *Fi Sabil Hizb Shuyu'i Lubnani Muhad,* 1.

38   *Fi Sabil Hizb Shuyu'i Lubnani Muhad,* 1.

39   Iyad Nuwayhid, email correspondence, June 15, 2017. While Iyad's timeline helped clarify the scope of Imad's life and work, most of the items were out of chronological order. Moreover, he merely indicated that Imad "translated a book," which he did not know the title of.

40   Walid Nuwayhid, WhatsApp correspondence, January 14, 2021.

41   Walid Nuwayhid, interview, Beirut, May 25, 2016.

42   Walid Nuwayhid, WhatsApp correspondence, February 16, 2021.

43   Ibid.

44   See Susie Linfield, *The Lions' Den: Zionism and the Left from Hannah Arendt to Noam Chomsky* (New Haven, CT: Yale University Press, 2019).

45   Maxime Rodinson, "*Israël, fait colonial?*" *Les Temps Modernes* 22 (1967), 17–90.

46   Maxime Rodinson, *Israel: A Colonial-Settler State?* (New York: Pathfinder Press, 1973).

47   Abram Leon, *La Conception Matérialiste de la Question Juive* (Paris: Études et Documentation Internationales, 1968).

48   Jawad Nuwayhid, interview, Beirut, May 30, 2018.

49   Jawad Nuwayhid, WhatsApp correspondence, April 12, 2021.

50   Gilbert Achcar, WhatsApp conversations, August 11, 2023.

51   See Di Capua, *No Exit.*

52   Nabil Khishin, WhatsApp interview, February 3, 2021. See Hendrickson, *Decolonizing 1968.* It is unlikely that Imad encountered Rodinson in Paris in September 1967—when he was living in Hanover, writing home to his family about his travels—given that it was a short, tourist trip and he doesn't mention anything like it in his letters.

53   Jawad Nuwayhid, WhatsApp correspondence, November 29, 2023.

54 Gilbert Achcar "doubt[s] very much" that Imad met Rodinson before translating Leon's book. Gilbert thinks "if [Imad] had met Maxime Rodinson he would have written that in the introduction" of his translation. But as I show later in this chapter, Imad was more interested in Leon's original text, not Rodinson's introduction of it. Gilbert Achcar, WhatsApp interview, April 9, 2024.

55 Abram Leon, *The Jewish Question: A Marxist Interpretation* (New York: Pathfinder Press, 1970). See Elmaliach, "The 'Revival' of Abram Leon."

56 Bardawil, *Revolution and Disenchantment*, 13–14 and 58.

57 Browers, "Beginnings, Continuities and Revivals," 2.

58 For a counterpoint, emphasizing the inability of 1960s leftist youth to produce new theoretical ideas on Zionism, see Elmaliach, "The 'Revival' of Abram Leon."

59 Unless noted otherwise, all biographical information on Leon comes from Ernest Mandel's (pen name of Ernest Germain) "A Biographical Sketch of Abram Leon," in Leon, *The Jewish Question: A Marxist Interpretation* (1970 English version), 13–31.

60 Zackary Lockman, *Comrades and Enemies: Arab and Jewish Workers in Palestine, 1906–1948* (Berkeley, CA: University of California Press, 1996), 174.

61 Cited in Dave Prince's introduction for the most recent edition of Leon's *The Jewish Question: A Marxist Interpretation* (New York: Pathfinder Press, 2020), 38.

62 Leon (1970 edition), 11.

63 Ibid., 85.

64 Ibid., 82.

65 Ibid., 262.

66 Stephen H. Norwood, *Antisemitism and the American Far Left* (Cambridge, UK: Cambridge University Press, 2013), 200.

67 Karl Marx, "On the Jewish Question" (1844), https://www.marxists.org/archive/marx/works/1844/jewish-question/.

68 Leon, *The Jewish Question*, 5.

69 Ibid., 266 and 264.

70 Ibid., 269–70.

71 Ibid., 279.

72 John Rose, "Liberating Jewish History from its Zionist Stranglehold: Rediscovering Abram Leon," *Holy Land Studies* 5, no. 1 (2006), 19.

73 Abram Leon, *al-Mafhum al-Madi lil-Mas'ala al-Yahudiyya*, trans. Imad Nuwayhid (Beirut: Dar al-Tali'a lil-Taba'a wa al-Nashr, 1969), 5.

74 Ibid., 6.

75 Ibid.

76   Iman Nuwayhid, interview, Beirut, May 13, 2016.

77   In turn, thinkers considered him an equal, worthy of critique. For one, Syrian
     scholar, Ilyas Murqus, starts the introduction of his 1970 book, *Naqd al-Fikr
     al-Muqawam, Criticism of Resistance Thought*, noting that in a later volume
     (one which was never released), he would take on the work of "first, Sadiq Jallal
     al-Azm, second Muhammad Suwaid [Lebanese thinker], Imad Nuwayhid." Ilyas
     Murqus, *Naqd al-Fikr al-Muqawam*, vol. 1 (Beirut: Dar al-Haqiqa lil-Taba'a wa
     al-Nashr, 1970), 17. I thank Walid Nuwayhid for this tip.

78   Leon, *al-Mafhum al-Madi lil-Mas'ala al-Yahudiyya*, 6–7.

79   Ibid., 7.

80   Ibid., 8.

81   Constantine Zurayk, *Ma'na al-Nakba* (Beirut: Dar al-'Alim lil-Malayin, 1948),
     7 and 24. See English translation (Beirut: Khayat's College Book Cooperative:
     1956).

82   Fayez A. Sayegh, *Zionist Colonialism in Palestine* (Beirut: Research Center,
     Palestine Liberation Organization, 1965), 1.

83   Ibid., 5.

84   Leon, *al-Mafhum al-Madi lil-Mas'ala al-Yahudiyya*, 8–9.

85   Ibid., 7.

86   Ibid., 9.

87   Zurayk, *Ma'na al-Nakba*, 76. Indeed, Sayigh's title starts with *Zionist* (not Jewish)
     Colonialism.

88   Jawad Nuwayhid, interview, Beirut, May 30, 2018.

89   Nabil Khishin, WhatsApp interview, April 14, 2021.

90   Nabil Khishin, WhatsApp interview, February 3, 2021.

91   Conversations with al-Tayyib al-Hosni, Beirut, June 2016 and Facebook
     Messenger correspondence, April 10, 2024.

92   Nabil Khishin, WhatsApp correspondence, May 5, 2023.

93   Nabil Khishin, WhatsApp interview, February 3, 2021.

94   Regarding lack of format, for example, when citing Adolphe Lods' *Israël, des
     origines au milieu du VIII° siècle, Israel: From its Beginnings to the Middle of the
     Eighth Century*, from the 1968 version, Imad only includes his Arabic translation
     of the title, not the original French one. This is unlike many citations above and
     below it that include both the titles in their original language and the Arabic
     translated ones. Leon, *al-Mafhum al-Madi lil-Mas'ala al-Yahudiyya*, 23–4.

95   Ibid., 147–8.

96   Nabil Khishin, WhatsApp correspondence, August 19, 2022.

97 Leon, *La Conception Matérialiste de la Question Juive.*

98 Nabil Khishin, WhatsApp interview, July 19, 2021.

99 There are many examples where the inclusion/style of translation meshes more with the 1968 version than the 1946 version, but I hope these two suffice: on page 22, citation #5, Imad cites Arthur Rubin's *The Jews in the Modern World*, which is not in the 1946 edition but is in the 1968 edition. And on page 185, Imad cites Böhm's *The Zionist Movement in Tel-Aviv and Jerusalem, 1935–1937* in the endnotes like the 1968 version, not in text, like the 1946 version.

100 Fadi Bardawil, "Dreams of a Dual Birth: Socialist Lebanon's World and Ours," *Boundary* 2, no. 43 (2016), 321.

101 One example is found on page 63: "Al-Asiniyun Esseniens [in Latin]: members of a Jewish religious sect, it originated in the second century BC, it is believed, and disappeared in the first century AD."

102 It is also plausible that the publisher, *Dar al-Tali'a*, crafted this list, whether in consultation with Imad or not. Nabil does not remember this process, so I cannot confirm or deny who created this list. Either way, it includes works that Imad was reading.

103 Võ Nguyên Giáp, "The Big Victory; The Big Task" (Reston [?], VA: Foreign Broadcast Information Service: October 16, 1967).

104 Liddel Hart, *A History of the World War: 1914–1918* (London: Faber and Faber Limited, 1948).

105 Leon, *al-Mafhum al-Madi lil-Mas'ala al-Yahudiyya*, 6.

106 Maha Nassar, *Brothers Apart: Palestinian Citizens of Israel and the Arab World* (Stanford, CA: Stanford University Press, 2016), 148.

107 See *The Arab Lefts: Histories and Legacies, 1950s–1970s*, ed. Laure Guirguis (Edinburgh, UK: Edinburgh University Press, 2020).

108 Gilbert Achcar, WhatsApp interview, April 9, 2024.

109 Nuwayhid, *Dossier de L'Élève.*

110 Letter of recommendation for Imad Nuwayhid, October 15, 1967.

111 Imad Nuwayhid, Resident Control Documentation in Lausanne, 1969–1971. Courtesy of the Libraries and Archives Services of the Ville de Lausanne and "Growth through innovation—Lausanne's new driverless metro," *Intelligent Transport* (October 31, 2011), https://www.intelligenttransport.com/transport-articles/5604/growth-through-innovation-lausannes-new-driverless-metro/.

112 *Encyclopedia Britannica*, "Lausanne," https://www.britannica.com/place/Lausanne.

113 *Encyclopedia Britannica*, "Nestlé, SA," https://www.britannica.com/money/ Nestle-SA.

114 Jawad Nuwayhid, WhatsApp correspondence, June 5, 2023.

115 Letter home, September 16, 1966.

116 There is a lack of literature on the Global Sixties and Lausanne. I have only seen one picture of protests in Lausanne in the 1970s, without reference to what they were about. See David Eugster, "The Great Liberalisation" (2018), https://blog. nationalmuseum.ch/en/2018/09/1968-the-great-liberalisation/.

117 Gindraux, *L'Art et La Manière*.

118 Ibid., 21.

119 Pamphlet, *École Hôtelière de la Société Suisse Des Hôteliers* (S.S.H) Lausanne-Cour, 1949, Course Programs and educational plans, 1949–1972.

120 "EHL History: 130 Years of Innovation," https://www.ehl.edu/en/about-ehl/our-history.

121 Pamphlet, *École Hôtelière de la Société Suisse Des Hôteliers* (S.S.H) Lausanne-Cour.

122 "Histoire de l'EHL" (1968), https://www.youtube.com/watch?v=S8c3FMOu8aE& feature=youtu.be.

123 Author conversation with Delphine Thonney, former head archivist at *École Hôtelière de Lausanne*, Lausanne, Switzerland, June 19, 2023.

124 *École Hôtelière de Lausanne*, Awards lists from 1968 to 1969, Imad's personal file.

125 Eugster, "The Great Liberalisation."

126 *École Hôtelière de Lausanne*, Information on Director Erich Gerber, excel spreadsheet.

127 Ibid.

128 EHL, "Top Reasons to Choose EHL for Your Future," https://www.ehl.edu/en/ why-ehl-is-the-best-hospitality-management-school-in-the-world.

129 *Vente de terrain à l'École Hôtelière*, February 4, 1972, Course Programs and educational plans, 1949–72.

130 *La Marmite* (The Pot, *École Hôtelière de Lausanne* student magazine), May/June 1970. EHL archives, digital collection.

131 Jawad Nuwayhid, WhatsApp correspondence, June 5, 2023.

132 Letter home, April 27, 1971.

133 Based on a detailed schedule from the summer of 1970, which would have been the term after Imad graduated. *Horaire des cours*, Imad's personal file.

134 Letter home, September 19, 1967.

135 Programmes D'Enseignement, 1966, Course Programs and educational plans, 1949–1972.

136 *Examen Final de mécanographie*, July 17, 1975, Graded Work and Exam, 1970–1975.

137 Nuwayhid, *Dossier de L'Élève*.

138 *Journées de formation des experts*, March 7–8, 1969, Operations EHL Gerber.

139 Nuwayhid, *Dossier de L'Élève*.

140 Nuwayhid, Resident Control Documentation in Lausanne. It is not outside the realm of possibility that the hours missed are a result of Imad being sick or traveling around Switzerland. Regarding the former, to miss two weeks of classes for sickness, even if on and off, seems serious. I at least assume it is something family and friends would have heard about, but I have no indication today that this was the case. The same goes for the possibility of traveling around the country—plausible, but no family can remember Imad speaking of such.

141 Letter home, January 9, 1967.

142 Nabil Khishin, WhatsApp interview, August 14, 2023.

143 Conversations with Jawad Nuwayhid and Nabil Khishin, Ras al-Matn, June 18, 2022. Through my own research, I could not confirm or deny this trip or its blocking.

144 Nabil Khishin, WhatsApp interview, August 14, 2023.

145 Ibid.

146 Conversations with Jawad Nuwayhid and Nabil Khishin, Ras al-Matn, June 18, 2022.

147 Nabil Khishin, WhatsApp interview, April 14, 2021.

148 In a 1969 edition of *La Marmite*, a student, signed H. Salloum, wrote an article about the Middle East. In it Salloum defends "citizens of Palestine" who are "trying by all means to liberate their land." It is the only article of its kind and Salloum (likely Lebanese) seems to have graduated before Imad. Still, it indicates there may have been those on campus, even if very few, who Imad could connect with. *La Marmite*, May 1969.

149 Eugster, "The Great Liberalisation."

150 *Indications relatives à la rétribution des élèves (salaries minimum)* 1968–9 [?], Operations EHL Gerber.

151 Nuwayhid, *Dossier de L'Élève*.

152 *Journées de formation des experts*.

153 Letter of recommendation for Imad Nuwayhid, September 30, 1970.

154 Nuwayhid, Resident Control Documentation in Lausanne.

155 Letter home, March 14, 1971.

156 Letter home, April 27, 1971.

157 John Darwin, *The Empire Project: The Rise and Fall of the British World System* (Cambridge, UK: Cambridge University Press, 2009), 611.

158 Roy Porter, *London: A Social History* (Cambridge, MA: Harvard University Press, 1994), 353–5.

159 Letter home, April 27, 1971.

160 Ibid.

161 Letter home, March 14, 1971.

162 Curriculum-Vitae, 1967, Operations EHL Gerber.

163 "Selim El Zyr," https://hospitality-on.com/en/contacts/selim-el-zyr.

164 While in a different course than Imad, El Zyr did have a higher composite score. *La Marmite*, May/June 1970.

165 Letter home, April 27, 1971.

Chapter 4

1   Lebanese Communist Party, *Shuhada' al-Hizb al-Shuyu'i al-Lubnani 1975–1980*.

2   *al-Nida'*, October 29, 1975.

3   I use this term and periodization in "Populism and War-Making: Constructing the People and the Enemy during the Early Lebanese Civil War Era," in *Mapping Populism: Approaches and Methods*, eds. Majia Nadesan and Amit Ron, pages 146–57 (New York: Routledge, 2020). Some of the argument, source work, and some prose are adapted from that chapter as well as research from my dissertation fieldwork circa 2013.

4   See Salibi, *Crossroads to Civil War* and Khalaf, *Civil and Uncivil Violence in Lebanon*.

5   Elizabeth Picard, *Lebanon: A Shattered Country Myths and Realities of the Wars in Lebanon*, trans. Franklin Phillip (New York: Holmes & Meier, 1996), 77.

6   See Richard Falk, "The Beirut Raid and the Law of Retaliation," in *The Arab-Israeli Conflict*, vol. II: Readings, ed. John Norton Moore (Princeton, NJ: Princeton University Press, 1974).

7   For text of the agreement, see Walid Khalidi, *Conflict and Violence in Lebanon: Confrontation in the Middle East* (Cambridge, MA: Harvard Center for International Affairs, 1979), 185–7.

8   Hussein Sirriyeh, "The Palestinian Armed Presence in Lebanon since 1967," in *Essays on the Crisis in Lebanon*, ed. Roger Owen (London: Ithaca Press, 1976), 79.

9   Rashid Khalidi, *Under Siege: P.L.O. Decisionmaking During the 1982 War* (New York: Columbia University Press, 1986), 22.

10   Khalaf, *Civil and Uncivil Violence in Lebanon*, 220 and Picard, *Lebanon*, 83.

11   See Baun, "Populism and War-Making."

12   See Hazran, "Lebanon's Revolutionary Era."

13   See Baun, *Winning Lebanon*, 135.

14   Kamal Jumblatt, *al-'Amal al-Fida'i wa Darura Tawjihahu*, February 20, 1969. Cited in Kamal Jumblatt, *Filistin: Qadiyya Sha'b wa Tarikh al-Watan*, ed. Susan al-Nijar Nasir (Moukhtara, Lebanon: al-Dar al-Taqadumiyya, 2006), 121.

15   While Deeb claims the front was in place since 1965, the first reference I see in *al-Nida'* for "The Progressive Parties and Forces in Lebanon" is November 1969. Marius Deeb, *The Lebanese Civil War* (New York: Praeger Publishers, 1980), 62.

16   See Nathaniel George, "'Our 1789': The Transition Program of the Lebanese National Movement and the Abolition of Sectarianism, 1975–1977," *Comparative Studies of South Asia, Africa and the Middle East* 42, no. 2 (2022), 470–88.

17   *Hawl Itihad al-Shuyu'iyyin al-Lubnaniyyin*, 5.

18   Ibid., 1.

19   Maasri, *Cosmopolitan Radicalism*. She borrows and develops this term from Fawwaz Traboulsi.

20   Ibid., 173.

21   Baun, "Populism and War-Making." I borrow and develop the term "the plot" from Robert Fisk.

22   Gilbert Achcar, WhatsApp conversation with author, August 11, 2023.

23   See Laure Guirguis, "'Dismount the Horse to Pick Some Roses': Militant Enquiry in Lebanese New Left Experiments, 1968–73" in *The Arab Lefts: Histories and Legacies, 1950s–1970s*, ed. Laure Guirguis (Edinburgh, UK: Edinburgh University Press, 2020).

24   Edito International, *Mausu'a al-Ahzab al-Lubnaniyya*, vol. 1 (Beirut: Edito International, 2006), 167–8.

25   Guirguis, "Dismount the Horse to Pick Some Roses," 188.

26   Rida Ismael, Interview, Beirut, June 22, 2022.

27   Ibid.

28   Jawad Nuwayhid, WhatsApp correspondence, November 29, 2023 and December 8, 2023.

29 *al-Nida'*, October 29, 1975. I could not find a union by this name in Buwari's
    book cited below. This leads me to believe one of two things: either the union
    designation is just a general phrase (even if a very specific one) or the party
    made it up. Given that the obituary does not mention his place of employment
    or job, it would seem odd for the party to fabricate union affiliation.

30 Ilyas Buwari, *Tarikh al-Haraka al-'Amaliyya wa al-Naqabiya fi Lubnan*, vol. 2
    (Beirut: Dar al-Farabi, 1980), 373.

31 Micha Tobia, "The Gandour Factory Worker Strike of 1972" (2020), https://
    www.youtube.com/watch?v=lR_enxea5UY.

32 Nick Chafic Kardahji, "A Deal with the Devil: The Political Economy of Lebanon,
    1943–75," Ph.D. Dissertation, University of California, Berkely (2015), 156.

33 Lea Bou Khater, *The Labour Movement in Lebanon: Power on Hold* (Manchester,
    UK: Manchester University Press, 2022), 32–3.

34 See Ibid and Kardahji, "A Deal with the Devil," 167–71.

35 Buwari, *Tarikh al-Haraka al-'Amaliyya wa al-Naqabiya fi Lubnan*, 373–4.

36 *Nidal al-'Ummal*, May 1973.

37 This is not to argue that student politics, like labor politics, did not also have
    their conservative counter-movements or pro-United States counterparts. See
    Rabah, *A Campus at War*.

38 Anderson, *The American University of Beirut*, 151–2.

39 Halim Barakat, *Lebanon in Strife: Student Preludes to the Civil War* (Austin, TX:
    University of Texas Press, 1977), 167. Iyad Nuwayhid, email correspondence,
    June 15, 2017.

40 Traboulsi, *A History of Modern Lebanon*, 169.

41 Barakat, *Lebanon in Strife*, 168.

42 Traboulsi, *A History of Modern Lebanon*, 170.

43 Fatima Fouad El-Samman, "The Student Movement in Lebanon, a Struggle
    Through Time," *The Public Source* (2022) https://thepublicsource.org/student-
    movement-mobilizations-lebanon.

44 Barakat, *Lebanon in* Strife, 121–2.

45 Halim Barakat, "Social Factors Influencing Attitudes of University Students in
    Lebanon towards the Palestinian Resistance Movement," *Journal of Palestine
    Studies* 1, no. 1 (1971), 110.

46 Lebanese Communist Party, *Jami 'a Dimuqratiyya* (1974). Linda Sadaqah
    Collection. Courtesy of the American University of Beirut.

47 Ibid.

48 Mahdi Amal, *Fi Qadaya al-Taribiyya wa al-Siyasa al-Ta'limiyya* (Beirut: Dar al-Farabi, 1991), 11.

49 Maurice Nahra, WhatsApp correspondence, August 24, 2023.

50 Maurice Nahra, interview, Beirut, June 15, 2022.

51 Maurice Nahra, WhatsApp correspondence, October 9, 2023.

52 *Sawt al-Sha'b*, January 7, 1944.

53 Gilbert Achcar, WhatsApp interview, April 9, 2024.

54 Lebanese Communist Party. *Barnamij al-Hizb al-Shuyu'i al-Lubnani*, 1968, 32. Linda Sadaqah Collection.

55 Ismael and Ismael, *The Communist Movement in Syria and Lebanon*, 40.

56 Lebanese Communist Party, *Nidal al-Hizb al-Shuyu'i al-Lubnani min khilal Watha'iqahu*, vol. 1 (Beirut: Manshurat al-Hizb al-Shuyu'i al-Lubnani, 1971), 98.

57 Lebanese Communist Party, *Barnamij al-Hizb al-Shuyu'i al-Lubnani*, 38.

58 Ismael and Ismael, *The Communist Movement in Syria and Lebanon*, 81.

59 Lebanese Communist Party, *al-Watha'iq al-Kamila lil-Mu'atamir al-Thalith lil-Hizb al-Shuyu'i al-Lubnani* (Beirut: Manshurat al-Hizb al-Shuyu'i al-Lubnani, 1972).

60 Ismael and Isamel, *The Communist Movement in Syria and Lebanon*, 96.

61 Lebanese Communist Party, *al-Watha'iq al-Kamila lil-Mu'atamir al-Thalith lil-Hizb al-Shuyu'i al-Lubnani*, 418.

62 Ibid.

63 Ibid., 684–5.

64 Ibid., 419.

65 Ibid., 482.

66 Ibid., 484.

67 *Fi Sabil Hizb Shuyu'i Lubnani Muhad*, 3.

68 See Farid el-Khazen, *The Breakdown of the State in Lebanon 1967–1976* (New York: I.B. Tauris & Co Ltd, 2000).

69 *Al-'Amal*, March 5, 1975. 5 soldiers were killed as well.

70 See Salibi, *Crossroads to Civil War*.

71 Traboulsi, *A History of Modern Lebanon*, 168.

72 Rida Ismael, interview, Beirut, June 22, 2022.

73 Walid Nuwayhid, WhatsApp interview, August 24, 2023.

74 Bou Khater, *The Labour Movement in Lebanon*, 40 and Mary Jirmanus Saba, "What's the Use of a Strike Archive? On Image Archives, Surplus, and Solidarity," *Critical Times* 5, no. 3 (2022), 672.

75 See Micha Tobia, "The Gandour Factory Worker Strike of 1972."

76 Mary Jirmanus Saba, *Shu'ur Akbar min al-Hub* (Beirut, Lebanon: Tricontinental Media, 2017).

77 Samir Khalaf, *Heart of Beirut: Reclaiming the Bourj* (London: Saqi Books, 2006), 89.

78 See Salim Nasr, "Backdrop to Civil War: The Crisis of Lebanese Capitalism," *MERIP Reports* 73 (1978), 3–13.

79 Saba, *Shu'ur Akbar min al-Hub*.

80 Rida Ismael, interview, Beirut, June 22, 2022.

81 I thank Mary Jirmanus Saba for the tip here.

82 Saba, *Shu'ur Akbar min al-Hub*.

83 *al-Nida'*, November 4, 1972. Per a new law, minimum wages were to rise by 5 percent across all sectors. Ghandour had yet to implement this law. Micha Tobia, "The Gandour factory worker strike of 1972."

84 *al-Nida'*, November 5, 1972.

85 Saba, *Shu'ur Akbar min al-Hub*.

86 *al-Nida'*, November 5, 1972.

87 Letter home, October 15, 1967.

88 *al-Nida'*, November 9, 1972.

89 *al-Nida'*, November 5, 1972.

90 *al-Nida'*, November 12, 1972.

91 See Tobia, "The Gandour Factory Worker Strike of 1972."

92 *al-Nida'*, November 12, 1972.

93 Ibid.

94 Saba, *Shu'ur Akbar min al-Hub*. It seems that the only thing that changed was the 5 percent wage increase, which had already been made law, but not implemented at Ghandour. Tobia, "The Gandour Factory Worker Strike of 1972."

95 Saba, *Shu'ur Akbar min al-Hub*.

96 Bou Khater, *The Labour Movement in Lebanon*, 31.

97 *al-Nida'*, November 21, 1972 and Tobia, "The Gandour Factory Worker Strike of 1972."

98 Saba, *Shu'ur Akbar min al-Hub*.

99 Rida Ismael, interview, Beirut, June 22, 2022.

100 Bardawil, *Revolution and Disenchantment*, 113.

101 George, "Jabal 'Amil between the Palestinian and Iranian Revolutions," 153.

102 This targeted attack was part of Israel's broader "Operation Wrath of God," following the massacre at the 1972 Munich Olympics. See Simon Reeve, *One Day in September: The Full Story of the 1972 Munich Olympics Massacre and the Israeli Revenge Operation "Wrath of God"* (New York: Arcade Publishing, 2000).

103 See Salibi, *Crossroads to Civil War*.

104 *al-Nida'*, April 12, 1973.

105 See el-Khazen, *The Breakdown of the State in Lebanon, 1967–1976*.

106 *al-Nida'*, April 12, 1973.

107 Ibid.

108 See Sayigh, *Armed Struggle and the Search for State*.

109 *al-Nida'*, May 4, 1973.

110 *al-Nida'*, May 3, 1973.

111 See Chamberlin, *The Global Offensive*.

112 Salibi, *Crossroads to Civil War*, 69.

113 See *al-'Amal*, April and May 1973 editions.

114 *al-Nida'*, October 29, 1975.

115 Bardawil, *Revolution and Disenchantment*, 117.

116 Walid Nuwayhid, WhatsApp correspondence, January 14, 2021.

117 Bardawil, *Revolution and Disenchantment*, 117.

118 Ibid.

119 Author conversations with Jawad Nuwayhid, Beirut, May 30, 2018.

120 Ibid.

121 Yezid Sayigh, email correspondence with author, 2021.

122 Jawad Nuwayhid, WhatsApp correspondence, April 12, 2021.

123 Gérard Chailand, *The Palestinian* Resistance, trans. Michael Perl (Middlesex, England: Penguin Books Ltd, 1972), 9.

124 Ibid., 97–8.

125 Ibid., 14.

126 Conversations with Jawad Nuwayhid, Beirut, May 30, 2018 and WhatsApp correspondence, April 12, 2021.

127 Rida Ismael, interview, Beirut, June 22, 2022.

128 See Baun, *Winning Lebanon*.

129 For a visual example of his place in the global Left, see Maasri, *Off the Wall*.

130 *al-Anba'*, May 1, 1975.

131 *al-Anba'*, December 12, 1975. Black Saturday was when members of the Kata'ib checked ID cards down by the port, and killed 300-plus Muslims. See Salibi, *Crossroads to Civil War*, 145–9.

132 Ibid., 99.

133 Letter home, February 19, 1967.

134 Nazih Richani, *Dilemmas of Democracy and Political Parties in Sectarian Societies: The Case of the Progressive Socialist Party of Lebanon 1949–1996* (New York: St. Martin's Press, 1998), 87.

135 Walid Nuwayhid, interview, Beirut, June 22, 2022.

136 Lebanese Communist Party, *Shuhada' al-Hizb al-Shuyu'i al-Lubnani 1975–1980*.

137 Jawad Nuwayhid, WhatsApp correspondence, November 29, 2023.

138 See Salibi, *Crossroads to Civil War*.

139 *al-Anba'*, May 1, 1975.

140 Salibi, *Crossroads to Civil War*, 101–2.

141 Ibid., 129.

142 Paul A. Jureidini, R. D. McLauren, and James M. Prince, *Technical Memorandum 11–79: Military Operations in Selected Lebanese Built-Up Areas, 1975–1978* (Aberdeen Proving Ground, MD: U.S. Army Human Engineering Laboratory, June 1979), B-6 and 7.

143 Maurice Nahra, interview, Beirut, June 15, 2022.

144 See George, "Jabal 'Amil between the Palestinian and Iranian Revolutions."

145 Salibi, *Crossroads to Civil War*, 132.

146 See Fregonese, *War and the City*.

147 Conversations with Walid Nuwayhid and comrades, Beirut, June 23, 2022.

148 Rida Ismael, interview, Beirut, June 22, 2022.

149 It appears Muhammad Maki, the third killed in Qantari, came from a different location than Muhammad and Diyab.

150 *al-'Amal*, October 28, 1975.

151 Jureidini, McLauren, and Prince, "Military Operations in Selected Lebanese Built-Up Areas, 1975–1978," B-8.

152 Conversations with Jawad Nuwayhid and Nabil Khishin, Ras al-Matn, June 18, 2022.

153 *al-'Amal*, October 28, 1975.

154 Conversations with Nuwayhids and friends, Ras al-Matn, June 3, 2018.

155 Nabil Khishin, WhatsApp interview, February 3, 2021.

156 Conversations with Nuwayhids and friends, Ras al-Matn, June 3, 2018.

157 Jureidini, McLauren, and Prince, "Military Operations in Selected Lebanese Built-Up Areas, 1975–1978," B-8.

Chapter 5

1   Much of the source work and some prose are adapted from my dissertation (completed in 2015) as well as the following articles: Baun, "Claiming an Individual," and "Populism and war-making."

2   Iman Nuwayhid, WhatsApp interview, January 13, 2023.

3   *al-Safir*, October 29, 1975.

4   *al-Nahar*, October 29, 1975.

5   At least one other obituary from that day in *al-Nahar*, not linked to a fighter or victim of the war it appears, included an address for the funeral.

6   *al-Safir*, November 1, 1975.

7   *al-Nahar*, October 29, 1975. At least one other obituary from that day, submitted by the executive committee of the Lebanese Communist Action Organization, did include the phrase "he was martyred." My assumption here is that the paper was less willing to do this for a member of the Lebanese Communist Party, submitted by a family member, not the party.

8   Iman Nuwayhid, WhatsApp correspondence, August 10, 2023, and WhatsApp interview, January 13, 2023.

9   *al-Nida'*, October 29, 1975.

10 Iman Nuwayhid, interview, Beirut, June 1, 2016. Iman tells me that the funeral started at their home, not Yusuf's because it had a bigger courtyard.

11 *al-Nida'*, October 30, 1975.

12 *Maurice* Nahra, interview, Beirut, June 15, 2022.

13 Information provided by Walid, Iman, and Jawad. The paraphrased quote is from my 2016 interview with Iman and was confirmed by Jawad in 2023 WhatsApp correspondence.

14 *al-Nida'*, October 30, 1975.

15 Ibid.

16 See Maasri, *Off the Wall* and Volk, *Memorials and Martyrs in Modern Lebanon*. Haugbolle's *War and Memory in Lebanon* reflects this trend as well (collective, party-centric), but his emphasis on competing nostalgias (state-sponsored amnesia vs. cultural producers and their ideal past) is similar to, and informs my approach regarding the battles over Imad's memory.

17 See Sami Hermez's book for an alternative, which I discuss at length in Chapter 6. *War Is Coming: Between Past and Future Violence in Lebanon* (Philadelphia, PA: University of Pennsylvania Press, 2017).

18 *al-Nida'*, October 29, 1975.

19 See Massri, *Off the Wall*.

20 See David Cook, *Martyrdom in Islam* (Cambridge, UK: Cambridge University Press, 2007).

21 See Tarif Khalidi, "Islamic Biographical Dictionaries: A Preliminary Assessment," *The Muslim World* 63, no. 1 (1973), 53–65. I thank Maryah Converse for this consideration.

22 See Baun, "Claiming an Individual."

23 See Baun, *Winning Lebanon*.

24 Fathi Abbas Khalaf Mahanna Al-Jabburi, *Nasha'a al-Hizb al-Taqadumi al-Ishtiraki wa Muwaqfahu al-Dakhiliyya wa al-Kharajiyya, 1949–1975* (Moukhtara, Lebanon: Dar al-Taqadumiyya, 2009), 269.

25 *al-Anba'*, April 19, 1958.

26 Maasri, *Off the Wall*, 89.

27 *al-Nida'*, October 29, 1975.

28 *al-Nida'*, February 1, 1976.

29 *al-Nida'*, October 29, 1975.

30 *al-'Amal*, December 4, 1975.

31 See Baun, "Populism and War-Making." To include one example here, the Progressive Socialist Party printed a cartoon in its May 1, 1975 edition of *al-Anba'* which compared the recent Ain al-Rummaneh massacre to that of the crucifixion of Jesus. It insinuates that the Roman executors were the Kataib and Jesus was the Lebanese worker and people.

32 See Steven M. Buechler, *Understanding Social Movements: Theories from the Classical Era to the Present* (Boulder, CO: Paradigm Publishers, 2011).

33 *al-Muharir*, October 29, 1975.

34 *al-Nida'*, October 29, 1975.

35 Ibid.

36 *al-Nida'*, December 10, 1975.

37 *al-Anba'*, December 12, 1975.

38 See Khalidi, *Conflict and Violence in Lebanon*.

39 *al-'Amal*, January 22, 1976.

40 *al-Nida'*, October 29, 1975.

41 Ibid.

42 *al-Anba'*, December 26, 1975 and *al-'Amal*, January 2, 1976.

43 Syrian Social Nationalist Party, *Sha'biyya al-Khidmat al-Ijtim'aiyya: al-Mustawsafat* (Beirut: Syrian Social Nationalist Party, 1974).

44 *al-Hurriya*, November 10, 1975.

45 *al-Nida'*, November 6, 1975.

46 *al-Hurriya*, November 10, 1975.

47 *al-Nida'*, November 6, 1975.

48 *al-Hurriya*, November 10, 1975 and *Al-Nida'*, November 6, 1975.

49 *al-Hurriya*, November 10, 1975.

50 Mentioned in several interviews in 2016.

51 *al-Nida'*, November 5, 1975.

52 Jawad Nuwayhid, interview, Beirut, May 30, 2018. See *Sawt Beirut International*, "Development stages of Lebanese pound against dollar in six decades" (March 23, 2021) https://english.sawtbeirut.com/lebanon/development-stages-of-lebanese-pound-against-dollar-in-six-decades/.

53 Baun, "Claiming an Individual," 364. See Melani Cammett, *Compassionate Communalism: Welfare and Sectarianism in Lebanon* (Cornell, NY: Cornell University Press, 2014).

54 Rida Ismael, interview, Beirut, June 22, 2022.

55 *al-Nida'*, October 29, 1975.

56 Rida Ismael, interview, Beirut, June 22, 2022.

57 *al-Nida'* October 29, 1975.

58 Rida Ismael, interview, Beirut, June 22, 2022.

59 Khalid al-Habre, WhatsApp interview, February 2, 2021.

60 Khalife was part of the Lebanese Communist Action Organization. I thank Nour Hodeib for his insight here.

61 See Baun, *Winning Lebanon*.

62 Khalid al-Habre, WhatsApp interview, February 2, 2021.

63 I thank Omar Deeb for this recording.

64 Khalid al-Habre, *Agniyya al-Qantari* (1975).

65 *Nuqatl,* "We fight" is the word used in the 2014 recording.

66 Khalid al-Habre, WhatsApp interview, February 2, 2021.

67 Walid Nuwayhid, WhatsApp correspondence, December 12, 2023.

68 Walid Nuwayhid, WhatsApp correspondence, January 30, 2023.

69 *al-Muharir*, November 4, 1975.

70 Ibid.

71 *al-Nida'*, December 9, 1975. This last part was a reference to the demands of the Lebanese National Movement, which included the disbandment of the Kataib and reformation of the political system.

72 *al-Nida'*, December 9, 1975.

73 Walid Nuwayhid, interview, Beirut, May 25, 2016 and *al-Nida'*, December 9, 1975.

74 Walid Nuwayhid, interview, Beirut, May 25, 2016.

75 Walid Nuwayhid, interview, Beirut, May 25, 2018.

76 Gilbert Achcar, WhatsApp conversations, August 11, 2023. Per Jawad, the *lycée* had a branch of the *Front des Forces Étudiantes,* which Imad was part of at Raml al-Zarif high school. Jawad Nuwayhid, interview, Beirut, May 30, 2018.

77 Iman Nuwayhid, interview, Beirut, June 1, 2016.

78 Jawad Nuwayhid, WhatsApp correspondence, December 13, 2023.

79 Iman Nuwayhid, interview, Beirut, June 1, 2016.

80 Baun, "Claiming an Individual," 366.

81 Jawad Nuwayhid, WhatsApp correspondence, December 13, 2023.

82 *al-Nida'* November 5, 1975.

83 Iman Nuwayhid, interview, Beirut, June 1, 2016.

84 *Al-Nida',* October 28, 1976.

85 Author conversations with Walid Nuwayhid, Beirut, May 25, 2018.

86 *al-Nida',* October 28, 1976.

87 Ibid.

Chapter 6

1   See UMAM's website, https://www.umam-dr.org/about/.

2   See exhibit explanation, https://www.umam-dr.org/event_detail/114/114/.

3   George, "Jabal 'Amil between the Palestinian and Iranian Revolutions," 154.

4   See Naomi Joy Weinberger, *Syrian Intervention in Lebanon: The 1975–1976 Civil War* (Oxford, UK: Oxford University Press, 1986).

5   See Khalidi, *Conflict and Violence in Lebanon.*

6   Hanf, *Coexistence in Wartime Lebanon,* 341.

7   Richard A. Gabriel, *Operation Peace for Galilee: The Israeli-PLO War in Lebanon* (New York: Hill and Wang, 1984).

8   See Andrew Arsan, *Lebanon: A Country in Fragments* (London: Hurst Publishers, 2018) and Jeffrey G. Karam and Rima Majed, eds., *The Lebanon Uprising of 2019: Voices from the Revolution* (London: I.B. Tauris, 2023).

9   See Barak, "Don't Mention the War?"

10 See Haugbolle, *War and Memory in Lebanon* and Volk, *Memorials and Martyrs in Modern Lebanon.*

11 Hermez, *War Is Coming*, 2.

12 Ibid., 144.

13 Much of this argument, the source work, and some prose for this chapter are adapted from Baun, "Claiming an Individual."

14 Cercas, *Lord of All the Dead*, 18–19.

15 For example, an entry for a six-year-old, named Jamal Mustafa, read that because of the inhumanity of the Kata'ib Party, who shot him dead, Jamal would not "grow up to be able to hold the rifle against their crimes." Lebanese Communist Party, *Shuhada' al-Hizb al-Shuyu'i al-Lubnani 1975–1980*, 44.

16 Hanf, *Coexistence in Wartime Lebanon*, 344.

17 See Maasri, *Off the Wall*.

18 Walid Nuwayhid, WhatsApp correspondence, October 10, 2023.

19 Maroun Baghdadi, *Ajmal al-Ummahat* (Lebanon, 1978).

20 Ibid.

21 *Behind the Scenes of Ajmal al-Ummahat* (Lebanon: Nadi li-Kul al-Nas, 2013).

22 See Lina Khatib, *Lebanese Cinema: Imagining the Civil War and Beyond* (London: I.B. Tauris, 2008).

23 *Behind the Scenes of Ajmal al-Ummahat*.

24 They were continued into the 1980s as well. See Maasri, *Off the Wall*.

25 *al-Hadaf*, January 17, 1976. December 1975 was a turning point in martyr narratives—after the events of Black Saturday—but the presence of this unique martyr narrative in early 1976 may be a result of its creator: a Palestinian organization, which had been making professional-level martyr narratives since the late 1960s. Maasri, *Off the Wall*, 38.

26 Baghdadi, *Ajmal al-Ummahat*.

27 Lebanese Communist Party, *Shuhada' al-Hizb al-Shuyu'i al-Lubnani 1975–1980*, 65.

28 Ibid.

29 Baghdadi, *Ajmal al-Ummahat*.

30 *al-Nida'*, October 28,1976.

31 Maurice Nahra, WhatsApp correspondence, January 11, 2023.

32 Lebanese Communist Party, *Shuhada' al-Hizb al-Shuyu'i al-Lubnani 1975–1980*, 6–9.

33 Ibid. See George, "Jabal 'Amil between the Palestinian and Iranian Revolutions."

34 Lebanese Communist Party, *Shuhada' al-Hizb al-Shuyu'i al-Lubnani 1975–1980*, 6–9.

35   I find the order and organization of the compilation of entries indiscernible.

36   Imad's brother Jawad thinks he may be in his mid-to-late 20s in the picture, placing it in the early 1970s. Jawad Nuwayhid, WhatsApp correspondence, August 7, 2024.

37   Author conversations with Walid Nuwayhid and comrades, Beirut, May 25, 2016.

38   Lebanese Communist Party, *Shuhada' al-Hizb al-Shuyu'i al-Lubnani 1975–1980*, 64.

39   As noted in Chapter 3, the timeline that Iyad gave me in 2017 was out of chronological order. Iyad Nuwayhid, email correspondence, June 15, 2017.

40   Lebanese Communist Party, *Shuhada' al-Hizb al-Shuyu'i al-Lubnani 1975–1980*, 64.

41   Leon, *al-Mafhum al-Madi lil-Mas'ala al-Yahudiyya*.

42   Lebanese Communist Party, *Shuhada' al-Hizb al-Shuyu'i al-Lubnani 1975–1980*, 64.

43   See Makram Rabah, *Conflict on Mount Lebanon: The Druze, the Maronites and Collective Memory* (Edinburgh, UK: Edinburgh University Press, 2020).

44   Lebanese Communist Party, *Difa'an 'an al-Jabal Difa'an 'an al-Watan* (Beirut: Lebanese Communist Party, 1985), 5–7.

45   Ibid.

46   See Hanf, *Coexistence in Wartime Lebanon*.

47   Lebanese Communist Party, *Difa'an 'an al-Jabal Difa'an 'an al-Watan*, 5–7.

48   Rida Ismael, interview, Beirut, June 22, 2022.

49   Walid Nuwayhid, WhatsApp correspondence, August 29, 2023.

50   Gilbert Achcar, WhatsApp correspondence, August 11, 2023.

51   Rida Ismael, interview, Beirut, June 22, 2022.

52   Nabil al-Khishin, email correspondence, November 22, 2018.

53   Nabil Khishin, WhatsApp interview, August 14, 2023.

54   Conversations with Nabil Khishin, Ras al-Matn, June 18, 2022.

55   Ibid.

56   Sfeir, "The Disenchantment of the Left."

57   Walid Nuwayhid, WhatsApp correspondence, August 29, 2023.

58   Ibid.

59   See Bashir Saade, *Hizbullah and the Politics of Remembrance: Writing the Lebanese Nation* (Cambridge, UK: Cambridge University Press, 2016), Bardawil, *Revolution and Disenchantment* and George, "Jabal 'Amil between the Palestinian and Iranian Revolutions."

60 See Miriam Cooke, *Wars Other Voices: Women writers on the Lebanese Civil War* (Cambridge, UK: Cambridge University Press, 1988).

61 Ziad Doueiri, *West Beyrouth* (Lebanon, 1998).

62 Ibid.

63 Najib Hourani, "The Militiaman Icon: Cinema, Memory, and the Lebanese Civil Wars," *The New Centennial Review* 8, no. 2 (2008), 299.

64 Conversations with the Nuwayhids, Ras al-Matn, June 3, 2018.

65 To prove that cleaning the slate is a society-wide phenomenon would take time I did not have for this project. However, I do provide examples of this phenomenon beyond Imad as a means of soft generalization.

66 Jawad Nuwayhid, interview, Beirut, May 30, 2018.

67 Jawad Nuwayhid, WhatsApp correspondence, December 13, 2023.

68 Conversations with Nuwayhid family and friends, Ras al-Matn, June 3, 2018.

69 Walid Nuwayhid, WhatsApp correspondence, January 21, 2021.

70 Conversations with Nuwayhid family and friends, Ras al-Matn, June 3, 2018.

71 Iman Nuwayhid, interview, Beirut, June 1, 2016 and WhatsApp correspondence, June 20, 2024.

72 Sune Haugbolle, "Entanglement, Global History, and the Arab Left," *International Journal of Middle East Studies* 51 (2019), 302.

73 Saba, *Shu'ur Akbar min al-Hub*.

74 Ibid.

75 Saba, "What's the Use of a Strike Archive?" 680.

76 Conversations with Nuwayhids and friends, Ras al-Matn, June 3, 2018 and Nabil Khishin, WhatsApp interview, February 3, 2021.

77 Conversations with Omar Deeb, Beirut, Lebanon, June 15, 2022.

78 Both Omar's story and the Nuwayhid story on Imad's death could coexist (Imad was trying to save the other two, he was shot, and then Marwan retrieved their bodies). But the fact that neither the Nuwayhid story nor the original party story mentions this adds a wrinkle.

79 Walid Nuayhid, WhatsApp correspondence, May 14, 2021.

80 Ibid.

81 Maurice Nahra, interview, Beirut, June 15, 2022.

82 Rida Ismael, interview, Beirut, June 22, 2022.

83 *al-Nida'*, December 9, 1975.

84 *al-Muharir*, November 4, 1975.

85 Author conversations with Jawad Nuwayhid, Beirut, May 30, 2018.

86 *al-Nida'*, October 29, 1975.

87 Jawad Nuwayhid, WhatsApp correspondence, June 21, 2024.

88 Walid Nuwayhid, WhatsApp correspondence, January 9, 2023.

89 Maurice Nahra, interview, Beirut, June 15, 2022.

90 Rida Ismael, interview, Beirut, June 22, 2022.

91 Conversations with Walid Nuwayhid and friends, Beirut, June 23, 2022.

92 Rida Ismael, interview, Beirut, June 22, 2022.

93 Conversations with Walid Nuwayhid and friends, Beirut, June 8, 2016.

94 Baun, "Claiming an Individual," 367.

95 See Marieke Krijnen and Mona Fawaz, "Exception as the Rule: High-End Developments in Neoliberal Beirut," *Built Environment* 36 (2010), 245–59.

96 Michael W. Suleiman *Political Parties in Lebanon: The Challenge of a Fragmented Political Culture* (Cornell, NY: Cornell University Press, 1967), 73–4.

97 Conversations with Nuwayhids and friends, Ras al-Matn, June 3, 2018.

98 Hanf, *Coexistence in Wartime Lebanon*, 341.

99 I first saw this on a visit in to Ras al-Matn in 2016.

100 See Saade, *Hizbullah and the Politics of Remembrance*.

101 Fieldwork notes, Beirut Lebanon, 2013.

102 Conversations with Iyad Nuwayhid, Beirut, June 5, 2018.

103 Conversations with Nuwayhids and friends, Ras al-Matn, June 3, 2018.

104 See Baun, *Winning Lebanon*.

105 Conversations with Nadim Nuwayhid, Huntsville, Alabama, September 2, 2022.

106 Nabil Khisin, WhatsApp correspondence, August 19, 2022.

Bibliography

Archives and Special Collections

Arab Center for Architecture, 1954–1956. Beirut, Lebanon.

Daniel and Emily Oliver Orphanage, Ephemera, 1921–1956. Friends Historical Library of Swarthmore College.

Daniel and Emily Oliver Papers, 1907–1960. Haverford College Quaker and Special Collections.

Écolé Hôtelière de Lausanne, Archival and Digital Collections.

Hannover City Archives.

Interviews with the Nuwayhids, friends and comrades, in person in Beirut & Ras al-Matn, Lebanon, WhatsApp, Facebook Messenger, and Email Correspondence, 2016–2024.

Lebanese Radical New Left of the late 1960s–1970s collection. International Institute of Social History. Amsterdam, Netherlands (online).

Linda Sadaqah Collection. Archives and Special Collections. American University of Beirut.

Ministry of National Education, Youth and Sports. *Philosophy and Civilizations*, Secondary Education, Second Year, Humanities Section. Sin El-Fil, Lebanon: National Center for Educational Research and Development, 1999.

Ministry of Tourism. Beirut, Lebanon, Archival Collections.

Nuwayhid, Imad. Personal Sources: Letters & Certificates, 1966–1971. Courtesy of the Nuwayhid Family.

Pan American World Airways, Inc. records. Special Collections, University of Miami Libraries, Coral Gables, Florida.

Resident Control Documentation for Imad Nuwayhid in Lausanne, 1969–1971. Libraries and Archival Services of the Ville de Lausanne.

Newspapers

al-ʿAmal

al-Anba'

al-Hadaf

al-Hurriyya
Miami Herald
al-Muharrir
al-Nahar
The New York Times
al-Nida'
Nidal al-'Ummal
al-Safir
Sawt al-Sha'b

Other Primary Sources

al-Azm, Sadik. *Self-Criticism after the Defeat*, translated by George Stegois. London: Saqi Books, 2011.

Al-Habre, Khalid. *Agniyya al-Qantari*, 1975.

al-Hassan, Hassan. *al-Siyaha fi Lubnan: Madiyyan wa Hadiran wa Mustaqbilan*. Beirut: Matba'a Salim, 1973.

Amal, Mahdi. *Fi Qadaya al-Taribiyya wa al-Siyasa al-Ta'limiyya*. Beirut: Dar al-Farabi, 1991.

Baghdadi, Maroun. *Ajmal al-Ummahat*. Lebanon, 1978.

Chailand, Gérard. *The Palestinian Resistance*, translated by Michael Perl. Middlesex: Penguin Books, 1972.

Giáp, Võ Nguyên. *The Big Victory; The Big Task*. Reston, VA: Foreign Broadcast Information Service, October 16, 1967.

Hart, Liddel. *A History of the World War: 1914–1918*. London: Faber and Faber, 1948.

"Interiors to Come," *Interiors* 116, no. 6, January 1955.

Jowitt, Lettice. *Quaker Biographies: Daniel Oliver and Emily, His Wife*. London: Friends Home Service Committee, 1955.

Jumblatt, Kamal. *Filistin: Qadiyya Sha'b wa Tarikh al-Watan*, edited by Susan Al-nijar Nasir. Moukhtara: al-Dar al-Taqadumiyya, 2006.

Jureidini, Paul A., R.D. McLauren, and James M. Prince. *Technical Memorandum 11–79, "Military Operations in Selected Lebanese Built-Up Areas, 1975–1978."* Aberdeen Proving Ground, MD: U.S. Army Human Engineering Laboratory, June 1979.

Kayser, Bernard. *Eyclically-Determined Homeward Flows of Migrant Workers and the Effects of Emigration*. Washington, DC: Organization for Economic Co-Operation and Development, 1972.

Lebanese Communist Party. *al-Watha'iq al-Kamila lil-Mu'atamir al-Thalith lil-Hizb al-Shuyu'i al-Lubnani*. Beirut: Manshurat al-Hizb al-Shuyu'i al-Lubnani, 1972.

Lebanese Communist Party. *Difa'an 'an al-Jabal Difa'an 'an al-Watan*. Beirut: Lebanese Communist Party, 1985.

Lebanese Communist Party. *Nidal al-Hizb al-Shuyu'i al-Lubnani min khilal Watha'iqahu*, vol. 1. Beirut: Manshurat al-Hizb al-Shuyu'i al-Lubnani, 1971.

Lebanese Communist Party. *Shuhada' al-Hizb al-Shuyu'i al-Lubnani 1975–1980: min Ajalak ya Watani*. Beirut: Manshurat al-Hizb al-Shuyu'i al-Lubnani, 1980.

Leon, Abram. *al-Mafhum al-Madi lil-Mas'ala al-Yahudiyya*. Beirut: Dar al-Tali'a lil-Taba'a wa al-Nashr, 1973.

Leon, Abram. *al-Mafhum al-Madi lil-Mas'ala al-Yahudiyya*, translated by Imad Nuwayhid. Beirut: Dar al-Tali'a lil-Taba'a wa al-Nashr, 1969.

Leon, Abram. *La Conception Matérialiste de la Question Juive*. Paris: Études et Documentation Internationales, 1968.

Leon, Abram *The Jewish Question: A Marxist Interpretation*. New York: Pathfinder Press, 1970 and 2020.

Marx, Karl. "On the Jewish Question," 1844. https://www.marxists.org/archive/marx/works/1844/jewish-question/.

Morineau, Raymond. *Lebanon Today*. Paris: Editions Jeune Afrique, 1974.

Murqus, Ilyas. *Naqd al-Fikr al-Muqawam*, vol. 1. Beirut: Dar al-Haqiqa lil-Taba'a wa al-Nashr, 1970.

Pan American Airways. *New Horizons World Guide: Pan American's Travel Facts about 138 Countries*. New York: Simon and Schuster, 1970.

Rodinson, Maxime. *Israel: A Colonial-Settler State?* New York: Pathfinder Press, 1973.

Rodinson, Maxime. "*Israël, fait colonial?*" *Les Temps Modernes* 22 (1967): 17–90.

Saba, Mary Jirmanus. *Shu'ur Akbar min al-Hub*. Beirut: Tricontinental Media, 2017.

Sayigh, Fayez A. *Zionist Colonialism in Palestine*. Beirut: Research Center, Palestine Liberation Organization, 1965.

Stone, Edward Durrell. *The Evolution of an Architect*. New York: Horizon Press, 1962.

Syrian Social Nationalist Party. *Sha'biyya al-Khidmat al-Ijtim'aiyya: al-Mustawsafat* Beirut: Syrian Social Nationalist Party, 1974.

U.S. Congress, House of Representatives, Committee on Foreign Affairs. H.J. Res. 350: To Promote the Foreign Policy of the United States by Fostering International Travel and the Exchange of Persons, 83rd Cong., 2nd sess., February 8–March 31, 1954.

Zurayk, Constantine. *Ma'na al-Nakba*. Beirut: Dar al-'Alim lil-Malayin, 1948.

Zurayk, Constantine. *The Meaning of the Disaster*. Translated into English by R. Bayly Winder. Beirut: Khayat's College Book Cooperative: 1956.

Secondary Sources

Adalet, Begüm. *Hotels and Highways: The Construction of Modernization Theory in Cold War Turkey*. Stanford, CA: Stanford University Press, 2018.

al-basha, Muhammad Khalil. *Muʿajim Aʿlim al-Druz fi Lubnan*, vol. 1. Beirut: Dar al-Taqadumiyya, 2010.

al-hakim, Karim. *Zokak el-Blat: Memories from a Beirut Neighborhood*. Beirut: UMAM Videotech, 2009.

al-jabburi, Abbas Khalaf Mahanna. *Nashaʾa al-Hizb al-Taqadumi al-Ishtiraki wa Muwaqfahu ad-Dakhiliyya wa al-Kharajiyya 1949–1975: Darasa Tarikhiyya*. Moukhtara: Dar al-Taqadumiyya, 2009.

Anderson, Betty. *The American University of Beirut: Arab Nationalism and Liberal Education*. Austin, TX: University of Texas Press, 2011.

Arsan, Andrew *Lebanon: A Country in Fragments*. London: Hurst Publishers, 2018.

Badran, Margot. *Feminism in Islam: Secular and Religious Convergences*. Oxford: Oneworld, 2009.

Barak, Oren. "'Don't Mention the War?' The Politics of Remembrance and Forgetfulness in Postwar Lebanon," *Middle East Journal* 61, no. 1 (2007): 49–70.

Barakat, Halim. *Lebanon in Strife: Student Preludes to the Civil War*. Austin, TX: University of Texas Press, 1977.

Barakat, Halim. "Social Factors Influencing Attitudes of University Students in Lebanon towards the Palestinian Resistance Movement," *Journal of Palestine Studies* 1, no. 1 (1971): 87–112.

Bardawil, Fadi. "Dreams of a Dual Birth: Socialist Lebanon's World and Ours." *Boundary 2* 43, no. 3 (2016): 313–35.

Bardawil, Fadi. *Revolution and Disenchantment: Arab Marxism and the Binds of Emancipation*. Durham, NC: Duke University Press, 2020.

Baron, Beth. *The Orphan Scandal: Christian Missionaries and the Rise of the Muslim Brotherhood*. Stanford, CA: Stanford University Press, 2014.

Baun, Dylan. "An Arab, Jewish, and Inter-Generational Tradition: The History of a Scholarly Critique against Israel," *Jadaliyya*, 2021. https://www.jadaliyya.com/Details/43141/An-Arab,-Jewish,-and-Inter-Generational-Tradition-The-History-of-a-Scholarly-Critique-Against-Israel.

Baun, Dylan. "Claiming an Individual: Party, Family and the Politics of Memorialization in the Lebanese Civil War," *Middle East Critique* 30, no. 4 (2021): 353–71.

Baun, Dylan "A Contentious Empire: Pan Am, Intercontinental, and Hotel Phoenicia in Beirut," *Journal of Tourism History* 16, no. 2 (2024): 191–206.

Baun, Dylan. "Populism and War-Making: Constructing the People and the Enemy during the Early Lebanese Civil War Era," 146–57. In *Mapping Populism: Approaches and Methods*, edited by Majia Nadesan and Amit Ron. New York: Routledge, 2020.

Baun, Dylan. *Winning Lebanon: Youth Politics, Populism, and the Production of Sectarian Violence, 1920–1958*. Cambridge: Cambridge University Press, 2021.

Behind the Scenes of Ajmal al-Ummahat. Lebanon: Nadi li-Kul al-Nas, 2013.

Bou Khater, Lea. *The Labour Movement in Lebanon: Power on Hold*. Manchester: Manchester University Press, 2022.

Browers, Michaelle. "Beginnings, Continuities and Revivals: An Inventory of the New Arab Left and an Ongoing Arab Left Tradition," *Middle East Critique* 30, no. 1 (2021): 25–40.

Brown, Timothy Scott. *West Germany and the Global Sixties: The Antiauthoritarian Revolt, 1962–1978*. Cambridge: Cambridge University Press, 2013.

Buechler, Steven M. *Understanding Social Movements: Theories from the Classical Era to the Present*. Boulder, CO: Paradigm Publishers, 2011.

Buheiry, Marwan. *Beirut's Role in the Political Economy of the French Mandate, 1919–1939*. Oxford: Centre for Lebanese Studies, 1990.

Burke III, Edmund and David Yaghoubian, editors. *Struggle and Survival in the Modern Middle East*, 2nd edition. Berkeley, CA: University of California Press, 2006.

Buwari, Ilyas. *Tarikh al-Haraka al-'Amaliyya wa al-Naqabiya fi Lubnan*, vol. 2. Beirut: Dar al-Farabi, 1980.

Byrne, Jeffrey James. *Mecca of Revolution: Algeria, Decolonization & the Third World Order*. New York: Oxford University Press, 2016.

Cammett, Melani. *Compassionate Communalism: Welfare and Sectarianism in Lebanon*. Ithaca, NY: Cornell University Press, 2014.

Cercas, Javier. *Lord of All the Dead*. London: MacLehose Books, 2019.

Chamberlin, Paul Thomas. *The Global Offensive: The United States, The Palestine Liberation Organization, and the Making of the Post-Cold War Order*. New York: Oxford University Press, 2012.

Chin, Rita C.K. *The Guest Worker Question in Postwar Germany*. Cambridge: Cambridge University Press, 2007.

Chin, Rita C.K. "Imagining a German Multiculturalism: Aras Ören and the Contested Meanings of the 'Guest Worker," *Radical History Review* 83 (2002): 44–72.

Conroy-Krutz, Emily. *Christian Imperialism: Converting the World in the Early American Republic*. Cornell, NY: Cornell University Press, 2015.

Cook, David. *Martyrdom in Islam*. Cambridge: Cambridge University Press, 2007.

Cooke, Miriam. *Wars Other Voices: Women Writers on the Lebanese Civil War*. Cambridge: Cambridge University Press, 1988.

Craig, Sir James. *Shemlan: A History of the Middle East Centre for Arab Studies*. London: Macmillan Press, 1998.

Creswell, Robyn. *City of Beginnings: Poetic Modernism in Beirut*. Princeton, NJ: Princeton University Press, 2019.

Daam, Jasmin. *Tourism and the Emergence of Nation-States in the Arab Mediterranean, 1920s–1930s*. Leiden, Netherlands: Leiden University Press, 2023.

Darwin, John. *The Empire Project: The Rise and Fall of the British World System*. Cambridge: Cambridge University Press, 2009.

de Grazia, Victoria. *Irresistible Empire: America's Advance Through Twentieth Century Europe*. Cambridge, MA: The Belknap Press of Harvard University Press, 2005.

Deeb, Marius. *The Lebanese Civil War*. New York: Praeger Publishers, 1980.

Deguilhem, Randi. "Turning Syrians into Frenchmen: The Cultural Politics of a French Non-Government Organization in Mandate Syria (1920–1967)—the French Secular Mission Schools," *Islam and Christian-Muslim Relations* 13, no. 4 (2002): 449–60.

Di-Capua, Yoav. *No Exit: Arab Existentialism, Jean-Paul Sartre & Decolonization*. Chicago, IL: University of Chicago Press, 2018.

Di-Capua, Yoav. "The Slow Revolution: May 1968 in the Arab World," *American Historical Review* 123, no. 3 (2018): 733–8.

Doueiri, Ziad. *West Beyrouth*. Lebanon, 1998.

El-Khazen, Farid. *The Breakdown of the State in Lebanon, 1967–1976*. New York: I.B. Tauris, 2000.

El-Kurd, Mohammed. *Perfect Victims and the Politics of Appeal*. Chicago, IL: Haymarket Books, 2025.

El-Samman, Fatima Fouad. "The Student Movement in Lebanon, a Struggle through Time," *The Public Source*, 2022. https://thepublicsource.org/student-movement-mobilizations-lebanon.

Elmaliach, Tal. "The 'Revival' of Abram Leon: The 'Jewish Question' and the American New Left," *Left History* 21, no. 2 (Winter 2017/18): 73–95.

Endy, Christopher. *Cold War Holidays: American Tourism in France*. Chapel Hill, NC: University of North Carolina Press, 2004.

Eugster, David. "The Great Liberalisation," 2018. https://blog.nationalmuseum.ch/en/2018/09/1968-the-great-liberalisation/.

Fahrenthold, Stacey D. *Between the Ottomans and the Entente: The First World War in the Syrian and Lebanese Diaspora, 1908–1925*. Oxford: Oxford University Press, 2019.

Falk, Richard. "The Beirut Raid and the Law of Retaliation." In *The Arab-Israeli Conflict: Readings*, vol. II, edited by John Norton Moore, 221–49. Princeton, NJ: Princeton University Press, 1974.

Favier, Agnès. "Logiques de l'engagement et modes de contestation au Liban: genèse et éclatement d'une génération de militants intellectuels, 1958–1975." Ph.D. Dissertation, Université Paul Cézanne Aix-Marseille III, 2004.

Featherstone, Mike. *Undoing Culture: Globalization, Postmodernism and Identity*. New York: Sage, 1995.

Firro, Kais. *A History of the Druzes*. New York: E.J. Brill, 1992.

Fregonese, Sara. "Between a Refuge and a Battleground: Beirut's Discrepant Cosmopolitanisms," *Geographical Review* 102, no. 3 (2012): 316–36.

Fregonese, Sara. *War and the City: Urban Geopolitics in Lebanon*. London: I.B. Tauris, 2020.

Gabriel, Richard A. *Operation Peace for Galilee: The Israeli-PLO War in Lebanon*. New York: Hill and Wang, 1984.

Gates, Carolyn. *Merchant Republic of Lebanon: Rise of an Open Economy*. London: I.B. Tauris, 1998.

Gelvin, James. *The Modern Middle East: A History*, 5th edition. New York: Oxford University Press, 2020.

Gendzier, Irene L. *Notes from the Minefield: United States Intervention in Lebanon and the Middle East, 1945–1958*. New York: Columbia University Press, 1997.

George, Nathaniel. "Jabal 'Amil between the Palestinian and Iranian Revolutions." In *The Fate of Third Worldism in the Middle East: Iran, Palestine and Beyond*, edited by Rasmus C. Elling and Sune Haugbolle, 145–69. London: Oneworld Publications, 2024.

George, Nathaniel. "'Our 1789': The Transition Program of the Lebanese National Movement and the Abolition of Sectarianism, 1975–1977," *Comparative Studies of South Asia, Africa and the Middle East* 42, no. 2 (2022): 470–88.

Gerber, David. *Author of Their Lives: The Personal Correspondence of British Immigrants to North America in the Nineteenth Century*. New York: New York University Press, 2006.

Ghobrial, John Paul. "The Secret Life of Elias of Babylon and the Uses of Global Microhistory," *Past & Present* 222 (2014): 51–93.

Gindraux, Philippe. *L'Art et La Manière: L' École hôtelière de Lausanne*. Lausanne: Editions Payot Lausanne, 1993.

Ginzburg, Carlo. *The Cheese and the Worms: The Cosmos of a Sixteenth-Century Miller*. Baltimore, MD: John Hopkins University Press, 1982.

Gomez-del-moral, Alejandro J. "Refashioning Spain: Fashion, Consumer Culture, Gender, and International Integration under the Late Franco Dictatorship." In *The Global 1960s: Convention, Contest, and Counterculture*, edited by Tamara Chaplin and Jadwiga E. Pieper Mooney, 159–76. New York: Routledge, 2018.

Guirguis, Laure. "Dismount the Horse to Pick Some Roses': Militant Enquiry in Lebanese New Left Experiments, 1968–73." In *The Arab Lefts: Histories and Legacies*, edited by Laure Guirguis, 187–205. Edinburgh: University of Edinburgh Press, 2020.

Hanf, Theodor. *Coexistence in Wartime Lebanon: Decline of a State and Rise of a Nation*. London: The Centre for Lebanese Studies, 1993.

Hanssen, Jens. *Fin de Siècle Beirut: The Making of an Ottoman Provincial Capital*. Oxford: Oxford University Press, 2005.

Hartman, Saidiya, "Venus in Two Acts," *Small Axe 26* (2008): 1–14.

Haugbolle, Sune. "Entanglement, Global History, and the Arab Left," *International Journal of Middle East Studies* 51 (2019): 302.

Haugbolle, Sune. *War and Memory in Lebanon*. Cambridge: Cambridge University Press, 2010.

Hazbun, Waleed. *Beaches, Ruins, Resorts: The Politics of Tourism in the Arab World*. Minneapolis, MN: University of Minnesota Press, 2008.

Hazran, Yusri. "Lebanon's Revolutionary Era: Kamal Junblat, The Druze Community and the Lebanon State," *Muslim World* 100 (January 2010): 157–76.

Hendrickson, Burleigh. *Decolonizing 1968: Transnational Student Activism in Tunis, Paris, and Dakar*. Ithaca, NY: Cornell University Press, 2022.

Hendrickson, Burleigh. "Finding Tunisia in the Global 1960s," *Monde(s)* 11 (2017): 61–78.

Hermez, Sami. *War Is Coming: Between Past and Future Violence in Lebanon*. Philadelphia, PA: University of Pennsylvania Press, 2017.

Herzog, Dagmar. "Between Coitus and Commodification: Young West German Women and the Impact of the Pill." In *Between Marx and Coca-Cola: Youth Cultures in Changing European Societies, 1960–1980*, edited by Axel Schildt and Detlef Siegfried, 262–86. New York: Berghahn Books, 2006.

Hobsbawm, Eric. *The Age of Extremes: A History of the World, 1914–1991*. New York: Vintage Books, 1994.

Hourani, Albert. "Ideologies of the Mountain and the City." In *Essays on the Crisis in Lebanon*, edited by Roger Owen, 33–41. London: Ithaca Press, 1976.

Hourani, Najib. "The Militiaman Icon: Cinema, Memory, and the Lebanese Civil Wars," *The New Centennial Review* 8, no. 2 (2010): 287–307.

Hyland, Steven. *More Argentine Than You: Arabic Speaking Immigrants in Argentina.* Albuquerque, NM: University of New Mexico Press, 2017.

Immerman, Richard H. *Empire for Liberty: A History of American Imperialism from Benjamin Franklin to Paul Wolfowitz.* Princeton, NJ: Princeton University Press, 2010.

Immerwahr, Daniel. *How to Hide an Empire: A History of the Greater United States.* New York: Farrar, Straus and Giroux, 2019.

Ismael, Tareq Y. and Jacqueline S. Ismael. *The Communist Movement in Syria and Lebanon.* Gainesville, FL: University Press of Florida, 1998.

Ivaska, Andrew. *Cultured States: Youth, Gender, and Modern Style in 1960s Dar es Salaam.* Durham, NC: Duke University Press, 2011.

Jobs, Richard Ivan. *Backpack Ambassadors: How Youth Travel Integrated Europe.* Chicago, IL: University of Chicago Press, 2017.

Johnson, Kay Ann. *Women, the Family and Peasant Revolution in* China. Chicago, IL: University of Chicago Press, 1983.

Johnson, Sylvester A. and Stephen W. Angell. "Quakers and Empire." In *The Creation of Modern Quaker Diversity, 1830–1937,* edited by Stephen W. Angell, Pink Dandelion, and David Harington Watt, 18–36. University Park, PA: The Pennsylvania State University Press, 2023.

Kanovsky, Eliyahu. "The Economy of Lebanon: Postwar Prospects," *Middle East Review* 16, no. 2 (1983): 28–37.

Karam, Jeffrey G., editor. *The Middle East in 1958: Reimagining A Revolutionary Year.* London: I.B. Tauris, 2020.

Karam, Jeffrey G. and Rima Majed, editors. *The Lebanon Uprising of 2019: Voices from the Revolution.* London: I.B. Tauris, 2023.

Kardahji, Nick Chafic, "A Deal with the Devil: The Political Economy of Lebanon, 1943–75." Ph.D. Dissertation, University of California, Berkely, 2015.

Kassir, Samir. *Beirut,* translated by M.B. DeBevoise. Berkeley, CA: University of California Press, 2010.

Kaufman, Asher. *Reviving Phoenicia: In Search of Identity in Lebanon.* London: I.B. Tauris, 2004.

Kerr, Malcolm H. *The Arab Cold War: Gamal Abd al-Nasir and His Rivals, 1958–1970,* 3rd edition. New York: Oxford University Press, 1971.

Khalaf, Samir. *Civil and Uncivil Violence in Lebanon: A History of the Internationalization of Communal Conflict.* New York: Columbia University Press, 2002.

Khalaf, Samir. *Heart of Beirut: Reclaiming the Bourj.* London: Saqi Books, 2006.

Khalidi, Rashid. *Under Siege: P.L.O. Decisionmaking During the 1982 War.* New York: Columbia University Press, 1986.

Khalidi, Tarif. "Islamic Biographical Dictionaries: A Preliminary Assessment," *The Muslim World* 63, no. 1 (1973): 53–65.

Khalidi, Walid. *Conflict and Violence in Lebanon: Confrontation in the Middle East.* Cambridge, MA: Harvard Center for International Affairs, 1979.

Khatib, Lina. *Lebanese Cinema: Imagining the Civil War and Beyond.* London: I.B. Tauris, 2008.

Khater, Akram Fouad. *Inventing Home: Emigration, Gender, and the Middle Class in Lebanon, 1870–1920.* Berkeley, CA: University of California Press, 2001.

Khuri-Makdisi, Ilham. *The Eastern Mediterranean and the Making of Global Radicalism, 1860–1914.* Berkely, CA: University of California Press, 2013.

Klimke, Martin. *The Other Alliance: Student Protest in West Germany and the United States in the Global Sixties.* Princeton, NJ: Princeton University Press, 2010.

Kramer, Paul A. "How Not to Write the History of U.S. Empire," *Diplomatic History* 42, no. 5 (2018): 911–31.

Krijnen, Marieke and Mona Fawaz. "Exception as the Rule: High-End Developments in Neoliberal Beirut," *Built Environment* 36 (2010): 245–59.

Lepore, Jill. "Historians Who Love Too Much: Reflections on Microhistory and Biography," *The Journal of American History* 88, no. 1 (2001): 129–44.

Levey, Zach. "The United States' Skyhawk Sale to Israel, 1966: Strategic Exigencies of an Arms Deal," *Diplomatic History* 28, no. 2 (2004): 255–76.

Linfield, Susie. *The Lions' Den: Zionism and the Left from Hannah Arendt to Noam Chomsky.* New Haven, CT: Yale University Press, 2019.

Little, Douglas. "The Making of a Special Relationship: The United States and Israel, 1957–1968," *International Journal of Middle East Studies* 25, no. 4 (1993): 563–85.

Lockman, Zackary. *Comrades and Enemies: Arab and Jewish Workers in Palestine, 1906–1948.* Berkeley, CA: University of California Press, 1996.

Longrigg, Stephen Hemsley. *Syria and Lebanon under French Mandate.* London: Oxford University Press, 1958.

Louis, Wm. Roger and Avi Shlaim, editors. *The 1967 Arab-Israeli War: Origins and Consequences.* Cambridge: Cambridge University Press, 2012.

Maasri, Zeina. *Cosmopolitan Radicalism: The Visual Politics of Beirut's Global Sixties* Cambridge: Cambridge University Press, 2020.

Maasri, Zeina. *Off the Wall: Political Posters of the Lebanese Civil War.* London: I.B. Tauris, 2009.

Maasri, Zeina. "Troubled Geography: Imagining Lebanon in 1960s Tourist Promotion." In *Designing Worlds: National Design Histories in the Age of Globalizations,* edited by Kjetil Fallan and Grace Lees-Maffaei. Oxford: Berghahn Books, 2016.

Mahler, Anne Garland. *From the Tricontinental to the Global South: Race, Radicalism, and Transnational Solidarity*. Durham, NC: Duke University Press, 2018.

Makdisi, Ussama. *Artillery of Heaven: American Missionaries and the Failed Conversation of the Middle East*. Cornell, NY: Cornell University Press, 2008.

Makepeace, Claire. "Correspondence as a Historical Source: Clare Makepeace on Researching the Experience of Prisoners of War," *On History*, 2018. *https://blog.history.ac.uk/2018/08/correspondence-as-a-historical-source-claire-makepeace-on-researching-the-experience-of-prisoners-of-war/*.

Marglin, Jennifer. *The Shamama Case: Contesting Citizenship across the Modern Mediterranean*. Princeton, NJ: Princeton University Press, 2022.

Markarian, Vania. *Uruguay, 1968: Student Activism from Global Counterculture to Molotov Cocktails*. Berkeley, CA: University of California Press, 2016.

Marwick, Arthur. *The Sixties: Cultural Revolution in Britain, France, Italy, and the United States c. 1958–1974*. Oxford: Oxford University Press, 1998.

Mehanna, Tania Hadjithomas. *Le Phoenicia un hôtel dans l'Histoire*. Beirut: Tamyras, 2012.

Merrill, Dennis. *Negotiating Paradise: U.S. Tourism and Empire in Twentieth Century Latin America*. Chapel Hill, NC: University of North Carolina Press, 2009.

Mikdashi, Maya. *Sextarianism: Sovereignty, Secularism, and the State in Lebanon*. Stanford, CA: Stanford University Press, 2022.

Miller, Jennifer A. *Turkish Guest Workers in Germany: Hidden Lives and Contested Borers, 1960s to 1980s*. Toronto: University of Toronto Press, 2018.

Nasr, Salim. "Backdrop to Civil War: The Crisis of Lebanese Capitalism." *MERIP Reports* 73 (1978): 3–13.

Nassar, Maha. *Brothers Apart: Palestinian Citizens of Israel and the Arab World*. Stanford, CA: Stanford University Press, 2016.

Norwood, Stephen H. *Antisemitism and the American Far Left*. Cambridge: Cambridge University Press, 2013.

Obeid, Anis. *Druze and their Faith in Tawhid*. Syracuse, NY: Syracuse University Press, 2006.

Parsons, Laila. *The Commander: Fawzi al-Qawuqji and the Fight for Arab Independence 1914–1948*. New York: Hill and Wang, 2016.

Picard, Elizabeth. *Lebanon: A Shattered Country Myths and Realities of the Wars in Lebanon*, translated by Franklin Phillip. New York: Holmes & Meier, 1996.

Porter, Roy. *London: A Social History*. Cambridge, MA: Harvard University Press, 1994.

Potter, James. *A Room with a World View: 50 Years of Inter-Continental Hotels and Its People 1946–1996*. London: Weindenfeld & Nicolson, 1996.

Prestel, Joseph. "A Diaspora Moment: Writing Global History Through Palestinian-West German Ties," *American Historical Review* 127, no. 3 (2022): 1190–221.

Quandt, William B. *Peace Process: American Diplomacy and the Arab-Israeli Conflict since 1967*. Berkeley, CA: University of California Press, 2005.

Rabah, Makram. *A Campus at War: Student Politics at the American University of Beirut, 1967–1975*. Beirut: Dar Nelson, 2009.

Rabah, Makram. *Conflict on Mount Lebanon: The Druze, the Maronites and Collective Memory*. Edinburgh: Edinburgh University Press, 2020.

Redford, Bruce. *The Converse of the Pen: Acts of Intimacy in the Eighteenth Century Familiar Letter*. Chicago, IL: University of Chicago Press, 1986.

Reeve, Simon. *One day in September: The Full Story of the 1972 Munich Olympics Massacre and the Israeli Revenge Operation "Wrath of God."* New York: Arcade Publishing, 2000.

Richani, Nazih. *Dilemmas of Democracy and Political Parties in Sectarian Societies: The Case of the Progressive Socialist Party of Lebanon 1949–1996*. New York: St. Martin's Press, 1998.

Rose, John. "Liberating Jewish History from Its Zionist Stranglehold: Rediscovering Abram Leon," *Holy Land Studies* 5, no. 1 (2006): 1–20.

Rothwell, Matthew D. *Transpacific Revolutionaries: The Chinese Revolution in Latin America*. New York: Routledge, 2013.

Rowbotham, Judith. "'Sand and Foam': The Changing Identity of Lebanese Tourism," *Journal of Tourism History* 2, no. 1 (2010): 39–53.

Saade, Bashir. *Hizbullah and the Politics of Remembrance: Writing the Lebanese Nation*. Cambridge: Cambridge University Press, 2016.

Saba, Mary Jirmanus. "What's the Use of a Strike Archive? On Image Archives, Surplus, and Solidarity," *Critical Times* 5, no. 3 (2022): 663–87.

Sabel, Charles. *Work and Politics: The Division of Labour in Industry*. Cambridge: Cambridge University Press, 1984.

Safieddine, Hicham. *Banking on the State: The Financial Foundations of Lebanon*. Stanford, CA: Stanford University Press, 2019.

Salibi, Kamal. *Crossroads to Civil War: Lebanon 1958–1976*. Ann Arbor, MI: Caravan Books, 1976.

Salibi, Kamal. *A House of Many Mansions: The History of Lebanon Reconsidered*. Berkeley, CA: University of California Press, 1988.

Sajdi, Dana. *The Barber of Damascus: Nouveau Literacy in the Eighteenth-Century Ottoman Levant*. Stanford, CA: Stanford University Press, 2013.

Santer, Janina. "'Open Your Eyes onto These Unexploited Treasures': *The Société d'Encouragement au Tourisme* and the making of a Lebanese nation in the 1930s," *Journal of Tourism History* 16, no. 2 (2024): 170–90.

Sayigh, Yezid. *Armed Struggle and the Search for State: The Palestinian National Movement 1949–1993*. Washington, DC: Institute for Palestine Studies, 1997.

Sbaiti, Nadya. "'If the Devil taught French:' Strategies of Language and Learning in French Mandate Beirut." In *Trajectories of Education in the Arab World: Legacies and Challenges*, edited by Osama Abi-Mershed, 59–84. New York: Routledge, 2010.

Schildt, Axel and Detlef Siegfried, editors. *Between Marx and Coca-Cola: Youth Cultures in Changing European Societies, 1960–1980*. New York: Berghahn Books, 2006.

Sfeir, Janet. "The Disenchantment of the Left: Two Memories of the Palestinian Struggle," *TRAFO – Blog for Transregional Research*, 2018. https://trafo.hypotheses.org/9905.

Shamir, Ronen. "British Interwar Airspace in the Middle East: The Forgotten Airport of Lydda," *Journal of Historical Geography* 76 (2022): 23–33.

Sirriyeh, Hussein. "The Palestinian Armed Presence in Lebanon since 1967." In *Essays on the Crisis in Lebanon*, edited by Roger Owen, 74–89. London: Ithaca Press, 1976.

Skwiot, Christine. *The Purpose of Paradise: U.S. Tourism and Empire in Cuba and Hawai'i*. Philadelphia, PA: University of Pennsylvania Press, 2011.

Slobodian, Quinn. *Foreign Front: Third World Politics in Sixties West Germany*. Durham, NC: Duke University Press, 2012.

Sneering, Julia. *A Social History of Early Rock'n'Roll in Germany: Hamburg from Burlesque to The Beatles, 1956–69*. New York: Bloomsbury Academic Press, 2018.

Stephens, Elizabeth. *US Policy towards Israel: The Role of Political Culture in Defining the "Special Relationship."* Brighton: Sussex Academic Press, 2006.

Stephens, Julie. *Anti-Disciplinary Protest: Sixties Radicalism and Postmodernism*. Cambridge: Cambridge University Press, 1998.

Stur, Heather. *Saigon at War: South Vietnam and the Global Sixties*. Cambridge: Cambridge University Press, 2020.

Suleiman, Michael W. *Political Parties in Lebanon: The Challenge of a Fragmented Political Culture*. Ithaca, NY: Cornell University Press, 1967.

Summerfield, Penny. *Histories of the Self: Personal narratives and Historical Practice*. London: Routledge, 2019.

Tantivejakul, Napawan. "The State Railway of Siam and the Origin of Tourism Public Relations in Thailand (1917–1941)," *Corporate Communications: An International Journal* 29, no. 1 (2024): 9–23.

Thompson, Elizabeth. *Colonial Citizens: Republican Rights, Paternal Privilege and Gender in French Syria and Lebanon*. New York: Columbia University Press, 2000.

Tobia, Micha. "The Gandour Factory Worker Strike of 1972," 2020. https://www.youtube.com/watch?v=lR_enxea5UY.

Traboulsi, Fawwaz. *A History of Modern Lebanon*. London: Pluto Press, 2007.

Traboulsi, Fawwaz. *Surat al-Fata al-Ahmar: Ayyam fi al-Salam wa al-Harb*. London: Riad El-Rayyes Books, 1997.

Van Vleck, Jenifer. *Empire of the Air: Aviation and the American Ascendancy*. Cambridge, MA: Harvard University Press, 2013.

Volk, Lucia. *Memorials and Martyrs in Modern Lebanon*. Bloomington, IN: Indiana University Press, 2010.

Von Bulow, Mathilde. *West Germany, Cold War Europe and the Algerian War*. Cambridge: Cambridge University Press, 2016.

Weinberger, Naomi Joy. *Syrian Intervention in Lebanon: The 1975–1976 Civil War*. Oxford: Oxford University Press, 1986.

Wharton, Annabel Jane. *Building the Cold War: Hilton International Hotels and Modern Architecture*. Chicago, IL: University of Chicago Press, 2004.

Whitley, Lauren D. *Hippie Chic*. Boston, MA: MFA Publications, 2013.

Zisser, Eyal. *Lebanon: The Challenge of Independence*. New York: I.B. Tauris, 2000.

Zolov, Eric. "Introduction: Latin America in the Global Sixties," *The Americas* 70, no. 3 (2014): 349–62.

Zolov, Eric. *The Last Good Neighbor: Mexico in the Global Sixties*. Durham, NC: Duke University Press, 2020.

Zolov, Eric. *Refried Elvis: The Rise of Mexican Counterculture*. Berkeley, CA: University of California Press, 1999.

Index